The Early Records

of the

First Presbyterian Church

at

Goshen, New York

from 1767 to 1885

Compiled by

Charles C. Coleman

HERITAGE BOOKS
2007

HERITAGE BOOKS
AN IMPRINT OF HERITAGE BOOKS, INC.

Books, CDs, and more—Worldwide

For our listing of thousands of titles see our website
at
www.HeritageBooks.com

A Facsimile Reprint
Published 2007 by
HERITAGE BOOKS, INC.
Publishing Division
65 East Main Street
Westminster, Maryland 21157-5026

Copyright © 1934 Charles C. Coleman

— Publisher's Notice —
In reprints such as this, it is often not possible to remove blemishes from the original. We feel the contents of this book warrant its reissue despite these blemishes and hope you will agree and read it with pleasure.

International Standard Book Number: 978-1-55613-222-3

Contents

RECORD OF MARRIAGES, 1776-1885 .... Page 9

REGISTER OF MEMBERS, 1767-1850 .... Page 48

RECORD OF DEATHS, 1805-1850 .... Page 79

REGISTER OF BAPTISMS, 1773-1851 .... Page 98

INDEX .... Page 149

Preface

This volume as published is not a history of the Presbyterian Church of Goshen, New York. The history of this Church would comprise a much larger volume.

It would not be entirely out of place to include some salient facts concerning the establishment of the Goshen Presbyterian Church. It has been said that religious services were held in Goshen as early as 1715 by an itinerant clergyman named Treat. Organization of the Presbyterian Church in Goshen took place in 1720. Under the agreement for the establishment of the church the proprietors of the land of Goshen were to give two hundred acres of land to the minister and one hundred forty acres to the Church. This was accordingly done and in 1721 the Rev. John Bradner became the first minister. Steps were taken immediately for the erection of a church building. Very little is known of this building which accommodated the congregation until 1810, when on the 16th of April in that year a favorable plan was reported for the erection of a new building. This, the second building, was among the best and most expensive church buildings of its time. It was dedicated in August 1813. On July 21st, 1866 the congregation resolved that a new church edifice be built. Accordingly one was built, the cornerstone laid on May 11, 1869 and the edifice dedicated to worship on November 22nd, 1871. This is the present edifice. Thus during these two hundred and twelve years there have been only three buildings and during the same time there have been thirteen pastors.

In this volume we are concerned with the vital statistical records of the church, regretting that they are not as complete as the early history. The original record is in existence and now shows the years of wear from use by those seeking genealogical data. Wisely the original record has been taken from circulation and a typewritten copy thereof used locally. To extend its usefulness this volume has been published. This publication has been undertaken to reproduce the original record in its complete form including all marks, omissions, additions, erasures and notations so that the context may be given the reader's version or interpretation when not made clear in the record.

As vital statistics were not required to be recorded in those early days this church record is the only record of such early vital statistics of Goshen and vicinity, and much valuable and authentic data will be found therein which can not be found elsewhere, and to the end that such data may become available for public use this volume is herewith published.

CHARLES C. COLEMAN.

March 1, 1933
Goshen, New York.

Printed by
THE DEMOCRAT PRINTING CO.
Goshen, New York

Record of Marriages

Oct 29 A D 1776 Married Elihu Marvin to Esther Youngs
Oct 29 Married Samuel Racket*to Rhoda Youngs
Nov 12 1776 Married James Everett*to Hannah Waters
*Novr 18 Henry Allison*to Hannah Jackson
Jany 12 A. D 1777 Married James Carpenter to Mary Wells
Jany 26 Married Moses Carpenter to Hannah Smith
*Jany 26 Hamilton Jackson to Abigail Dains
*Jany 30 James Little to*Phebe Youngs
*Feby 13 Married Francis Burns*to Mary McBride
Feby 13 Married John Roads to Elizabeth Green
Feby 16 Married James Babcock to Temperance Decker
*Feby 17 Married Solomon Finch to Deborah Duning
*Feby 20 Married Asa Vail to Sarah Smith
*March 2 Married Wm Carpenter to Hannah Vail
Mar 9 1777 Married*Silas Horton to Mary Dains
*Mar 15 Married Samuel *Carpenter to Sarah Smith
*Mar 23 Married Christopher Springsteen to Susanna Cortwright
*Mar 25 Married John Beekman to*Christian Gale
Apl 3 Married Andrew Willson to Unice Cooly
Apl 24 Married Danniel Horn to Elizabeth Seewright
May 4 1777 Married Jabez Knap to Hannah Holly
June 30 Married Israel Smith & Tabitha Bourlen
July 13 Married Albert Foster &*Abigail Coleman
July 14 Married Allexander Bodel*to Charity Vantyle
*July 17 Married Peter Arnout to Mary Knap
*July 22 Married Samuel Smith & Abigail Web
Augt 17 1777 Married Matthew Wickham & Anna Horton
Septr 8th Married John Simonton &*Ruth Ryan
Septr 15th Married Richard Allison & Amy Case
Septr 26 1777 Married Nathan Reeves to Mary Shepard
Septr 28 1777 Married Isreal Wickham to Abigail Knap
Novr 5 1777 Married Daniel Rumsey to Mary Cooly
Novr 16 1777 Married Jonathan*Thomson & Hannah Thomson
Novr 18 1777 Married Jeremiah Jesup & Hannah Gale
Decemr 2 1777 Married James De Frees & Sevier Rise
Decemr 25 Married Daniel Shepard & Cloe Burr
*Decemr 28 Married Michael Carpenter & Dolle Smith
December 31 Married John Green & Cloe Brockway
Jan 3 A D 1778 Married Benjamin Goble & Elizabeth Beetman
Jan 18 Married Nathaniel Owen& Nancy Darby
Feby 9 Married Archibd Little& Susanah Horton
Feby 12 Married John McCambly& Elizabeth Crawford
Feby 19 A D 1778 Married Samuel Bodle & Catharine Vantile
Feby 26 1778 Married John McBride & Martha Hill
Mar 5 1778 Married Elias Clark & Hittye Cole
Married Peter Kimble & Elizabeth Clark
Married John Reed & Rebecah Rogers
Mar 11 Married Joseph Hulse & Margarett Williams

RECORD OF MARRIAGES

*Mar 17 Married John Slott &*Ruth Drake
Mar 24 Married William Cooly & Elizabeth Hopkins
Apl 2 Married Thaddeus Sealy &*Joannah Sealy
*Apl 8 Married Peter Hill & Isable Trimble
Apl 16 1778 Married John Willkin & Hannah Weller
Apl 18 Married Thomas Williams & Catharine Higgins
Apl 25 Married William Stephenson & Aulle Cluff
May 7 Married Sam a Negro of Mr. William Thompson & Caty Elias a free woman
*May 14 Married James More & Charity Newkirk
May 20 1778 Married Duncan McConnely & Mary Whitaker
*June 14th Married Jacob Arnout & Millecent Weily
June 22 Married Gideon Mace & Catharine Ridman
June 31 Married Jacob Hulse & Rhebeckah Vantassel
July 21 Married David Lynch & Catharine Knight
Augt 2 Married Robert Cochron & Charity Clarewater
Augt 13 Married Caesar a Negro of Michael Jacson's, Esq & Suk a wench of Mr. Peter Townsend's
Septr 10 Married James Forguson & Lydia McCurdy
Septr 10 Married Abraham Huff & Milly Spreag
Septr 26 Married Pet a Negro of Henry Wisner's Esqr & Dina a woman of John Everetts.
Octr 13 Married Silas Holly & Hester Holly
Octr 17 Married Cyrus a Negro & Dine a woman of Mr. Danniel Everett's
Octr 19 Married Joshua Hubard & Catherine Strong
Octr 20 Married Michael Crons &*Hester Smith
Novr 8 A D 1778 Married*Daniel Jackson & Elizabeth McCoun
*Novr 12 Married Samuel Moffatt & Sarah Wilkins
Novr 12 Married Isaac Corey & Tabitha Deans
Novr 30 Married Samuel Parshill & Sarah Megee
Decmr 3 Married Solomon Rogers& Ann Humphry
*December 17 Married Clark McNish *& Elizabeth Davies
Decemr 20 Married Thomas Vanbumel & Hannah Chandler
Decemr 27th Married Saml More & Elizabeth Love
Decemr 27th Married Isaac Dunning & Mary Foster
Jan 4 A D 1779 Married Samuel Sealy & Mary Bartlet
*Jan 10 Married Richard Wood & Christian Finch
Jan 10 Married John Owen & Elizabeth Boyle
Jan 10 Tobias Feller & Isabella Neely
Jan 17 Married Daniel Conkling*& Suzanah Roe
Jany 24 Married Jonathan Rogers*& Martha Smith
Jany Married Daniel a Negro of John McCamly & Serena a Woman Samuel Gale's
Jany 31 A. D. 1779 *Married John Carpenter & Abigail More
Feby 8 Married David Mapes & Mary Cornwall
Feby 10 Married Smith Mapes & Rachel Knight
Feby 15 Married James Dunning & Sarah Wells
*Feby 23 Married Elihu Horton & Johanah Coleman
Feby 25 Married Micha Coleman & Elizabeth Powell
Feby 25 Married Moses Thomson & Sarah Wood
Mar 28 Married Ephriam Marston & Ruth Carpenter
Mar 30 Married Able Kimble & Syble Chapman
Apl 1 Married Hezekiah Woodward & Ellinor Vail
Apl 6 Married John Wood & Sarah Hulse
*Apl 18 Married Benjn McVeagh & Phebe Brinson

RECORD OF MARRIAGES

Apl 18 Married William Monnel & Francis Tuthill
Apl 22 Married Wm. Duglass &* Janett McBride
Apl 29 Married James Mapes & Anna Manny
May 5 A D 1779 Married Samuel Rogers*& Jane Agur
May 13 Married James Ensighn & Mary Carpenter
Moses Son of Coe Gale& Hannah Carpenter his Wife, Born
Baptised May 16 1779 (This insertion is crossed out)
Mary Daughter of Silas Stewart-Born Jany 31 1779 Baptised May 16 1779
*May 17 Married Jeremiah Tuthill & Ann Hulse
Ellinor Daughter of Alexander McVaugh & Hannah Maypes, his wife Born
Baptised May 23, 1779 (This insertion is crossed out)
May 26 Married Thos Oliver & Keziah Wood
May 31 Married James Drake & Mary Holly
*June 3 Married John Faulkener & Bathia Reeves
June 9 Married John Lamoreaux & Jemimah Stephens
June 16 Married Cornelius Mieres & Coykendall
June 29 AD 1779 *Married Wm Elmer & Mary Allison
* July 11 1779 Married Joseph*Coleman & Mary Salmon
*John Lhomedieu & Mary Horton were married Augt 7 1779
July 28 Married James Ward & Leah Mace
Aug 15 Married William Miller   Sarah Cooly
Augt 22 Moses Swarthout & Martha Holly were married.
Augt 31 Married Moses Hallett & Phebe Fuller.
Septr 2 Married Ezra Keeler& Elizabeth Goldsmith
Sept 15 Married Adam Muskinnos & Catherine Culp
Sept 21 Married Matthias Quick & Rhoda Carpenter
Septr 30 Married Henry Jackson& Ellinor McDougall
*Octr 2 Married Eliud Tryon & Bethiah Aldrich
Octr 3 AD 1779 Married Allexander Trimble*& Keziah Oldfield
Octr 3 Married Isaac Witter & Margrett Owens
Octr 7 Married Josiah Vail &*Meriam Smith
*Octr 10 Married Thos Horton & Hannah More
Octr 14 Married Chales Webb & Martha Vectur
Octr 28 Married Charles Boorland & Rebeckah Mac Neal
Octr 31 Married Benjamin Hulse & Abigail Everson
Novr 2 Married Philips Hohamer & Mary Peck
Novr 2 Married Francis Popham & Martha Denton
Novr 9 Married Levi Man & Anna Cooly
Novr 13 Married Abraham Rand & Elizabeth Lane
Novr 14 Married John Osborn & Esther Farrier
Novr 14 Married Zacceus Case & Hannah Salmon
Novr 14 Married David Case & Mary Wells
Novr 18 1779 *Married James Foster &*Mary Drake
*Novr 18 Married William Holley & Hannah Dun
*Novr 21 Married Carman Carpenter & Mary Webb
*Novr 22 Married John Chandler & Rebeckah Dougherty
23 Married David Smith & Mary Owens
*Married Danniel Dains & Mary Parish
*Decemr 5 Married Colville Steward & Joana Brown
6 Married Ashkenar Shappe & Mary Couly
*9 Married Theophilus Howell Parson & Elizabeth More
Married James Reed & Abigail Johnson
20 Married Moses Kellum & Mary King
22 Married James Smith & Ruth Carpenter
Jany 16 AD 1780 Married Caleb Goldsmith*& Rhoda Finch

RECORD OF MARRIAGES

17 Married Samuel Chandler & Phebe Reed
Married Daniel Bull & Catherine Miller
January 18th AD 1780 Married Peter More & Elizabeth Cary
Feby 1 Married Aaron Vanatta & Elizabeth Yerks
Feby 10 Married Joel Brigs & Esther Pain
15 Married James Young &*Mary Newkirk
21 Married Jeremiah Kinner & Sarah Knap
Mar 2 Married William Brand & Elizabeth Evans
7 Married Jeremiah Oakly & Mary Vantassal
8 Married David Hawkins & Sarah Horton
12 Married James Dolson & Elinor Carpenter
14 Married Francis Tuthill & Francess Conkling
Apl 2 Married Luther Steward & Keziah Carpenter
6 Married Daniel Skinner & Mary Smith
11 Married John Tuthill & Millescent Sealy
12 Married Richard Davies & Catherine Christ
Apl 25 1780 *Married Jonathan Owen & Mary Dunning
Married John King & Mary Teed
Married Angus Munroe & Margret Homes
May 2 *Married John Reid &*Irene Parish
21 Married Isaac Kinney & Margarett Brunning
25 Married Abijah Wells & Phebe Coleman
June 6 Married Bazaleel Seely & Rachel Tuthill
10 Married John Mosier & Mary Harden
22 Married Gabriel Connel & Abigail Knap
25 Married Gabriel Cory & Esther Manroe
29 Married Ebenezer Griffin & Mary Clintock
July 5 Married James Denton*& Temperance Tusteen
14 Married Lemuel Allen & Johannah Deans
17 Married Edward Campbel & Deborah Ellis
*23 Married Isaac Vanduser & Martha Tusteen
Augt 22 1780 * Married Richard Gale*& Experience Couly
Septr 17 * Married James Murdock Mary Campbel
24 Married James Kid & Elizabeth Byard
Novr 6 * Married John Knap & Unice Willcox
8 * Married Charles Giles & Janat Armstrong
13 * Married Daniel Denn Jemima Decker
16 * Married Reeves Cox & Elizabeth Weeb
Decmr 4 Married Samuel Seely &*Catherine Cox
Married Enos Smith*& Phebe Vail
Decmr 24 Married John McNeal &*Mary Allison
26 * Married Nathan Jones &*Temperance Sawer
28 * Married Charles Tinley & Mary Lewis
Married Clement King & Mary Woodward
31 Married Abraham Osbourn & Patience Roe
Married Ezekiel Roe*& Mary Budd
January 15th AD 1781*Married Benj Carpenter & Eunice Steward
16 Married James Crawford & Charity Sands
18 Married David Glaspay & Abigail Maypes
25 Married Abraham Letts & Abigail Garrisson
30 Married William Jackson & Abigail Pearson
Feb 12 Married Samuel Pain & Patience Oldfield
22 Married Alsup Vail & Francess Saybolt
Mar 4 Married Marcum Sha & Sarah Hennison
* Married John Jackson & Elener Whitman

RECORD OF MARRIAGES

11 Married John Dains & Dorothy Thomson
22 * Married George Smith & Mary Tylar
Apl 11 Married Joseph Coddington & Elizabeth Jones
16 * Married Joseph Smith*& Sarah Barker
25 Married John Knap &*Elizabeth Kellum
May 15 1781 Married*Usher Hampton More & Patience Vail
21 * Married James Peirson &*Anna More
22 James White & Elizabeth*Carpenter
June 19 William Wilkins & Catharine Miller
* James Monnel & Mary Miller
28 Married Stephen Barton & Mary Thomson
July 17 Married Nicholas Knight & Elizabeth Case
26 * Married Solomon Smith*& Phebe Dunning
Augt 16 Married Elijah Seely &*Mary Goldsmith
Septr 4 * Married Allexandr Smith*& Mary Tuthill
6 Isaac Carpenter &*Suzannah Little
11 * Kadmiel More & Julianah Wickham
12 George Gershimer & Lucy Ellis
18 * John Thompson &*Margrett Thompson
23 * Nehemiah Carpenter &* Elizabeth Thompson
Octr 11 1781 Married Stephen Crane & Mary Arnout
17 John Manhcart & Martha Lyon
21 * Jabez Noble & Lois Dunning
Novr 1 James Miller & Elizabeth Brown
8 *Benjamin Gale & Mary Bradner
13 Benjamin Himson & Elizabeth Price
Decmr 3 Theophilus Howell &*Susannah Carpenter
William Little & Meriam Cooly
11 Isreal Green & Tabithy Owen
18 Samuel Finch & Hannah Macdeugal
20 *Thomas Watkins &*Lydia Eager
27 Elisha Reeve & Temperance Reeve
Jany 10 AD 1782 *Married Anthony Yelverton*& Elizabeth Dunning
15 Nathaniel Knap & Margrett Rowlin
16 Russel Buckbee & Hannah Maypes
29 Danniel Popyno &*Mary Sayre
Feby 11 John Cory & Ruth Hawks
12 *Danniel Case &*Phebe McCune
28 William Tylar & Mary Vail
Asa Chapman & Abigail Thomas
Mar 7 Jesse Carpenter & Sarah Seely
12 David Owen & Martha Armstrong
14 David More & Tabitha Smith
29 *Nathaniel Baily &*Margrett Wickham
Apl 25 *Jepthah Fuller & Mary Godfry
May 6 AD 1782
Married William Hodge& Sarah Coleman
7 Jesse Case &* Sarah Solomon
16 Israel Maypes & Jemimah Maypes
June 23 William More & Elizabeth Howell
25 Daniel Holly & Sarah West Broock
Augt 11 *Stephen Smith & Margarett Buttler
24 Allexander Eaten & Esther Martin
Septr 15 David Cooly & Hannah Smith
23 John Penny & Sarah Simmers

RECORD OF MARRIAGES

26 Jedediah Fuller & Sarah Wisner
Octr 3 Henry Spencer & Mary Huff
Nov 2 Richard Welling & Mary Denton
3 Moses Rogers & Susanna Hill
Nvr 4th AD 1782 *Married John Denton * Abigail Scoit
14 John Short & Margrett Oakly
24 *William Knap & Mary Holly
Ralph Swarthout & Lois Halsteed
Decemr 5 Daniel Bailey & Mary Tuttle
Moses Latty & Elizabeth Carman
11 Joseph Denton & Hannah Yelverton
16 *Nathaniel Ludlum & *Catharine Wells
26 John Taylor & Sarah McCamly
31 William Millar &* Elizabeth Crawford
Jany 6th AD 1783 Married Allexander McCory & Eunice Armstrong
8 Peter Randall &* Mary Cooly
23 Andrew Rickey & Elenor Neely
27 *Benjamin Ludlum & Christian Bradner
Feby 3 Jonathan Knap & Amy Smith
6 Israel Seely & Sarah Gale
13 Charles Tucker & Mary Hunnell
Mar 3 *Benjamin Lathrop & Abigail Cooly
9 Henry Conklin Smith & Juliana Vail
10 Benjamin Hulse & Keziah Parshall
19 *Rev Andrew King &* Jane Trimble
24 John Bradner & Margaret Howell
27 Enos Maypes & Irene Vail
Apl 13 AD 1783 Married Benjamin Whitaker * Abigail Pellett
June 10 James Jackson & Rebeckah Arnout
16 John Vanorsdoll & Mary Crawford
Hugh Connely & Mary Pauly
17 Nathan Arnout & Margrett Stewart
24 *Ebenezer Dunning & Martha Danes
*Nail Brown &*Elizabeth McVaegh
July 17 Caleb Smith & Hannah Drake
29 *Henry Abraham Williams*& Elizabeth Mathews
31 Nathan Rumsey   Lydia McGowen
31 Thomas Ray & Abigail Brown
Augt 1 Benjamin Simson & Mary McClintock
Augt 21 1783 Married Archbald Thomson & Mary Thomson
29 Phineas Salmon &*Phebe Bingham
James Rumsey & Rachel Smith
Septr 6 William Steel & Deborah Dorson
Septr 11 *Jonathan Bayley &*Keturah Dunning
Octr 6 Hugh Greag & Triphenah Mathews
9 Benjamin Waldron & Melesent Maypes
13 Stephen Maypes & Suzanah Carroway
14 Samuel Vail & Hannah Dunning
20 Danniel Cooly &*Sybill Biells
28 Nathan Hallet & Huldah Vantassel
Novr 3 Amos Park &*Margarett More
Decmr 10 Eli Corwin & Mary Wickham
17 Nathaniel Hunt & Azubah Kimbel
Jany 1st AD 1784 * Married Daniel G. Rogers & Elizabeth Wilkins
8 David Vail & Elizabeth Smith

RECORD OF MARRIAGES

Mehitable Tuttle & Samuel Boyd
11 James Hulse & Phebe Denny
14 * Jonathan Tuthill &*Sarah Wadkins
28 Samuel Denton & Juliana Roe
29 Aaron Swort-Hout & Lydia Wells
Henry Yongs & Deborah Howell
Feby 2 * Abiel Fry & Abigail Owen
* George Sullivan &*Sarah Traverse
13 * William Walker & Jane Neely
19 Samuel Raner & Fanny Brown
Mar 4 Moses Reed & Agness Symons
March 13 AD 1784 * Married Ichabod Winan & Elizabeth Drake
15 Laban Landon & Elizabeth Gillis
30 Benjamin Howell & Sarah Webster
Apl 19 Samuel Horton Mehatable Hulse
June 17 Enoch Jackson & Mary Armstrong
July 26 John Oakly & Mary Holly
Augt 9 * Uriah Terry & Elizabeth Peirson
26 Jesse Garner & Martha Carpenter
Septr 8 William Shippy & Naomi Westover
14 * Benjamin Jenings &*Mary Jenings
Octr 25 * Benjamin Drake &*Elizabeth Roe
Decmr 2 Joseph Webb & Esther Cooper
6 David Dains & Phebe Borland
Decemr 14 1785 Married Thomas McHenry & Mary Reed
Jany 11 1785 Married Freegift Couly & Experience Little
William Gidney & Elizabeth Knap
Feby 24 Andrew Hart & Elizabeth Trimpon
28 Archbald Cunningham & Phebe Kimble
Mar 1 William Falls & Elsy Davies
Samuel Crawford & Margarett Gallispy
Abraham Bennet & Lydia Shults
2 * Cornelius Bruyn & Sarah Morris
17 Peter Johnson &*Isabel Lackey
31 * Elisha Goldsmith & Sarah Dunning
Apl 4 Francis Craig & Anna Forsythe
6 Henry Bush &*Esther Wilkison
Apl 19 AD 1785 William Smith & Rachel Newkirk
21 Anthony Dobbins &*Hannah Jones
28 John Bell &*Keziah Maypes
May 23 Benjamin Smith & Catherine Kearney
30 * Cornelius Janson & Christian Morris
June 12 John Seward & Mary Butler
Augt 14 George Boials & Rachel Samson
25 * William Eager &*Elizabeth Slott
Septr 16 * William Arnold &*Elizabeth Hopper
Octr 13 Ephriam Blanchard & Mary Rogers
16 John More & Mary Hulse
Octr 30 * James Thompson & Keturah Tucker
Nov 3 Allexander Cory & Martha Wells
Novr 24 AD 1785 Married Peter Poff & Mary Imbler
Decmr 16 William Graham &*Mary Moffat
29 John Smith & Esther Little
Jany 17 1786 * Frederick Saybolt and Abigail Reeve

RECORD OF MARRIAGES

Jonathan Tuthill & Mary Harlow
Feb 9 * Thomas Curtis &*Juliana Coleman
*William Eager &*Elizabeth Watkins
23 Joseph Coddington & Unis Mott
Mar 11 Robert Morris & Francess Ludlum
13 William Plummon & Sarah Hull
Apl 13 * Charles Bull &*Elizabeth Mains
Erastus Porter &*Hannah Denton
Apl 27 1786 Joshuah Reeve &*Abigail Haff
May 14 Hugh Polley & Jane Polley
June 8 Silas Peirson & Abigail More
15 Stephen Allison & Suzanah Brunson
20 * William Cooke & Mary Howell
July 28 Martin Decker & Hannah Odell
Augt 17 * John Tucker & Anna Soper
21 * Peter R. Ludlow &* Christian Beekman
Septr 3 *Thomas Bull & Sarah Gale
14 Benjamin Moore & Hannah Gillis
Octr 15 Ananias Volentine & Elizabeth Meeker
31 Caleb Goldsmith & Elizabeth McWilliams
Novr 9 Stephen Harden and Jane Ray
Goshen Novr 19 1786, Married William Oldfield & Mary Avery
22 Eleazar Fairchild & Elizabeth Weeks
26 * Jeremiah Schenkling & Hannah Reeves
Decmr 3 Isaac Coleman & Martha Smith
7 Benjamin Jennings &*Sarah Smith
Jany 2 1787 * Married John Saybolt &* Sarah Little
*Nathaniel Vail & Mary Little
11 John Dill & Martha Stott
18 * Joseph Archer &*Ann Comstock
29 David Rumsey & Abigail Monger
Feb 1 Ichabob Blackman & Elizabeth Franklin
21 John McKinstry & Sibyl Smith
22 James Bowhanon & Elizabeth Galaway
Mar 6 1787 Married Ebenezer Mills & Abigail Vail
13 * George Clark & Naney Swales
Apl 15 Samuel Bull & Margaret Gale
17 Joseph Vail & Juliana Smith
May 24 John Knap & Sarah *Sawyer
27 Joshua Brown & *Temperance Wisner
June 4 Peter Vaness & Hannah Fort, Washington County
12 David Thomas & Jane Turner, Washington County
Walter Martin & Sarah Turner, Washington County
July 19 Samuel Maypes & Luciana Cory
Augt 27 Thomas Barnea & Elizabeth Carpenter
Septr 11 David Wells & Sarah Knap
Octr 11 1787 James Jackson & Phebe Totten
25 Samuel Gardner & Hannah Owens
Novr 15 Joseph Smith & Lenah Smith
18 * Joshuah Case & Patience Van Scoit
Decmr 13 * Nathan Tuttle & Jane Brown
15 James Doyle & Deborah Meddaugh
24 Tilton Hill & Esther Cooly
26 John Carmichal & Hannah Howell
31 Terry Owen & Mary Finch

RECORD OF MARRIAGES

Moses Pauly & Millecent Vanscoit
Jany 3 1788 Married Andrew Davies & Mary Ketcham
Elisha Reeve Junr. & Phebe Saybolt
John Gold & Mary Avery
12 *Theodorus Van Wyck & Hannah Ker, by Rev. Andw King
13 Samuel Harlow & Phebe Vail
21 Vincent Clark & Patience*Stringham
24 Israel Wood & Anna Randel
26 Ezra Horton & Hannah Gardner
Feby 27 *Benjamin Hallsey &*Millicent Forgerson
Mar 5 Robert Thomson & Phebe Watkins
6 James Brewster & Mary Tuthill
John Tuthill & Fanny Brewster
Erastus Maypes & Phebe Vail
16 William Crane & Mary Couley
Mar 19th A. D 1788 Married Daniel Wilkin & Mary Stott
Apl 3 * William Faulkner & Agness McWilliams
20 Robert Dolph & Jane Jackson
29 Peter Stagg & Ruth Marston
May 1 Henry Huffman & Mary Griffin
4 Benjamin Webb & Sarah Vail
12 John Hoery & Unis Pain
June 5 William Armstrong & Keziah Finch
Constance Terry &*Hephzibah Case
*Nathaniel Conkling & Margrett Bradner
July 6 Allison Finch & Sarah Owens
13 * Nathaniel Tuthill & Abigail Smith
Augt 15 Joseph Gallaspy &*Anna Gary
Richard Garner Forgerson & Juliana Davies
Septr 25 1788 Married Peter Davies & Martha Eager
Octr 16 David Clark & Ann Bigger
19 Ephriam Hulbert & Jemima Rumsey
31 *George Trimbel & Mary McCobb
Nov 2 Alexander Wood &*Lucretia Tusteen
3 *Waight Carpenter &*Elizabeth Clark
4 Daniel Jessup &*Mary Denton
27 *John McGloughlin & Martha Hulse
Decmr 8 Daniel Mosher &Margret Randle
9 James Wisner & Elizabeth Runyen Carpenter
11 *Jacob Tears & Sunanah Puff
Benjamin Lardon & Suzanah Crance
John Tuthill & Ann More
30 Archibald McCurdy & Mary Libolt
George Fleming & Phebe Yelverton
January 8th AD 1789 Married William Mulock & Rebeckah Saybolt
10 *William Allison &*Mary Graham
11 *Chounrod Foulprouck & Abby Conly
24 Jesse Booth & Dolly Watkins
26 Moses Reed & Permela Corwine
27 John Everett & Suzannah Erwinton
29 James Eager & Arabella Bohanen
Feb 8 *David More 3rd & Marion Butlar
11 Elisha Ames & Elizabeth Crance
John Taylor & Mary Devoe
28 John Johnston &*Margret Townshend

RECORD OF MARRIAGES

Apl 16 *Enos Case & Anna Clark
26 *William Stringham &*Priscilla Carpenter
James Smith & Sarah Totten
May 3 Cornelius Vanosdol & Margarett Robinson
May 22 1789 Married Henry Tucker & Rebeckah Gale
John Boreland &*Suzannah Dier
27 Abel Gale Smith & Mary Smith
June 7 Benjamin Sawer & Hannah Wood
*Edward Handley & Unice Toppen
30 *Joel Smith & Judah Russel
July 9 Benjamin Cleveland &*Mary Gardiner
16 Benjamin Bradner & Mary Wickham
27 Coe Gale & Elizabeth Wisner
30 Abraham Vail &*Esther Rockwell
Augt 25 Peter Holbert & Rozanah Durland
Novr 1 1789 Married Norton Terry & Catharine Tents
8 Stephen Salmon &*Catherine Carr
14 Abel Watkins & Submit Reeve
Decmr 6 Jacob Denton &*Mary Wyley
12 John McCurdy & Margaret Carnagen
13 Henry Youngs & Christian Ivery
15 Robert Rogers & Mary Brown
30 Gilliam Bartolf & Jane Wood
31 Thomas Caldwell &*Elizabeth Steward
Jany 2nd AD 1790 * Married Prosper Pain & Rachel Earles
12 Edward McHenry & Sarah Stott
21 Samuel Watkins Junr & Mary Booth
28 Absolon Vail & Keziah Kinner
Feb 4 Richard Clark &*Lydia Totten
6 Robert Thomson Junr & Agnis Lyby
8 *Hamilton Morrison & Lydia Bemer
9 Benjamin Goldsmith & Elizabeth Jackson
17 Jesse Jennings & Elizabeth Curtice
28 William Thomson Wood & Margrett Smith
Mar 7 William Roe & Phebe Thomson
Ananias Whitman & Esther Smith
10 Phinehas Osbourn & Abigail Copse
11 Caleb Smith & Anna Gale
March 11 1790 Married David Riker Oliver & Phebe Vail
20 William Stringham Sarah Carpenter
Apl 6 Samuel Belknap   Mary Goldsmith
9 *James Horton &*Abigail Tuthill
26 *Nathaniel Harrison &*Mary Allison
May 2 Curtice Drake & Jemimah Pain
10 Benjamin Smith &*Eleoner Dunning
June 3 Richard Popyno & Hannah Jackson
17 Samuel Drake & Unice Carpenter
20 *Ebenezer Cutter & Chatharine McGloughlin
Octr 20 Simon Hosack &* Catharine Ker by Rev. Mr. King
Novr 4 James Buchanan & Martha Eager
11 Levi Terwillager & Hannah Johnson
Novr 17 1790 Married Allexander Forguson & Anna Rice
21 Samuel Brunson & Sarah Crane
Decmr 5 Benjamin Tuthill & Ruth Knap
14 John Mellony & Rachel Hart

RECORD OF MARRIAGES

16 Peter Milspaugh & Mary Berkley
21 Frederick Smith & Hannah Niver
Jany 6 1791 John Weed & Rhodana Anderson By Rev. Simon Hosack
Jany 11 AD 1791 Married David Miller & Anna Wilkins
13 *John Ingram & Christien Horse
19 *John Wood &*Hannah Carpenter
Feb 7 Isaac Thompson &*Sarah Bradner
24 Samuel Mott & Sarah Waugh
25 James Harrington & Mary Cory
26 William Macclure & Sarah Farnam
March 5 *Andrew Johnes & Sarah Denton
15 Benjamin Simons & Isabel McWilliam
24 James Campbell &*Azuba Reed
27 John Jarvis & Doreas, neagroes
31 *Obediah Howell & Julianah Everett
Apl 2 Richard Wood & Mary Conkling
7 Wilmot More and Azuba Knap
Apl 21st 1791 Married Henry Weller &*Letty Thomson
30 George Phillipes & Mary Wells
June 9 Salmon Wheat & Hannah Maypes
19 Daniel a negro of Samuel Gale & Bathina a negro woman of Jacob Decay
July 2 Henry Wells &*Mary Hulse
14 Robert Bell & Nancy Roy
Augt 7 David Hammon & Catherine Johnson
9 *John Bran & Rachel Thacker
15 *Roger MacDaniel   Margrett Burns
16 Samuel Doty & Hannah Storm
Septr 3 Jonathan Owen & Johannah Wood
Octr 22 Thomas Moffatt Clark &*Rebekah Carpenter
Octobr 24 AD 1791 *Married Samuel Bouton & Lucy Tracy
25 *Dan'l Osborn & Catharine Saybolt
29 James Finch & Hester Vail
Novr 1 Hanes Bartlet & Hannah Couley
8 Selah Arnout & Prudence Knight
Decemr 22 Benjamin Crane &*Assenath Pellet
31 *John Gale & Abigail Bradner
Jany 5 1792 Married Edward Eager & Susanah Milegan Barker
7 Peter McInnes & Phebe Maypes
8 Silas Moon & Sarah McCormick
12 Andrew Walker &*Sybilla Couly
15 John Gilbert Burtis & Abigail Arnout
Feb 16 Wilmott Halstead &*Deborah Nealy
26 Nathaniel Tuthill &*Martha Wickham
Mar 4 James Penney & Mary Osbourn
8 Benjamin Rogers & Elizabeth Puff
15 John White & Effy Brown
Apl 15 Isaac Hangan & Leah Galloway
22 Isaac Johnson & Jane Howell
25 Francis Courtney & Sarah Mott
May 28 *Elisha Comstock & Asenath Reed
31 Elijah McMun & Ann Eager
June 7 AD 1792 Married Henry Redner & Caty Persal
10 Isaac Smith Junr. & Elizabeth Davies
11 *John Galaspsy & Martha Crawford
14 John Linderman & Margrett Puff

23 John Henry & Huldah Mansor
28 David Patten & Rachel Henry
July 7 John Smith & Suzanah Smith
15 Joshua Rapalya & Keziah Finch
Augt 28 *James McBride & Sarah Eager
Septr 8 John Van Lever & Mary Shaw
11 Joseph Belknap & Sarah Clement
13 *Thomas Cunningham & Jane McCormick
23 Daniel Seward & Juliana Rumsey
24 John Jackson & Mathetable Terry
Octr 6 *William Blosdoll & Mary Tucker
21 John Smith &*Lydia More
Oct 27 1792 Married Theophilus Howell & Hannah Denton
30 Allexander Murray & Abigail Tryon
Novr 17 Jonathan Bennett & Abigail Smith
Decmr 31 William Burns & Martha McHugh
Aprl 6 1793 *Married Charles Conner & Agness Gilchrist
May 18 John Totten & Lydia Jack
Jesse Crocker & Fanny Decay
20 Jonathan Burrill &* Frances Wickham
26 Joseph Conkling & Ellienor Vail
June 20 *George Barkley &*Jane Crawford
30 George Galloway & Rebekah Hizar
July 2 Israel Wickham & Mary More
Augt 17 Hugh Lindsey & Dorothy Booth
18 Oliver Hawkins & Elizabeth McCormick
24 Cadwallader Bull & Submit Watkins
Septr 25 Daniel Snyder & Mary Bennet
26 Nathaniel Boyd & Judah Stott
Octr 21 Samuel Vail &*Hilah Gale
Decmr 2 1793 Married Benjamin Garey & Sarah Gellispy
23 Rev. Jonathan Freeman & Margaret Clark Ker
January 12 1794 Married David More, Junr & Abigail McCain
Feb 4 *Richard Coleman & Hannah Sweet
8 Charley Jeffry Smith & Mary Coddington
22 *John Cook & Hannah Vail
26 Gilbert Terry & Temperance Baily
Mar 1 Jason Eager & Jane Taylor
15 James Potter & Elizabeth Gerrey
Apr 5 Henry B Wisner & Ruth Carpenter
10 Joseph Beatey & Mary Smiley
12 Richard Jackson & Mary Jackson
19 Henry Wisner Denton & Juliana Dunning
26 John Miller &*Ellioner Smith
May 24 1794 *Married Andrew Weller & Anna Stott
John Knap & Unice Smith
June 9 William Bennett & Jane Feltman
15 George McClintock & Mary Nickolson
21 Francis Berger & Jane Kimble
July 8 George Arnout &*Mary Camble
15 *John Conkling & Elizabeth Jackson
31 James Johnson & Jemimah Stagg
Augt 30 William Tuthill & Anna Terry
Septr 4 Joseph Case & Elizabeth McCord
Novemr 5 Benjamin ClareWater & Mary Young

RECORD OF MARRIAGES

Decmr 4 *William Baird & Elizabeth Vail
6 Robert Townsend & Susanah Seely
Decembr 9 1794 Married James Baily & Phebe Wood
11 James Husten &*Abigail McNeal
John French &*Mary Scoit
13 Jonathan Drake & Mary Shonch
23 Ezra Smith & Diantha Farris
January 13th A.D 1795 Married Peter Bloom & Elizabeth Prindel
24 *Daniel Thorn & Mary Johnes
Feb 18 *Joseph Rose & Elizabeth Dunning
22 Stewart Garry & Miriam Lee
Apl 25 George Bucannan & Sarah Eldred
Samuel Barclay &*Esther Van Keuren
Augt 22 Joshua Roe & Hannah Cook
Septr 4 William Bache & Christian Eliza Cooper
Octr 3 Thomas Sooden & Juliana Budd
8 David Ayres & Jane Savage
16 John McNeal & Patience Gooldsmith
Novr 4 1795 *Married David Edmonson & Margarett Dunning
7 Zechariah Youngs &*Mary Caldwell
Jany 10 1796 Married Thomas Tuthill & Mary Cooper
30 Henry Savage & Rachel Reed
Cornelius Decker &*Hannah Duryea
31 Peter Hammon & Elioner McCarty
Feby 8 William Hays & Margeret McHanney
Mar 28 Hezekiah Freedinburgh & Mary Smith
Apl 7 *John Harlow &*Sarah Webb
12 Frederick Horton & Elizabeth Reed
16 William Maurice Thompson &*Sarah Gale
May 14 Joseph Totten & Mary Medaugh
28 William Morrison & Affai Crane
June 4 *Stephen Lynch & Fanny Jackson
July 10 Isaac Smith & Elizabeth Day
Septr 1 1796 Married Charles Smith & Hannah Sayre
10 John Finch & Phebe Ozbourn
Octr 29 Peter A Terwilliger & Mary Decker
Novr 29 Saml Dunning & *Easter Eager
Decemr 15 Abraham Dunning & Elizabeth Conkling
16 John Budd Horton & Hannah Webb
January 7th 1797 Married Enos Case &*Christian Dekay
9 William Rayney & Martha Caldwell
Feby 12 * Revd. John Joline & Mary Gale
19 Joseph Conkling & Helen Conkling
23 Daniel W. Sackrider & Dorothy Gale
Mar 6 James Neely & Elizabeth Carpenter
13 Benjain S Carpenter & Catherine Solomon
Apl 11 Silas Wood & Elioner Hanyan
May 21 John Nicoli & Hannah Albertson
22 John McCarthy & Elizabeth Ker married by Rev. Andrew King
30 Joshuah Tuthill & Catherine Smith
Sept 2 * Nehemiah Denton & Louis Carpenter
Novemr 20th AD 1797 Married Wate Smith & Rachel Butler
28 * Nathaniel Wells & Abigail Wickham
Decemr 6 James Brown & Elizabeth Dunning
9 * Obediah Pellett & Mary Crane
Feby 20th AD 1798 Married Jonathan Estill & Elizabeth Gallespy

RECORD OF MARRIAGES

Mar 3 Isaac Williams & Rebeckah Rodgers
May 6 * John D Willoughby & Mary Hoffman
June 5 John Savage &*Martha McNeal
12 John Dicky & Servia Stanbraugh
July 11 Henry Smith & Alletta Lewis
28 Abimel Youngs & Mary Harlow
Augt 25 John Wells & Sarah Everett
Sept 9 * Nathaniel Bayley & Bathia Tryon
Novr 3 Jesse Belknap & Sussanah Eldred
4 Simeon Wood & Charity Hulse
Novr 10 1798 Married Benjamin Howell &*Elioner Webb
*Everet Eldred & Mary Denton
John Carpenter & Sarah Nobel
22 John Bodle & Deziah Palmer
January 15th 1799 Married William Thom &*Sarah Wisner
19 John Brewster &*Mary Harrison
Abel Birdseye Watkins & Hannah Harlow
Feb 2 Amos Gates White &*Abigail Marvin
13 Hugh Gauly & Margaret Sincebaugh
23 Peter Milspaugh & Hilah Duryea
Mar 3 Christopher Vanorsdol & Margarett Campble
9 Asa Jennings & Elioner Thomson
18 Thomas Carmer & Mary Gale
May 25 Daniel Fullerton & Anna Bull
June 1 Allexander Brown & Mary Milspaugh
July 13 Francis Drake & Hannah Dekay

Thus far examined & approved.
By order of the Presby.
John Joline, Moderator

Octr 22nd 1799 Married Nathaniel Row , Esq & Mary L'Homideau
Novr 5 * David Southerland & Mary Dunning
Decmr 28 * Phinehas Redding & Juliana Cory
Feby 1st 1800 Married George Williams & Bathia Conkling
15 John Gale Junr. &* Fanny Dunning
18 Isaac McNeal & Anna Mandevill
Mar 4 William Conner &* Sarah Roe
Apl 12 Richard Bull & Sarah Harlow
May 3 David Webb & Fanny Smith
17 * Moses Utter & Elizabeth Brundage
June 18 Jared Mosier & Sarah Smith
28 Stephen Goldsmith & Deborah Vail
Augt 12 * Jacob Dewitt Rose & Elizabeth Butler
Septr 13 1800 Married William Goorley & Susannah Bodel
23 John Thursteen Wood & Catherine Seely
Decemr 6 Stephen Jackson & Abigail Denton Jackson
Jany 5 1801 Married Freegift Tuthill & Elizabeth Swezy
8 Joseph Wilkin & Elizabeth Moffat
31 William Bodle & Hannah Smith
Feby 7 Reuben Moore & Margaret Hosier
10 Joshua Wells &* Jemima Sayre
Apl 25 * Daniel Wells & Abigail Wickham
Augt 29 Manuel Smelliger &*Juliana Ploughman
Septr 29 George Carr & Sarah Owen
Novr 23 Richard Graham & Ann Moffat
Decemr 19 Timothy Wood & Dorothy Carpenter

RECORD OF MARRIAGES

Jany 14 1802 * Married Archibald Strain &* Hannah McNeal
Feby 3 Archibald Sayre & Martha Sayre
6 Jackson McCord & Sarah McClear
13 William Foster & Phebe Pain
Mar 2 Ieronimus Johnson & Mary Carpenter
6 Joseph Holly & Huldah Benjamin
13 Michael (A) Jones & Mary Everett
Apl 17 Stephen Marvin & Martha Duryea
James Lewis & Jane Denton
May 19 Joshua Green & Jane Cunningham
20 Richard Merrill & Margaret Boreland
Ju y 31 1802 Married Thomas Thorn & Mary Seely
Augt 15 David Webb & Suzannah Moffitt
21 * Henry Jackson & Elizabeth Conkling
Septr 4 Samuel Jackson & Sarah Moore
Ebenezer Augur & Elizabeth Southerlin
11 James Jones& Abigail Clark
28 William Buckle & Sarah Dunning
Decemr 4 James Clearman & Elleoner Higby
13 William Wilson & Margaret Rogers
18 Jonathan Swezy & Elizabeth Griffen
1803 Jany 15 Married James Vanduser & Elizabeth Smith
29 Peter Lish & Mary Lyon
John Barker & Prissylla Smith
Feb 5 William McCoy & Abigail Holley
Mar 5 * Dan Hartheway& Sarah Jackson
8 William Popyno & Hannah Foster
May 11 William Sidway & Elizabeth Dains
Jun 4 Elisha Smith &*Dolly Boreland
28 Samuel Hull & Adelaide Hopkins
July 28 John Slowwater & Lueia Youngs
Augt 24 Samuel Millar & Hannah Meeker
Septr 3 Robert Smith & Esther Beach
Septr 13 1803 Married William Henry Welsh & Temperance Helm
Novr 28 Robert Moore Potter & Sarah Wycoff
January 12th 1804 Married Andrew Wood & Julia Popyno
29 Samuel Hunt &Abigail Jackson
Feby 4 Michael Allison Elmer & Eliza Allison
18 Obediah Tibbits & Margaret DeKay
Mar 13 James Carpenter & Juliana Owens
Apl 7 Peter Gale & Juliana L'Homideu
May 5 *David Conger & Abigail Smith
June 2 Edward Hulse & Elizabeth Tucker
14 Enos Smith & Phebe House
July 14 James Seely & Sarah Townsend
1804 Septr 11 Married James Steward Arnout & Julia Terry
Hezekiah Watkins & Elizabeth Sayre
23 John Clark & Ida Mosier
Octr 20 John Whitney & Susannah Smith
Nvr 11 Samuel Holmes & Jane Absley

> The Revd Nathan Ker died, who married all the persons mentioned in the foregoing pages and no record of Marriages in this Congregation was kept until the Revd Isaac Lewis was installed Pastor who married the following persons.

RECORD OF MARRIAGES

Rev. Isaac Lewis was installed pastor of this Church Jany 1st, 1806
1805 December 10th Andrew Morrison & Mary McClare
1806 Jany 16 Benjamin Everett & Letty Faulkner
23 Daniel Case & Julia Knight
25 Zarah Taylor & Nancy Rogers
27 Archibald Smith & Abigail Sayres
March 22 John Owens & Mary Goldsmith
April 3 Charles Tredwell & Jemimah Quick
9 Anthony Dobbins & Nancy Board
May 17 Samuel S. Seely & Rebecka Hopkins
24 Joshua Wells Wood & Eleanor Brown
June 25 James Gale & Elsa Wood
July 31 Isaac Reeves & Abigail Tusten
August 28 Peter Quick & Phebe Sprought
Sept 6 Isaac Ludlum & Anna Pierson
11 Patrick McBride & Elizabeth Toulon
20 Henry Johnson & Sally Little
21 Thomas Lewis & Elizabeth Patten
Oct 4 Jonathan Jackson & Mary McCorkey
Nvr 1 Joseph Wickham & Amelia Carpenter
Decr 3 Joshua Crosby & Mary Salmon
6 Asa Jennings & Hannah Thompson
6 William Lewis & Helen Case
11 Thomas W. Goble & Maria Green
13 John W. Birdsley & Elizabeth Tuthill
13 Lewis Hall & Mary Corey
20 Frederick Dolsen & Margaret Moore
27 Andrew Noble & Eleanor McLaughlin
1807 Jany 3 Abijah Dunning & Nancy Smelliger
3 William Hinchman & Sarah Crowell
21 Samuel G. Lewis & Mary Young
24 Nathan Wheeler & Christian Miller
31 Gilbert Horton & Sally White
March 5 John Boyd & Eleanor Adams
June 6 Stephen Jayne & Sally Marvin

1806 July 5 Peter Servt of Wm Wickham Esq. & Peggy
    servant of Revd Isaac Lewis
1807 Jany 10 Zadock servant of William Hudson & Amy
    servant of Phinehas Rumsey

July 25 1807 Jabez Mitchell & Phebe Springer
Sept 3 Cornelius Quick & Margaret Sprought
26 John A Smith & Abigail Foster
30 John Roe & Julia Armstrong
Oct 17 William Willson & Elizabeth Moore
Nov 14 Barna Horton & Anna Hawkins
14 James Turner & Lydia Sodon
18 Lina Birdsley & Mary Gardner
28 Horace Elmer & Susan Steward
Decr 5 Daniel Foster & Sally Newton
8 William McPherson & Nancy Willson
11 Ambrose Jones & Hannah Gale
11 Jacob Vanderhoof & Sally Holly
24 Samuel Buckbee & Nancy Roy
1808 Feb 13 Joseph Brown & Anna Wood

RECORD OF MARRIAGES

20 Richard A Holly & Lydia Kortright
March 2 William A Smith & Eunice Howell
5 David Dunning & Margaret Lusk
6 William Brewster & Hannah Salmon
12 William Taylor & Margaret Jackson
April 30 James Wood & Charlotte Dunning
May 2 Col. John Cowdrey & Christian Thompson
June 18 William Vanduzer & Sally Maria Wheeler
21 Benjamin Smith & Sarah Bull
July 7 John Coleman & Letty Thew
16 Michael Jackson & Annis Foster
Oct 5 Dr John De Normandie Gillespy & Susan Bedford
Novr 5 William Stephens & Frances Baldwin
19 Robert Blakely & Anna Lusk
20 Simon Yonker & Jemimah Horton
Decr 24 Stephen Valentine & Elizabeth Knapp
24 Daniel Carpenter & Sarah Thompson
31 Jacob Tears & Jane Graham

1807 Decr 26 Daniel Servt. of Joseph Wood to Marget Servt of A Hetfield
1808 Jany 30 Oliver Servt of Jno. G. Hurtin to Matilda a free woman
Sept 24 Peter Servt of John Duer to Mary Servt of Joseph Wood
Decr 24 Dick Servt of Daniel Seward to Debby Serv B. Bradner

February 8th 1809 Joel Wheeler & Elizabeth Rogers
15 David Watkins & Julia Conkling
March 15 James Robinson & Ruth Conkling
25 George Hamilton Jackson & Elizabeth Sawyer
April 5 Nathaniel Carpenter & Phila Coleman
15 Benjamin Wood & Avis Harding
15 Thomas Mills & Deborah Ball
May 13 Enoch Reeves & Ila Brown
28 James McGee & Mrs. Mary Smith
June 3 Thomas Denton & Elizabeth Sodon
Joseph McCollum & Elizabeth Haslett
Aug 5 John L' Hommidieu & Dolly Vail
Sept 2 John Horton & Katy Salmon
16 James Howell & Ann Thompson
17 Rumsey Mapes & Mary Rumsey
30 Benjamin Vanduzer & Elmira Tooker
Oct 14 Jonas Satterly & Betsey Hetfield
28 John Gregg & Margeret Conkling
Dec 16 Thomas Bull & Hannah Smith
30 Jason W. Rogers & Hannah Bull
1810 Jany 25 Edward Ely Esq. & Dolly Wells
Feby 22 Vincent Strong & Hester Rose
March 24 Nathaniel Tuthill & Mary Bodle
24 Peter Plowman & Julia Coleman
April 7 Benjamin Crane & Sally Lusk
May 24 John Decker & Christian Wells
August 2 Thomas Goldsmith & Catharine Gale

1810
Feby 3 Charles Servt of Geo D Wickham & Jane servant of James Watkins
7 Peter servant of Solomon Carpenter & Lucy servant of Joseph Denton

RECORD OF MARRIAGES

March 17 Ellick servant of Henry Denton & Judah servant of John Stewart Esq.
17 James servant of Maj John Wood & Dinah servant of Dr. David R Arnell

January 19th 1811 Daniel Payne & Mary Valentine
24 William Sayre & Martha Jackson
Feby 7 Gabriel Goldsmith & Christian Coleman
March 9 George Smith & Harriett Smith
21 David Case & Julander Case
June 5 William Carr & Anna Moffatt
July 20 William Mapes & Phebe Plowman
Aug 31 Youngs Bull & Rebeckah Laroe
Sept 11 Phillip Geatty & Mary Moore
19 Lewis Roe & Sarah King
Oct 3 Samuel McElroy & Esther Porter
10 Joshua Burnham & Phebe Bodle
Nov 16 Samuel Lane & Charlotte Case
23 Peter M. Bull & Jane Bull
Decr 17 Asa Dunning & Hetty Kelsey.
19 John Eager & Della Case
1812 Jany 2 Oliver Thompson & Sally Mathews
11 William Case & Jane Houston
29 Grant Smith & Miriam Smith
Feby 8 John M. Satterly & Frances Barker
29 Robert Boak & Mary Eldred
March 28 John Jackson & Julia Armstrong
April 25 George Moore & Maria Dunning
June 11 Dr. David Hanford & Margaret Bailey
July 11 Dr Eusebius Austin & Mary Joline

1811
June 3 Jonathan Hoglan & Rechel Bags
Sept 8 Prince, Servant of Benjamin Strong Esq & Rachel, Servant of Joseph Denton
21 John Bartholf & Nancy Cable

The Revd Isaac Lewis was dismissed from his pastoral relations to the Congregation of Goshen July 12 1812 and no record of Marriages kept untill September 1813 when the Revd Ezra Fisk took the pastoral charge of the Congregation, who married the following persons.

September 4th 1813 Thomas Gale & Juliana Moore
Oct 11 Gilbert Hopkins & Mary Smith
16 Nathaniel Conkling & Deborah Young
16 William Townsend & Azuba Vail
Nov 4 Festus Dunning & Mary Elliott
18 Benjamin W. Case & Polly Salmon
27 Jonathan Swezy White & Dolly Swezy
Dec 11 John Ludlum & Ila Pierson
18 Thomas Miller & Abigail Conger
18 Coe Smith & Susan Howell
23 Walter T. Miller & Eliza Drake
30 Joshua Smith & Sarah Smith
1814 Jany 20 William H. Reeder & Mary Smith
20 James Tuthill & Sarah Wells
Feby 3 Giles Goodrick & Sarah Ball

RECORD OF MARRIAGES

5 Barna Horton & Sarah Hawkins
March 2 Dr Joseph R. Andrews & Julia Clark
3 Epinetus H Jackson & Harriett Mills
22 Epinetus Howell & Fanny Coleman
April 2 John Johnson & Orpha Little
14 William Otis & Clarissa Gale
Aug 6 Silas Insign & Julia White
Sept 23 Silas Hawkins & Mary Harlow
25 John McDonald & Abby Whitney
Nvr 5 Horace Carpenter & Mehitable Graham
24 Richard S Horton & Kezia Valentine
24 John Bailey & Margaret Crabtree
Dec 22 Benjamin Bull & Eliza Wade
February 4th 1815 David Farrand & Nancy Kitchell
22 Gilbert B. Jackson & Olivia Skellinger
March 2 Allen Wilmot & Maria Pierson
April 15 John Cunningham & Phebe Maria Hetfield
May 13 John Budd Junr. & Frances Ball
June 3 George Luckey & Sally Hutchins
July 22 James Horton & Mary Clason
Aug 5 Peter Higby & Julia Cleves
Septr 12 Joel Coleman & Sally Harlow
Oct 3 Asa Dunning & Mary Kelsey
Feby 6 1816 Thomas W. Bradner & Susan Smith
10 Elijah Knapp & Polly Lewis
10 Harry Gale & Wid. Phebe McKoy
17 Calvin Wade & Melinda Moore
March 7 Thomas Ogden Kelsey & Jane Dunning
April 22 John Rodgers & Hester Smith
June 8 Samuel Hulse & Mary Smith
July 18 Samuel Jones Wilkin & Sarah G. Westcott
Aug 10 David Barnum & Jane Sodon
16 Jesse Marvin & Olivia Brewster

Jany 29 1814 Sam, Sevrt. of the Revd Ezra Fish to Patience servant of Benjamin Strong Esq.
June 18 Morris Van Horn, Servant of Thos. Waters Esq to Jane Dill, free woman
July 30 1815 Phillip Servant of John Crane to Mary Servant of Thos. Water Esq.
Feby 2 1816 Peter Servant of Gilbert B Jackson to Juda a free woman
10 Morris, Servant of Joseph Wood, Junr. to Juda Servant of Geo. D. Wickham
17 Joe, Servant of Richard Jackson to Hester, Servant of Freegift Tuthill

---

No Record of Marriages Kept for 3 months during the absence of the Revd. Mr. Fisk on a journey to Georgia.
January 2nd 1817 Doctr. Egbert Jansen & Frances Carpenter
16 Gilbert B Gale & Maria Gale
17 Morris Barker & Betsey Crabtree
Feby 6 John Budd & Widow Elizab'th Smith
8 William McBride & Elsa Eager
27 Jonathan Bodle & Eliza Taylor
March 6 Benjamin G Smith & Mary Gale
11 William Noble & Mehitable Jessup
April 12 Eleazer Hudson & Elizabeth Connor

RECORD OF MARRIAGES

19 Isaac Banker & Sarah Denton
June 5 Samuel Reynolds & Florinda Hanehett
7 Adin McVey & Harriet Tuthill
14 James Denton & Martha Lewis
July 16 Moses D. Bennett & Margaret Barber
Sep 16 Benjamin Gildersleeve & Sarah Elliott
Oct 30 Abraham Vail & Harriet Coleman
Wheeler Case & Elizabeth Wilkin
Nov 13 David Hammond & Amelia Kitchel
20 Uzal Harrison Wade & Rebeca Monnell
Dec 9 Gabriel Dunning & Keziah Case
11 William Everett & Cornelia Townsend
24 Jabez Knapp & Clarissa Drake
30 James D Wilkin & Clarrissa Jones
Jan 24 1818 Benjamin Hawkins & Melinda Knapp
Feb 5 Joseph W. Tuthill & Catherine Denton
19 Walter B. Strong & Frances Bradner
March 28 Hirman Ackley & Peggy Case
April 9 John A. Smith & Jane Bull
May 23 Hamilton Morrison & Maria Miller
Oct 8 J. Cooper Reeve & Hannah Watkins
10 Samuel Wiggins & Nancy Horton
Nov 26 Theodorus Denton & Elizabeth Denton
28 John Price & Julia Conner

Jany 25 1817 Charles Jarvis, a Freeman to Hannah Phillips a free woman of colour
June 21 John Stephens & Betsey Peterson
Oct 7 Benjamin Wright & Maria Cortland
June 20 1818 Isaac Cortland,free & Rosanna,servt. of James Everett Esq.
Sept 1 Ephriam Sert. of Jonah Decker & Rebeca Warner, free.
Oct 4 Andrew servt of D. Tooker & Maria servt of Judge Steward

---

Dec 22 1818 John Heros Tuthill & Sarah Youngs
29 Colvin Bradner & Sarah Denton
Jan 3 1819 Samuel Wright & Dolly Connor
21 Jacob Vail & Hila Ann Smith
Calvin G. Sawyer & Hannah Valentine
27 Stephen Clark & Prissilla Smith
28 Anthony D. Jones & Dolly Smith
Feb 18 Benjamin Lusk & Martha Laughlin
Nathan H. Corwin & Olive B. Case
May 8 Jesse Rhodes & Maria Bennet
June 26 John Haynes & Sally Miller
Oct 26 David Sans & Sally Maria Booth
Dec 13 Abner Clark & Mary Lewis
18 George Evertson & Lois Salmon
23 Stephen Smith & Hannah Gardner
1820 Augt 9 John Wells & Mary Ann Eldred
Nov 19 Gabriel Thompson & Ruth Wood
Dec 6 Hezekiah Watkins & Saly Ann Seely
27 Thophilus Arnout & Mary Ann Phillips
1821 Jan 31 William R. Gale & Cynthia Moore
Feb 8 John Boak & Julia Arnout
15 Ira Coleman & Emily Dunning
April 7 Charles Chandler & Catherine Pool (Montgomery)

RECORD OF MARRIAGES

May 2 John Everett & Hannah Jones
12 Richard Adams & Letitia Griffin — (Fishkill)
17 Ira Hawkins & Hannah Vail
June 9 James Watson & Ruth Smith
Augt 18 Henry Bugsby & Sarah McVey
Oct 27 Selah S Goble & Jane Neely
Nov 9 John Egbert & Abigail Drake

July 19 1819 Caesar Servt of G. D. Wilkham & Tamer Servt of Coe Smith
Jan 22 1820 Charles Call free man of Color & Peggy Decker, free woman of color
Dec 15 Samuel Cable & Silvia Dobbins, free.
Feb 15 1821 Thomas Brown & Lydia Clinton, free
July 14 James Brown & Rosanna Ouerman
Dec 6 David Dean & Amanda Crane, free.

1822 Jan 1 John Manny & Jane Johnson
3 William Bradner & Frances E. Wood
3 Wilmot Willis & Mary A. Wood
24 Stephen Millspaugh & Wid. Maria Cunningham
29 Oliver Teller & Juliet Braustead
March 12 William W. Caldwell & Elizabeth Ward
April 11 Abel Gale Smith & Cornelia Tusten
11 Benjamin Strong Jur. & Frances Smith
17 John J Ross & Mary Reynolds
18 John Sears Crane & Sarah Smith
25 Hannibal M. Hopkins & Mary Steward
May 15 Ellis Strong & Mary Jackson
16 William Arnout & Rebecca Hill
June 11 Thomas Boak & Sheba Ann Dunning
26 Eli Starr Benedict & Mary Egbert
July 30 John McVey & Catherine Case
Sep 12 Gilbert Budd & Charity Davis
Nov 5 James J. Craig & Harriet Phillips
Dec 9 John Smith & Ann Dougherty
19 Stephen Smith, Jr. & Matilda Wood
21 Andrew Webb & Julia Edsall
Jan 19 1823 Aaron Gleason & Fanny William, (Bathary, Penn.)
22 Robert Finn & Mary W. Taylor
28 Horace Tittyball & Hannah Cory
30 Moses Sawyer & Elizabeth Valentine
Feb 6 Richardson Hayes & Hannah Edsall
27 Gabriel Jackson & Nancy Conkling
March 8 James Gardner & Adeline Popino
13 Hiram Vail & Phebe Gardner
April 3 Solomon C Wood & Susan McKoy
7 William H. Wiggins & Catherine Lewis
June 4 Galen Terry & Eunice Youngs
11 John Wallace & Elizabeth Denton
Augt 6 Alfred S. Benton & Emily Jackson
Sept 11 James Norris & Phebe Good

Oct 12 1822 Jeffrey Green & Hannah Servt. Joshua Goldsmith
June 21 1823 Robert Heard & Peggy Tuthill
July 26 Stephen Hathorn & Mary Fields.

RECORD OF MARRIAGES

Sep 20 1823 Hudson L'Hommidieu & Julia Ann Vail
Jan 21 1824 Jonathan Hudson& Sarah Reeve
22 Hector Seward & Phebe Smith
Feb. 7 Jared Connor & Caroline McChord
March 11 Jonathan Davy & Mehitable Whitman
May 1 Lockwood Barnum & Thania Lockyer
10 Asa Dunning &Sarah Kelsey
29 Anthony Wood & Elizabeth Sawyer
31 William Jackson & Mary Tuthill
June 19 Lewis H. Hobby & Lucretia Vanduzer
Dec 15 Samuel Hawkins & Emeline Webb
16 Daniel C. Owen & Juliann Hulse
19 Hezekiah Hoyt & Rachel D.Southerland
Jan 19 1825 Milton McVey & Margaret Smelliger
Feb 9 James Brown & Fanny Corey
April 21 Sidney S. Fitzgerald & Hannah Conkling
June 11 John Ploughman & Eliza Estell
11 Archibold B Bodle & Eliza Smith
14 Jonathan B Dunning & Hannah Vail
Nov 2 Hezekiah Denton & Christiana Ludlum
29 William Robinson & Catherine Barker
Dec 20 John Moore & Maria Corey
24 John Barnes & Mary Ploughman
29 Henry J. Smith & Emily Rumsey
Feb 15 1826 Samuel Dusenbury & Jane Barker
March 23 Noah Gregory & Sally Maria Smith
May 4 George Stevens & Julia Vail
June 5 Zechariah N. Hoffman & Elizbeth Elliott
Sep 14 Jacob Crosby & Maria Case
20 William Dusenbury & Adeline Bodle
Nov 7 Henry Barker & Antoniette Drake
Dec 12 Daniel Hull Tuthill & Caroline Wilkin
14 William Hawkins & Elizabeth Hawkins
14 Ebenezer Seely & Maria Bradner

1824 April 10 Henry Smith & Hannah Bays, free
1827 July 5 Edward Holmes & Jane Elizabeth Bartholf, free.

Dec 21 1826 Oliver Budd & Milicent Ball
Jan 4 1827 Jonah Cooper & Emily Drake
March 27 Hudson Webb & Parmelia Ingersol
April 5 Jesse Holbert & Maria R. Whitman
10 Jeremiah D. Kelsey & Jane Hathaway
11 Henry Smith & Keturah Thompson
May 5 Hiram Smith & Sally Jane Bull, By Rev George Stebbins
June 14 John Summers & Sarah Elizabeth Butler
14 John Tompkins & Orphia McInnis
28 Obadiah Rumsey of Bloomingrove & Mary Saveny of New Windsor
Augt 8 Samuel Matthews & Fanny Fields
Oct 6 William Smiley & Christiana Smith
Nov 17 Benjamin Decker & Adeline Hill
Dec 31 Rev. Robert Roy of Warwick & Sarah Trimble of Minisink
Jan 16 1828 Jonathan Smith & Caroline Horton
Feb 7 John Jefferson Lusk & Letitia Hetfield
28 Samuel Owen & Elizabeth Goldsmith
April 23 Charles Doolittle & Maria Wade

RECORD OF MARRIAGES

July 17 Chauncy H. Smith & Rachael Egbert
Augt 28 Isaack P. Odle & Sally Dunn
Sep. 7 Constantine Conoly & Rachael McLaughlin
13 Hiram Burdsiel & Sally Tallmay
Oct 4 Elijah Broadman of New York City & Hannah Upson of Lexington, Georgia.
16 Hector C. Smith & Harriet Crabtree
21 George M. Newman & Sarah Rumsey
30 Daniel Brush & Clarissa Sturge
Nov 12 Horace Vail & Ann Joline Thompson
26 John Payne & Deby Ann Watkins
Dec 11 Daniel H. Keeler & Jenet Horton
18 Henry Moore & Caroline Foster
Jany 15 1829 Bradner Popino & Francis Goldsmith
27 Dr. Lewis Dunning & Sarah Jackson
April 30 Moses Webb & Mary Gale
May 7 William Barker & Elizabeth Seward
June 4 Benjamin Coulter of Cornwall & Wid. Ann Drake of Legrange, Wallkill.
June 24 1829 David W. Hoyt & Jane Kitchel
Jul 18 John M. Gillispie & Harriet Fisk
Nov 4 William Roe & Mary McLaughlin
Nov 19 Edward Mapes & Deborah Ann Wood
Dec 17 Gabriel Bennett & Mary Ann Jones
Jan 18 1830 Franklin Reeve & Mary Moore
19 Phineas Rumsey & Eliza Duryea
March 4 John D. Miller & Clarrissa Goble

REGISTER OF MARRIAGES ACCORDING TO THE REVISED STATUTES

NEW YORK

Dec 31 1829 John McLaughry & Rosetta Smith, free persons of color
Feb 11 1830 Hiram Thompson aged 19 & Amy Jennings aged 22, Witnesses John Wallace & Pierson Wilson
Jan. 18 1830 Franklin Reeve, Marlboro, Ulster Co. N. Y. age 25, manufactor &Mary Moore, Bloomingrove, Orange Co N. Y., 27 seamtress, proved by Joseph Brooks & Jon Moore, Bloomingrove O.Co N Y
Jn 19 Phineas Rumsey, Goshen, O. C. N. Y. 22, farmer, & Eliza Duryea, Bloomingrove, 21 daugh. Henry Duryea, farm. personally known, witnesses Henry Seward& Virgil Seward, Goshen, OCN. Y
Feb. 11 Hiram Thompson, Goshen Orange County, N. Y. 19, laborer, & Amy Jennings Goshen Orange County, N. Y., 22, spinster, personally known, witnesses John Wallace & Prime Wilson, Goshen, O. C. N. Y. (Colored persons)
March 4 John D. Miller, Blooming Grove, 25 farmer, proved by Levi Van Cleft & Clarrissa Goble, Goshen, O. C. N. Y. 22, Mantau maker, known, witnesses, Levi Vancleft, Henry Pearson, Blooming Grove, O. C. N. Y.
March 11 Thomas J. Whitman, Goshen Orange, 29, farmer, &Martha Conkling, 30, dau. Joseph Conkling, far. personally known, witnesses, Jesse Holley & Daniel Conkling, Goshen, O. C., N. Y.

RECORD OF MARRIAGES

May 1 Hamilton Dunning, Montgomery, mason & Sarah McChord, Wallkill Orange Co, lawful age, spinster, personally known, Dr. Millspaugh, Montgomery, & David Redfield, Goshen, witnesses.
Augt 4 Victor M. Watkins, Goshen, Orange Co. N. Y. lawful age teacher, & Juliet Egbert, Goshen, Orange Co. N. Y. lawful age, seamstress, personally known, witnesses Daniel Warden & Charles T. Jackson, Goshen, Orange Co.
Sep 9 Samuel D. Jones, Goshen Orange Co. New York, lawful age, farmer personally known & Cornelia Bennet, Goshen, Orange Co. New York, lawful age, spinster, personally known, witnesses Andrew Jones & Charles T. Jackson, Goshen Orange Co N. Y.
Oct 9 John Carpenter, laborer & Jane Brown, spinster, Goshen Or Co. N. York, lawful age, personally known, witnesses Isaac Moffatt & David Redfield, Goshen, Or Co N. Y. (Colored)
Nov 6 George Bayard & Violet Morrision, Goshen, Or Co. N. York, lawful age, laborer, spinster, personally known, witnesses Hiram Thompson & George Smith, Goshen Or Co. N. Y.
Nov 17 Wiliam S. Conkling, farmer & Sarah T. Wood, spinster, Goshen, Or Co N. Y. lawful age, personally known, witnesses Enos S Conkling, Alfred Harris, Goshen, Or Co. N. Y.
Nov 25 Abraham Perry, carpenter & Hannah Gardner, spinster, Goshen Or Co, N. Y., lawful age, personally known, witnesses Franklin Sawyer & John Gale, Goshen, Or Co. N. Y.
Dec 30 William B Morris, Newark, N. J. farmer & Emeline Benjamin, spinster Goshen, Or Co N. Y. lawful age, personally known, witnesses James R Reeves & Thomas Reeves, Goshen, Or Co N. Y.
Dec 30 Charles Clinton, mason & Clarrissa Crabtree, seamstress, Goshen Or Co N. Y. lawful age, personally known, witnesses, Jesse Smith & Wm. Smiley, Goshen, Or Co N. Y.
Jan 22 1831 David Dean, Goshen laborer & Emeline Smith, spinster, Warwick, Or. Co N. Y. lawful age, personally known, John Carpenter & David Redfield, witnesses, Goshen, Or Co N. Y. (colored)
Jan 26 Thomas Smith, Goshen, Orange Co., farmer & Hannah Moore, spinster Goshen Orange Co., lawful age, personally known, witnesses Andrew Jones & Elihu Moore, Goshen Or County
March 8 Crynus Laroe, Hamptonburgh, Orange Co. N York, farmer & Nancy Tuthill, Hamptonburgh, Orange Co N York, spinster, lawful age personally, witnesses John Barker & — Bedford, Hamptonburgh Or Co N. Y.
March 17 1831 James S. Banker, farmer & Mary Ann Denton, seamstress, Goshen Orange Co New York, lawful age, personally known, witnesses John Augustus Smith and Michael C. Denton, Goshen, Or. Co N. Y.
March 23 James Monell, farmer & Harriett McCarter, spinster, Hamptonburgh, Orange Co N. Y., lawful age, pesonally known, witnesses John B. Monell & Tuthill Ploughman, Hamptonburgh Or Co N. Y.
June 23 Dr. Hudson Kinsley, New York City, physican & Frances M Elliott seamstress Goshen Orange Co. N. Y., lawful age, testimony of H. W. Elliott, personally known, witnesses Horace W. Elliott & Saml. G. Wilkin Goshen, Orang Co New York
Sep 7 John Mapes, Wallkill, farmer & Mary W. Finn, Hamptonburgh, seamstress, lawful age, personally known, witnesses Andrew Wilson & John Wilson, Goshen ,Orange Co. N. Y.
Sept 13 Robert C. S. Hendrie, Goshen, editor, & Mary Caroline Watkins, seamstress Goshen, N Y lawful age, personally known, Saml. J. Wilkin & Phineas Rumsey, Goshen Orange Co N. York.

RECORD OF MARRIAGES

Dec 1 Benjamin C. Sherwood, farmer & Abigail Ann Strong, seamstress, Goshen, N. Y. lawful age, personally known, witnesses Benjamin Strong & Hezekiah H. Strong, Goshen Orange Co N York.

Jan 12 Christopher C. Graham, Montgomery N. Y. farmer & Sarah Dusenberry, spinster, lawful age, personally known, witnesses William & Daniel Dusenberry, Goshen Orange Co N. York

Jan 18 Virgil S. Seward, Goshen, farmer & Sarah Duryea, Blooming Grove seamstress, lawful age, personally known, witnesses Henry Seward & Samuel Rumsey, Goshen Orange County N Y.

Jan 19 David H Brewster, Monroe, Or Co N Y. ,physican & Sally Maria Watkins, Hamptonburgh, seamstress, lawful age personally known witnesses, Hezekiah Watkins & James Strong, Hampton Boro

Feb 7 Abraham Smith farmer, &— Abigail Tupper, spinster, Goshen Orange Co N. Y., lawful age, personally known, witness Colvin B Ludlum & David Redfield, Goshen, Or Co

March 1 Benjamin F. Sawyer, farmer & Louisa Valentine, spinster, Goshen Orange Co. N. Y., lawful age, personally known, witnesses Moses Sawyer & Robt W. Sawyer, Goshen Or. Co.

March 10 George Newton, wagonmaker & Sally Connor, spinster, Goshen Orange Co. N. Y., lawful age, personally known, witnesses, George W. Connor & Thomas McGonagel, Goshen, Or Co

March 22 Lewis H. Parsons, Blooming Grove & Juliana Jump, Wallkill, lawful age, known by testimony of credible witnesses, Ezra S. Fisk & Francis L. Upper, Goshen, Orange

May 10 Andrew Jones, mechanic & Almeda Edsall, seamstress, Goshen, Orange Co. N Y., lawful age, known personally, witnesses Selah Edsall & John J Smith, Goshen Orange Co

Sep 19 Josiah S. Jackson, farmer, Monroe, & Susan S. Brown, spinster, Hamptonboro, lawful age personally known, witnesses James Strong & John Payne, Hamptonboro Or Co

Rev. Dr. Fisk being obliged to spend the winter of '32, '33 at the South for the benefit of his health— His pulpit was supplied during his absence by Rev. John N. Lewis —— who soleminzed the following marriages.

That portion of the Revised Statues which required the record of the occupation of the Respective Parties, was repealed by an act of the Legislature— passed—

REGISTER OF MARRIAGES ACCORDING TO THE AMENDED REVISED STATUTES OF THE STATE OF NEW YORK

Nov. 15th 1832 Nehemiah Denton and Harriet Hall, residence, Goshen, Or. Co. N. Y. lawful age, idenity certified by Wm. Rysdek, witnesses Thomas W. Bradner and Stephen Smith, Goshen,Orange Co. N. Y.

Dec 13 William Millspaugh and Cornelia Hetfield, Goshen Or Co, N. Y. lawful age, certified by David Barnum, witnesses, Chaplin S Reeves and Stephen Millspaugh, Goshen OrCoN.Y.

Jany 2 1833 Henry Merriam and Ann Eliza Reeves, Goshen, Or Co, lawful age identity certified by John Wilson; Henry H Van Dyck, Goshen Or Co, N. Y.and Anthony Houston, Ramapo Rockland Co. N. Y., Goshen, Orange Co. N. Y.

Jany 30 Albert G. Watkins and Milicent S. Jackson, Hamptonburgh, Orange Co N. Y. lawful age, identity certified by Benjm Strong, witnesses, James Strong and Charles Heard, Hamptonburgh, Orange Co, N. Y., **Hamptonburgh, Orange Co, N. Y**

RECORD OF MARRIAGES

Feby 7 Philander Banker and Harriet Conkling, Gosehn, Or Co N. Y. lawful age, identity certified by Benjn Strong, witnesses Michael C. Denton and Abraham Banker, Goshen Or Co N. Y.

Feby 28 Derick B. Banker and Phebe Ann Cabrey, Goshen Or Co, N. Y., lawful age, identity certified by Usher H Case, witnesses Samuel Hawkins and Henry I Smith, Goshen Or Co N. Y.

May 1 Samuel H Corwin, Wallkill Or Co N. Y. and Adaline A Swezy, Goshen, Or Co N. Y., lawful age, indentity certified by John C. Wallace, witnesses Nathan Westcott and Hamilton J Jackson, Goshen Or Co, N. Y.

May 14 Joseph Weeks, Cornwall, Or Co N. Y. and Dorinda Shaw, Goshen Or Co N. Y. lawful age, identity certified by Prosper E. S. Payne, witness Prosper E. S Payne, Goshen Or Co. N. Y.

May 15 Usher H Case and Frances Emily Thompson, Goshen, Or Co N. Y. lawful age, personally known certified by Joseph Sayre, witnesses Henry W. Thompson and John S. Crane, Goshen Or Co.

June 12 John Borland New York City and Sophionia G Arnell, Goshen Or Co., lawful age, personally known, witnesses John Wilson & Wm W Arnell, Goshen Or Co, N. Y.

Augt 3 Reuben Miller Goshen Or Co. N. Y. and Catherine Knapp, Warwick, Or Co, N. Y. lawful age, personally known, witnesses, William Dusenbury and Zeno Dusenbury, Goshen, Or Co. N. Y.

Sept 17 George M. Halsted, and Wid. Ann Oakley, Goshen Or Co N. Y. lawful age, personally known, witnesses Chauncey H. Smith, Goshen Edward Jackson, New Burgh, Or. Co. N. Y., Goshen, Or. Co. N. Y.

Oct 2 John J Thompson, Hamptonburgh and Frances Wilkin, Goshen, lawful age, personally known, witnesses Saml. J Wilkin, & Charles Arnill, Goshen, Or Co. N. Y.

Oct 26 John M. Miller & Sally Jane Smith, Hamptonboro, lawful age, personally known, witnesses Henry Houston, Wallkill Or Co & Freegift Tuthill, Hamptonboro, married in Hamptonboro, Or. Co.

Oct 29 Henry Denton & Esther Vail, Goshen, Orange Co. lawful age, personally known witnesses William Denton & Peter Vail, Goshen, Or Co. N. Y.

Record of marriages continued by the Revd. Jas. R. Johnston subsequent to the dissolution of the pastoral relation of the Revd Dr. Fisk to the congregation of Goshen.

RECORD OF MARRIAGES ACCORDING TO THE REVISED STATUTES OF THE STATE OF NEW YORK

Nov 18 1834 Dr. Jerome Wells, Goshen, & Charlotte Horton, Goshen, lawful age, personally known, witness Dr. William Horton & Dr. James Horton, Goshen, Orange Co., Goshen N. Y.

Dec. 23 Philip Crist, Goshen, & Matilda Hawkins, Hamptonburgh, lawful age, personally known, witness, John Willson & Dr. James Horton Goshen, Or, Co N. Y.

Jany 17 1835 Thomas Pound, Warwick & Sally Ann Smith, N. York, lawful age, certified by C. Smith & S. Carp, witnesses Caleb Smith & Samuel Carp, Warwick, N Y.

Feby 19 William Wood, & Juliett Wood, Goshen, lawful age, personally known, witnesses Alfred Harris & Benjamin Gale, Goshen, N. Y.

July 31 John Silsby, Goshen & Hannah Vanderwort, Florida, lawful age

Sept 1 Austin Irving & Zube Corey, both of Goshen, lawful age, personally known, witness John Wilson, & — Goshen

RECORD OF MARRIAGES

Nov 24 Myndert Van Guishing, Schenectady Co & Eve Fisher, Schoharie Co., lawful age, witnesses Dr William Horton & Dr. Jerome Wells both of Goshen, Goshen, Or Co N. York
Jan 21 1836 John F. Steppenfield & Kezia Wood, Goshen, lawful age, witness Nathan Wescott Esq., & William T Little, Goshen, Goshen Or Co
Feby 24 Richard Hurton & Rachel Phillips, coloured people, Goshen, Or. Co. N. Y. lawful age, witnesses Sylvester Jervis & Chapman Miller, coloured people, Goshen, Or Co, N. Y.
March 9 Hamilton Jackson & Clarissa Webster, Goshen, Or Co, N Y. lawful age, personally known, witnesses, George Howell & Jas. Jackson, **Goshen, Or. Co., N. Y.**
May 12 Walter Scudder, Islip, Suffolk Co., & S. Frances Little, Goshen, Or. Co. N. Y. lawful age, witnesses Charles Little & Joseph Wood, New York City, Goshen, Or. Co.
Sept 1 Henry Gale & Mrs Sally Colwell, Goshen Or. Co New York, lawful age, witnesses George Howell & William Everett, Goshen, Or. Co.
Sept 10 Hosea Clark & Lydia Ann Bull, both of New York city, lawful age, witnesses Dr. J. S. Crane & John A. Smith, both of Goshen.
Oct 6 Daniel G Armstrong & Mary Ann Knapp, both of Goshen, lawful age, witnesses Ruben C. Miller & James Sloat, Goshen & Wallkill
Oct 11 Jas. A. Jackson & Catherine Blain, Goshen, personally known.
Oct 13 William Burgoyne & Mrs. Diana Goldsmith, colored people, Goshen.

REGISTER OF MARRIAGES ACCORDING TO THE REVISED STATUTES OF THE STATE OF NEW YORK

1837 Jany 18 Richard S. Denton, Vernon, Sux. Co. N. J. & Elizabeth Smith, Goshen, Or. Co. N. Y., lawful age, personally known, witnesses Samuel Denton, Warwick, Or. Co. & Joshua Smith, Goshen.
28 Daniel Potts & Sally Jane Bedford, Hamptonburgh, personally known, witnesses Dr. Wright & Philip Crist, Hamptonburgh
Feb 21 Samuel Foster & Mary Crist, both of Hamptonburgh, personally known.
Sep 23 William Little & Mary Block, widow, both of Hamptonburgh, personally known.
Nov 9 Robert Emmel Potter & Mary Egiles, widow, Goshen, personally known
December 7th, Harrison Thompson, & Abby Jane Foster of Goshen, personally known.
19th Theophilus Dolson & Cecelia Hathaway, of Goshen, personally known.
Feby 7th 1838 Colvin G. Gale & Dolly Knapp of Goshen, personally known.
March 13 Newton Randolph & Malinda Goldsmith, of Goshen, personally known.
14 Gabriel Goldsmith & Mary Priscilla Case, of Goshen, personally known.
15 Lemuel Palmer & Mary Jane Goldsmith, of Goshen, personally know.
June 11 Matthew Newkirk & Hannah Thompson, of Goshen.
26 James Palmer of New York & Catherine Westcott, of Goshen,
July 4th, Wm L. Wells of Minisink & Amelia J. Brown,
24 George W. Lord of Mount Hope & —— Stackhouse of Bloomingburgh
Sept 5 Moses Sweezy of Goshen & Mrs Jane Hoyt of Conn.
Nov 15 George W. Crans & Maria Owen both of Goshen
April 1839 John Little of New York & Mary Jane Hanis of Goshen.
Octr 24 Elmore Harlow & Melinda Newman.

RECORD OF MARRIAGES

Record of Marriages, under the following Pastorates, Viz. Rev Mr. Ker; Rev. Isaac Lewis; Rev. Ezra Fisk, (Rev. J. N. Lewis, stated supply) Rev. James R. Johnston, and Rev. Dr. McCartee; from 1776 to Feby 1844; with the following exceptions,—from Nov. 1804 to Jany 1806—from July 12, 1812 to Sept 1813—from Oct 29th 1833 to Nov. 1834; and from April 1839 to Sept. 1840

N. B. The Marriage Record from 1840 to 1844; Rev. Dr. McCartee, Pastor is in Volume 3 of the Minutes of Session.

Marriages by Robert McCartee, Pastor of the 1st Presbyterian Church, Goshen, Or. Co. N. Y.

Septr A. D. 1840 Ezra Thompson of Newburgh to Phebe Ann Jones of Goshen, witnesses William Wells, James Jones, Hannah Jones

Oct 17th John Strong of Goshen, Colored to Mary Ann Cortland, do. colored, witnesses, Francis Van Dyke, Mary Coe

Dec 24 George Castle to Deliah Wilson, both of Goshen, witnesses H Ball & wife, John W. Budd, Harriett Budd, Cornelia Hawkins .

Feb 1st A. D. 1841 Thomas J. Jackson of Chester to Margaret Stewart of Goshen, witnesses, George Whitman, Saml. Smith, Cornelia Stewart, Oliver B Tuthill

April 6th James Cooper Reeve of Goshen to Adeline Wells, of do, witnesses, Joshua Wells & daughters T. T. Reeve & wife, Alfd Harris, Luther Harris & wife.

Sept 15th Samuel W. Leddel of Mendham N. J. to Margaret Horton of Goshen, N. Y., witnesses, Dr. Wm. Horton & wife, Nathan Hooper, Silas R. Horton, Henrietta M. Leddel.

Sept 23d Sylvester Jervis of New York City to Sarah Jane Lowe, coloured people of Goshen, witnesses Hosea Lowe & wife, Mrs. Thomas Wilkins & daughters

Sept 21st Robert W. Sawyer, missionary to Aferica to Cathr. A. Hammond, in the Presbyterian Church Goshen, before the Congreation on the evening of Ordination.

Oct 14th William C. Foster of Goshen to Betsey Ann Satterly, of Goshen witnesses, Horace S. DeKay, Margaret Brooks, Mrs. Robinson, Frances B. Wallace, Mr. & Mrs. Chebee.

Nov. 15th Henry Halfheider of Goshen to Sarah Jane Carpenter, Goshen, witnesses Mary Ellen McLaughlin, Joseph Bugy.

Novr Andrew Hulse to Esther Smith, all of Goshen, witnesses Mrs. McCartee, J. G. McCartee, Miss Harris

Jan 6th A. D. 1842 Lewis E. Hulse of Goshen to Harriet E. Smith, Goshen, witnesses, widow Hannah Smith, Thomas J. Smith, Gabriel E. Smith

Jan 11th Henry I Duryea of Bloomingrove to Ann Eliza Wilkin of Hamptonburgh, witnesses. Gen. Henry Duryea & Lady Mrs. Wilkin, Mr. Phins. Rumsey & Lady, Virgil Seward & Lady.

Jan 13 Gilbert H. White, Philipsburgh to Margaret Brooks of Goshen, witnesses Noah Carpenter & wife Benj. B. Strong, Mary, Jane Horton, Mrs. Robinson, &c &c.

April 25 Edmund Seely of Goshen to Eliza Miller of Goshen, witnesses Col. Wm. Little & lady Mr. J. Little, Sen. Mrs. Banker.

Augt 16 Samuel D. Bathrick, West Milford, Passac Co. N. Jersey to Alvira Hall, Witnesses John S. Van Duzer, Mary Ann Sandford Lewis Hall & Rosanna, his wife.

Sept 7 Thomas Murtha of Goshen to Ann Maria McElroy, Goshen, witnesses Jonas Holbert, P. M. McCartee

Sept 7th James S. Tuthill of Goshen to Harriet Smith of Goshen, witnesses Benj. B. Strong, Sarah E. Smith, Mr. & Mrs. Henry Smith.

RECORD OF MARRIAGES 37

Sep 22 Charles N. Jayne of Florida to Ann Ella Thompson, Goshen, witnesses Dewitt C. Jayne, M. D. Charles H. Thompson, Sarah Y. Reeve. Emily Jayne

Jan 1843 Alfred Booth of Hamptonburgh to Dolly Reeve of Goshen, witnesses, James Cooper Reeve, T. T. Reeve.

March 16th William Everett of Goshen to Rebecca Matthews of Rochester, witnesses Jonas Seely & wife Col. Wm. Little, Robert Hathaway.

May 3rd John S. Clarke of Goshen to Jane Hammond of Goshen, witnesses Benjn. Ketchell, Emily Hammond, Wm. Everett, Mrs. Hammond.

May 18 Alexander H. Bailey, Catskill, Greene Co. to Mary E. Howell, o' Goshen, witnesses, Dr. J. Hall, Dr. J. S. Horton, Mrs. S. Howell, Arron Van Duzer, John B. Booth, Robt. A. Smith.

June 7 James Edward Serrell, N. Y. City to Margaret Ann Maginness, of New York city, witnesses Sydney Genin, P. Mc Bryson, Mrs. Maginness, Mr. Mrs. Serrell, the parents.

June 8th Oscar Brudinell of Goshen to Harriet Dill (coloured people), witnesses, T. S. Bradner, Cecilia Westcott, (colored)

June 14 E. Worden of Goshen to Emily Smith of Goshen, witnesses, Robt. A. Smith, Chas. Monell & wife, John Monell.

Aug 31st Joseph Maginness of Goshen to Rosella Thomas of Goshen, Mr. ——Edsall (witnesses) & wife, Mr. Seely Edsall & wife

Sept 3d George W. Lowe, Hamptonburgh, to Jane Simmons of Hamptonburgh, colored people Witnesses Mr. & Mrs. Lowe, Sylvester Jarvis & wife.

Sept 20 John B. Thompson of Warwick to Francis A. Gardner of Warwick, Witnesses, Capt. Sears, Francis E. Monell, John Monell.

Sept 23d Wm Henry Brewster of Goshen to Helena Loise Clay, of Long Island, (coloured people) Witness David Dean

Novr 8th Christopher P. Moeild of Montgomery to Sarah Maria Eager, of Hamptonburgh, witnesses, Willm. Shafer, Letty McCord, Joseph Case.

Novr 14th James T. Black, of Hamptonburgh to Martha Robinson of Hamptonburgh, witnesses, Virgil Milspaugh & wife, Andrew L. McCord, George Robinson.

Jan 3d 1844 Hezekiah D. Ludlum of Goshen to Julia H. Little of Goshen, Witnesses, James Stewart, Eliza J. Stewart.

Jan. 11th Henry Puff, Wallkill to Mary Elizah Owen Wallkill, witnesses Harriet E. Owen, Oscar Owen, Mrs. Owen, John Valentine.

Jan 24th Nathl. Ludlam Case of Goshen to Susan Hudson Goldsmith of Goshen, witnesses, Mary Goldsmith, Keziah Goldsmith, Jesse A. Case, Francis J. Tuthill.

Jan 25th Jesse A. Case, Goshen to ——— Romaine of Goshen, witnesses, Mr. John Romeyn Mrs. Romeyn Hannah Jones.

Feb 1st Henry W. Elliott of Goshen to Sarah W. Hulse of Wallkill, witnesses Wm. Jackson & wife, Edward Hulse & wife, Ethelinda Elliott.

Dec. 20, 1849 Hiram F. Farrand, of Goshen, Sarah J. Rankin of Goshen, Witness John C. Wallace.

Dec 27 1849 David Ayres, of Mount Hope, Margaret E. Sayre, of Goshen Witnesses, John S. Crans & Alex. Wilkin.

Jan 1 1850 Robert Freeman, of Orange Co. Sarah Carr of Orange Co. Witnesses, James Snodgrass & Wm. Simonton.

Jan 24 1850 Oliver D. Corey, of Pierpont Emiline Smith of Goshen Witnesses Dr. Ostrom & Horace Smith

Feb 28 1850 William T. Wynkoop, Bellevue, Iowa, Sarah Jane Booth, Goshen, Witnesses, Alfred Harris & Judge Jones

RECORD OF MARRIAGES

March 9 1805 George D. Van Kleeck, of Chester, Henrietta L. Youngs, of Goshen, Witnesses, Charlotte H. Snodgrass & El. K. Snodgrass

March 21 1850 William Allen Butler, N. York, Mary Russell Marshall, N. York witnesses, Martin Vanburen, Peletiah Perrit.

April 3 1850 William B. Sinsabaugh, Athens, Pa., Elizabeth B. Sinabaugh, Goshen, witnesses Alexander Payne, John Scofield.

May 22 1850 Rev. Thomas S. Bradner, Milford, Pa., Agnes Wilson, Goshen witnesses, Dr. John S. Crane, Walter Strong.

May 28 1850 John Amory of New York, Jane Smith of Goshen, witnesses Dr. Ostrom & Solomon Smith.

May 30 1850 Isaac Decker, of Bloomingrove, Elizabeth Mullign, of Bloomingrove witness, Charlotte H Snodgrass.

June 13 1850 James Oliver, Goshen, Sarah Sears, Goshen, witnesses, William M. Sayer, Alexander Payne.

August 30 1850 James Lawrence, Mt. Hope, Ann Norris, Mt. Hope, witnesses, Rev John M. Krebs, D. D. & Alex. Snodgrass.

May 28 1850 L. O. Tiffany &Susan Gregg, witness, James Gregg.

Oct. 3 1850 John S. Martin & Sarah E. Vail, Goshen, witnesses, Capt, J. Thompson & Capt. J. Andrews.

Nov. 20 1850 Solomon Smith, Goshen, Mary Tuthill, Goshen, witnesses William B. Tuthill, Willm. Jackson.

Jan, 15 1851 John G. Houston, of Scotchtown, Mary W. Bradner, of Goshen. witnesses, Benjamin Strong, Aaron VanDuzen

Jan 21 1851 Joseph D. Stage & Mary J. Gregory, Goshen, witnesses, James Tuthill, Smith.

May 11, 1851 John S. Wood, of Manaeating, Amelia A Ferguson, of Ulster witnesses, Odgen Edwards, Jr. A. A. Snodgrass.

Sept. 16, 1851, John Wesley Green — Christina Johnson, —; Colord.

Oct 14 1851 John N Budd, of Goshen, Phebe C. Case of Goshen, witnesses, Walter Anderson, Daniel Case.

Oct 18 1851 Tip Miller & Lydia DeWitt, Colord. witnesses, Charles Drawer, Chas. P. Thomson.

Nov. 5, 1851 Charles King of Goshen, Sarah Van Dyke, of Goshen, Colord. witnesses, Charles Drawer, George V. Snodgrass.

Nov. 11 1851 John Shaw of Minisink Mary Carters, of Minisink, witnesses JohnConners, Charolette H. Snodgrass.

Jan. 1 1852 Albert Wickam, of Waywayanda, Harriet Budd, of Goshen witnesses Horace Ball, Walter Anderson

Jan 8 1852 Archibald Bodle of Goshen, Harriet E. Sweezy, of Goshen, witnesses James Hopkins, Virgil Seward.

Jan 30, 1852, William H. Davis of Goshen, Ann Eliza Dill of Goshen, Colord. witnesses Mary Delancey, Elizabeth K. Snodgrass.

Feb 5 1852 Alonzo C. Wall, of Luzerne Co. Pa. Sarah M. Denton, of Goshen, witnesses William Denton, Benjn. Strong.

Feb 11 1852 Randolp Ayres, N. Jersey, Harriet E Goldsmith, Goshen, witnesses William B. Tuthill, A. H. Sinsabaugh.

March 6 1852 William Smith, Warwick, Mary Ann Furman, Warwick, witnesses — Thompson, — Budd.

April 3 1852 Joseph S. Martin, Vernon, Mary Casterling, Warwick, witnesses, Moses Sweezy, S. R. Owen.

Oct 14 1852 Joseph S. Young, Chester, Harriet A. Conklin, Goshen, witnesses, Nathaniel Conklin, — O'Neal.

Dec. 15, 1852 Willm. Henry Newman, Goshen, Eliza Bennet, Goshen, witnesses Theodore Wilkin, Edmund Seely.

RECORD OF MARRIAGES 39

Dec. 23 1852 George Tuthill, Bloomingrove, Jane A Purdy, Goshen witnesses James Gregg Benjn. F. Purdy.
Jan 7 1853 Wm. Henry Wilcox, Minisink, Eliza Eaton, Minisink witnesses James N. Eaton, Nicholas E. Williams.
March 16 1853 John H Thompson, Goshen, Emily Poppino, Goshen, witnesses Saml. R. Owen, Dr. Thompson.
May 11 1853 James Riker, Jr. Harlem, Vashti W. Horton, Goshen, Josephus Terbell, Dr. Clarke, Elizabeth K. Snodgrass
July 7 1853 Aaron Burr Guy — Goshen, Margaret Ann Peterson, Goshen, colored, witnesses George V Snodgrass, Thomas Snodgrass
August 10 1853 Robert Beebe, Middletown, Orange Co. N. Y. Frances Concklin, Middletown, Orange Co. N. Y. witnesses, George V. Snodgrass, Charolette, H. Snodgrass
Oct 15 1853 William Seargeant & Harriet Clark, Wawayánda, witnesses, Sally Ann Clarke, Elizabeth K. Snodgrass
Dec. 14 1853 Jason W. Corwin, Goshen, Sarah A. Howell, Jersey City, N. Jersey, witnesses, Levi L. Lockwood, Dunning.
April 27 1854 Cornelius J. Sip, Brooklyn, L. I., Susan Purdy, Goshen witnesses, James Gregg, Benjn. F. Purdy.
July 6 1854 Hosea Webster, Brooklyn, L. I., Margaret W. Warner, Goshen witnesses, Hannibal H. Hopkins, John Stewart.
Sep 5 1854 Archibald Alex. Snodgrass, N. York, Fanny Maria Hutchings. N. York, witnesses E. W. Hutchings, Saml. S. Snodgrass.
Sep 20 1854 Asaph L. Green, Jersey City, Julia Scofield, Goshen witnesses A. H. Sinnsabaugh, James H. Schofield.
Nov 8 1854 James Downie, Williamsburgh, L. I. Sarah Kitchell, Goshen witnesses Moses L. Sweezy, Hiram Farrand.
Dec. 1, 1854 John Petit, Hamptonburgh, Margaret Johnson, Hamptonburgh.
Dec 19, 1854 Thomas Welling, Warwick, Caroline Van Duzer, Goshen, witnesses Harvey Wallace DeWitt Howell
Dec. 21 1854 Henry C. Conkling, Michigan, Sarah F. Carpenter, Goshen witnesses Benjamin Strong, Daniel Carpenter
Jan 3 1855 Theodore Dusenbery, Scotchtown, Tillah Duryea, Goshen witnesses A. H. Sinsabaugh, Solomon Smith
March 29 1855 Hiram F. Farrand, Goshen, Conelia Waters, Goshen, witnesses John Houston, John Waters.
May 3 1855 Lewis Edson Coleman, Deposit, Pa. Mary Frances Wells, Goshen, witnesses Gabriel Wood, Schuyler Owen.
June 12 1855 James W. Taylor, Goshen, Caroline Wilson, Goshen, witnesses Andrew Wilson, David Redfield.
July 23 1855 John Northy, Munroe, Jane Kitner, Munroe, witnesses, Theodore Wells, George V. Snodgrass.
July 26 1855 William P. Thurston, Florida, Joanna Owen, Goshen, witnesses, Nathaniel Conkling, Schuyler P. Owen
Oct 30 1855 Maurice Faucon ,N. York, Elizabeth Brewster, Goshen, witnesses, John Wallace, Charles Elliott.
Dec 4 1855 Thomas B. Jackson, Hamptonburgh, Mary A Jones, Hamptonburgh, witnesses, Theodore Wilkin, Horace Tuthill
Dec. 18 1855 Alexander T. McLaughlen, Newton, N. Jersey, Sarah C Kortright Goshen, witnesses Willm. H. Tinkey, Thos. Mapes.
——— Wood, New York ——— Smiley, Goshen, witnesses, Saml. J. Wilkin, Martin L. Thompson.
Jan. 7 1857 John Webb, Goshen, Fannie Jones, Goshen, witnesses, Gabriel Bennet, Hiram Farrand.

RECORD OF MARRIAGES

Jan. 22 1857 John L. Welling, Warwick, Martha Van Duzer, Goshen, witnesses, Harvey Wallace, John Cooper.
Feb 25 1857 Henry A Sheldon, Rutland, Vermont Sarah F. Marvin, Goshen witnesses John C. Wallace, Asa Janson
March 4 1857 John Wood, Goshen, H. Elizabeth Smith, Goshen, witnesses, Jesse Smith, Solomon Wood.
March 19 1857 Samuel Beyea, Goshen, Mary Jones, Goshen, witnesses, David Redfield, Gabriel Bennet.
Sep 30 1857 Cornelius H. Loockee, Chester, Mary E. Helims, Chester, witnesses, Charlotte H. Snodgrass, Geo. V. Snodgrass
Oct 8 1857 Virgil S. Seward, N. York, Cornelia Duryea, Hamptonburgh witnesses Alpheus Duryea, Henry I. Duryea
Oct 22 1857 James S. Watkins, Hamptonburgh, Ann Eliz. Price, Hamptonburgh witnesses William Sayer, Ezra Sandford.
Nov 2 1857 William Sinnsabaugh, Goshen, Isabella Courtier, Goshen, witnesses Wickam Moffet, Dr. Townsend
Nov 7 1857 WilliDegroot, Chester, Rosanna Bartow, Chester, witnesses, (Colored) Charlotte H. Snodgrass, E. K. Snodgrass.
Nov 12 1857 Dr. Willm. P. Townsend, Goshen, Elizabeth Thew, Goshen, witnesses John E. Howell, Charles H Winfield.
Dec. 16 1857 Jesse O. Hoyt, Jane N. Ludlum, Goshen, witnesses John Cooper, Dr. Ostrom
Dec 23 1857 Oliver B Vail, Middletown, Sarah E. Smith, Goshen, witnesses Harvey Wallace, James S. Tuthill.
Feb 18 1858 J. Edward Wells, Goshen, Fannie E. Conkling, Goshen, witnesses, George Conkling, Dr. Ostrom
Feb 19 1858 Goldsmith Gregory, Goshen Kate Sinsaubaugh, Goshen, witnesses, Chas. T. Reevs, Alfred Harris.
Carrie A. Freeligh, Passaic, N. Jersey, Jewett T. Davis, Montgomery, Alabama, witnesses Saml. J. Wilkin, John C. Wallace.
Ap 21 1858 William Sawyer, La Crope, Wisconsin, Susan Wood, Goshen witnesses Thomas Smith, Robert Young.
May 15 1858 Richard T. Webb, Goshen, Bridget Delencey, Goshen, witnesses Thomas Snodgrass, Mrs. W. C. Smith.
June 15 1858 Floyd A. Crane, Goshen, Melissa Jennings, Goshen, witnesses.
June 21 1858 James Dill, Goshen, Julia Ann Thompson, do, colored. Witnesses. Francis Lowe, Elizabeth K. Snodgrass
June 22 1858 David Redfield, Goshen, Eliza Bradner, do, witnesses John S. Crane, George M. Grier
Augt. 18, 1858 Floyd Marvin, Goshen, Jane Strong, do, witnesses John C. Wallace, James Strong
Augt. 21, 1858 Michael Coan, Bloominggrove, Julia Falin, do, witnesses, Geo. V. Snodgrass, Thomas Snodgrass
Sept. 9, 1858 Edward Rine, Chester, Mary McNaughton, do, witness, Elizabeth K. Snodgrass
Sep. 21, 1858 John Wallace, Goshen, Mary Strong, do, witnesses, John C. Wallace, W. M. Sayer
Oct. 6, 1858 John H. Thompson, Goshen, Adeline L. Post, do, witnesses, R. M. Vail, Saml. J. Wilkin
Nov. 25, 1858 Warren Murray, Brookhaven, L. I., Sally Ann Vail, Goshen, witnesses, Nathaniel Tuthill, John Tuthill
March 17, 1859 James B. Sinsabaugh, Goshen, Frances Scofield, do, witnesses, John J. Heard, John S. Crane
June 7, 1859 David Courtier, Goshen, Ellen Cronk, do, witnesses, John Hawkins, Richard Webb

RECORD OF MARRIAGES 41

Augt. 6, 1859 Robert Wisner, Warwick, Sarah N. Clarke, do, witnesses, Thomas Snodgrass, E. K. Snodgrass
Sep. 22, 1859 John A. Mapes, N. York, Sarah S. Strong, Goshen, witnesses, Rev. Floyd A. Crane, John Wallace
Nov. 2, 1859 William E. Mapes, Newburgh, Sarah Owen, Goshen, George Crans, John Wallace
Nov. 17, 1859 Benjamin S. Smith, Goshen, Emma E. Sanford, do, witnesses, Gabriel Smith, Capt. Sanford
Dec. 7, 1859 Willm. Henry Bennet, Goshen, Lydia Ann Smith, do, witnesses, Chas. H. Winfield, Richard Sears
Dec. 20, 1859 Joseph R. Andrews, Munroe, Fanny E. Budd, Goshen, witnesses, Horace Ball, William Budd
Jan. 11, 1860 Charles B. Tuthill, Goshen, Lizzie B. Doughty, do, witnesses, Thomas B. Jackson, J. C. Andrews
July 15, 1860 John Shine, Goshen, Ellen Mulvey, do, witnesses, Charlotte H. Snodgrass, Mary Delancey
Oct. 10, 1860 Richard Sears, Goshen, J. Augusta Smith, do, witnesses, William Sayer, Geo. Millspaugh
Nov. 1, 1860 John A. Ballard, Chester, Catherine Price, Goshen, witnesses, William P. Smith, Denton Jones
Nov. 15, 1860 Rev. Oscar Harris, Centreville, Sarah E. Smith, Goshen, witnesses, Solomon T. Smith, Charles E. Merriam
Dec. 11, 1860 Alfred L. Gilson, Hamptonburgh, Angeline Banker, Goshen, witnesses, James S. Hopkins, Geo. V. Snodgrass
Dec. 6, 1860 Nathan R. Wheeler, Warwick, Frances C. Johnson, Goshen, witnesses, D. H. Haight, James C. Johnson
Feb. 5, 1861 Daniel Jessup, Jr., Florida, Nancy Reeve, Goshen, witnesses
June 25, 1861 Jerome Briggs, Newburgh, Sarah Wilcox, do, witnesses, S. P. Wright, Mrs. Helen Wright
Sep. 12, 1861 William A. Lawrence, Chester, Susan T. Holbert, do, witnesses, John Lawrence, Mary E. House
Sep. 18, 1861 John A. Wallace, Middletown, Abbe M. Wood, Goshen, witnesses, Nathan B. Wheeler, John Wallace
Sep. 26, 1861 John Bell, Middletown, Teressa S. Vanort, Goshen, witnesses, Horace Jones, John Moore
Oct. 23, 1861 Samuel Slaughter, Wallkill, Kate R. Wells, Goshen, witnesses, Lewis Wood, Stephen Smith
Nov. 7, 1861 William H. Henderson, Warwick, Mary Ann McGlauchlin, do, witnesses, Samuel Carson, Mary Jane Tilson
Nov. 7, 1861 Franklin Lamaline, Warwick, Ann Carson, do, witnesses, Samuel Carson, Mary Jane Tilson
Feb. 3, 1862 James E. Polhemus, Susan Brooks, Colored, witness, Elizabeth K. Snodgrass
Feb. 12, 1862 John I. Barr, Wallkill, Hattie Randolph, Hamptonburgh, witnesses, Peter Haynes, Solomon T. Smith
March 13, 1862 Louis Goldsmith, Walkill, Sarah A. Gregory, Goshen, witnesses, George H. Crans, Stephen Smith, Jr.
July 2, 1862 Daniel D. Banker, Goshen, Hannah L. Banker, Goshen, witnesses, Philander Banker, Jr., Schuyler Owen
Sep. 3, 1862 Wm. B. Wood, Chester, Jennie F. Gilmore, Hancock, N. Y., witnesses, Mr. & Mrs. M. P. Ross, Chester
Dec. 23, 1862 Edward Clissold, N. York, Annie E. Clark, Goshen, witnesses, John A. Moore, Thoms. T. Hetfield
Jan. 7, 1863 Joseph Ketcham, Canterbury, Joanna Reeve, Goshen, witnesses, Charles A. Reeve, Caroline Johnson
Ap. 8, 1863 R. D. Snodgrass, Harriet O. Hutchins

RECORD OF MARRIAGES

Aug. 20, 1863 John D. Tuthill, Goshen, A. Addie Van Sickel, do, witnesses, Joseph Tuthill, Danl. D. Banker

Oct. 21, 1863 Horatio Gates Gilbert, N. Y., Susan M. Dougall, do, witnesses, Capt. Wise

Oct. 21, 1863 Charles A. Wells, Waverly, N. Y., Angeline Fullerton, Goshen, witnesses, Jacob Haynes, Daniel Fullerton

Nov. 10, 1863 Henry Spencer Murray, Goshen, Sarah Dunning, witnesses, David Redfield, Levi L. Lockwood

Nov. 25, 1863 Hudson K. Hulse, Walkill, Annie Thompson, Goshen, witnesses, James S. Hopkins, John J. Thompson

Dec. 2, 1863 Ranselaer Knapp, Sugar Loaf, Mary H. Whitman, Goshen, witnesses, Samuel Whitman, Schuyler Owen

Jan. 21, 1864 Hiram T. Stage, Goshen, Catharine E. Gregory, do, witnesses, Joseph D. Stage, James Tuthill

March 23, 1864 Charles E. Merriam, Goshen, Jennie E. Wells, do, witnesses, Henry Merriam, Charles E. Millsapaugh

April 14, 1864 Anson Clarke, Munroe, Eunice Fortner, do, witnesses, Abraham Letts, Martin I. Thompson

John J. Thompson, Goshen, Mary Ada McNally, do, witnesses, Charles E. Merriam, Saml. J. Wilkin

Oct. 5, 1864 Henry Hosford, Brooklyn, L. I., Fannie E. Lockwood, Goshen, Witnesses, Jason W. Corwin, John E. Howell

Nov. 23, 1864 Henry Ball, Wayne Co., Pennsa, Margaret E. Reed, Goshen, witnesses, Nathl. Vansickle, John D. Tuthill

Jan. 25, 1865 John Earles, Munroe, Clara W. Clarke, do, witnesses, Thaddeus Banker, Anson Clarke

Feb. 25, 1865 William Brien of Wawayanda, Caroline Barrett of do, witnesses

Ap. 12, 1865 Roswell C. Coleman, Gohsen, Sarah W. Wilkin, do, witnesses, John E. Howell, Charles H. Winfield

July 19, 1865 Festus A. Webb, Elmira, Cornelia Ann Smith, Goshen, witnesses, Will. H. Bennet, Theodore Smith

Sept. 13, 1865 Charles Muth, Goshen, Sarah M. Pierson, do, witness, James Wood, Anna Sinsabaugh

Sep. 26, 1865 Charles E. Millspaugh, Goshen, Martha Sayer, do, witnesses, Charles E. Merriam, George M. Sayer

Augt. 7, 1865 James Mapes, Goshen, Sarah Jane Doly, do, colored, witnesses, Mary Jennings, George Jennings

Oct. 18, 1865 Samuel S. Snodgrass, N. York, Annie T. Morgan, New Rochelle, witnesses, George V. Snodgrass, John Traphagen

Nov. 14, 1865 Robert Osborn, Goshen, Anna A. Coleman, do, witnesses, Archibald Beyea, John Knapp

Dec. 6, 1865 Joseph S. Young, Goshen, Emily Bradner, do, witnesses, David Redfield, Daniel Vansickle

Dec. 13, 1865 Henry T. Van Duzer, Goshen, Sarah Bradner, do, witnesses, John Bradner, John Cooper

Feb 28 1866 Andrew Jones, Goshen, Maggie J. Owen, do, witnesses, Charles J. Everett, Josephus Terbell

Feb 28 1866 Uriah Terry, Warwick, Catharine Ann Thompson, Goshen, Witnesses, Adrian Holbert, Mrs. A. Holbert

June 7 1866 Alfred D. Hopkins, Goshen, Frances J. Anderson, do, witnesses, Horace Sweezy, James Delancey

June 7 1866 Charles H. Miller, Middletown, Sarah E. Jervis, Goshen, Colored, witnesses, Mary Banks, Chas. H. Robbins

Oct 2 1866 Dr. J. B. Van Hoosen, Delaware Co. N. Y., Lottie Brewster, Goshen, witnesses, Charles H. Winfield, John E. Howell

RECORD OF MARRIAGES 43

Oct 17 1866   John A. Smith, Goshen, Abbe A. Bennet, do, witnesses, Andrew Jones, John Webb
Oct 31 1866   Wm. S. Tuthill, Walkill, Hattie H. Vandewater, Goshen, witnesses, Mandeville Westcott, Elizabeth Drake
Nov 13 1866   Charles E. Balcom, Elmira, Jane E. Cheeseman, Sanford, Broome Co., N. Y., witnesses, William Philcox, J. Seely Edsall
Nov 29 1866   Thomas Jefferson Brown, Goshen, Jane Simmons, do, colored, witnesses, Sarah Youngs, Sarah Ellen Miller
Jan 23 1867   George Gouge, Hamptonburgh, Matilda Booth, do, witnesses, Vincent Booth, Rev. S. C. Hepburn
Ap 16 1867   William Sing, New York, Jane Griffin, do, witnesses, Charlotte H. Snodgrass, Robt. D. Snodgrass
June 12 1867   William B. Royce, Middletown, Mary E. Roe, Goshen, witnesses, Charles E. Merriam, Floyd A. Crane
June 26 1867   Roswell M. Sayer, Middletown, Mary B. Wright, Goshen, witnesses, Chas. H. Winfield, Dr. D. C. Winifield
Oct 5 1867   John Steiner, Montgomery, Lizzie McMinn, Goshen, witnesses, Peter Zimmer, Mrs. McDonald
Oct 16 1867   Gabriel B. Jones, Goshen, Jane Elizabeth Tuthill, do, witnesses, William H. Newman, John A. Smith
July 4 1868   Milton Morgan, Monroe, Martha Hall, do, witness, C. H. Snodgrass
July 4 1868   Nicholas Hillman, Munroe, Elizabeth Morgan, do, witness, C. H. Snodgrass
Nov 4 1868   Andrew Connover, Passaic, N. Jersey, Phoebe Thompson, do, Colored   Sarah Vandyke, C. H. Snodgrass
Nov 19, 1868   Jacob W. Hayne, Goshen, Jennie W. Strong, do, witnesses, John Wallace, G. W. Ostrom
Dec 3, 1868   John C. Lamb, Springfield, Illinois, Annie Plougher, do, witnesses Saml. S. Snodgrass, Annie Snodgrass
Dec 16 1868   Nathaniel J. Kelsey, Goshen, Carrie D. Post, do, witnesses, John E. Howell Chas. E. Merriam
Dec 17 1868   William Smith, Goshen, Margaret De Frees, do, witnesses, Colored Louis Bayard, Bridget Cunningham   ,
March 17 1869   Andrew J. Jessup, Florida, Ameilia Mc Cain, Goshen, witnesses, De Witt Howell, Dr. Rumsey
Nov 25 1868   Seneca Jessup, Florida, Sarah Delia Mc Cain, Goshen
March 24 1869   Charles T. Dunning, Goshen, Georgee Thompson, do, witnesses, Mrs. Denton Young, Miss Edna J. Thompson
April 10 1869   Joseph H. Daly, Middletown, Josephine Moore, do, witness, Robert D. Snodgrass
July 11 1869   Patrick Sullivan, Goshen, Johanna Donnelly, do, witness, Robert D. Snodgrass
Augt 4 1869   James Mapes, Goshen, Susan De Frees, do, witnesses, Henry Colored Williams, Susan E. Williams
Sep 8 1869   Nathaniel M. Jay, Goshen, Elizabeth C. Wilkin, do, witnesses, Henry & DeWitt Wilkin
Oct 6 1869   Edwin L. Roys, Goshen, Mary L. Coleman, do, witnesses, R. C. Coleman, W. M. Sayer
Jan 3 1870   J. Howard Clarke, Newark, N. Jersey, Cornelia A. Hunt, do, witnesses, J. H. Bertholf, Mrs. J. H. Bertholf
Feb 10 1870   Hezekiah Watkins, New York, Edna J. Thompson, Goshen, witnesses, Uriah Terry, James C. Coleman
April 12 1870   Richard A. Kipp, Goshen, Mary A. Dalley, do, witnesses, Richard Kip, Sr., Mrs. Duer

RECORD OF MARRIAGES

May 25 1870 James C. Coleman, Jr., Goshen, Ann Eliz. Hulse, Walkill, witnesses, Rev. Floyd S. Crane, Mrs. E. K. Huffnagle

Sep 21 1870 George W. Green, Middletown, Carrie Jenkins, do, Robt. D. Snodgrass, W. H. Redfield

Dec 22 1870 Adrian Holbert, New York, Frances Wells, Goshen, witnesses, Lewis Wood, John Wells

Dec 28 1870 Gilbert H. Hopkins, Goshen, Suzie R. Howell, do, witnesses, Charles E. Millspaugh, Willm. Jackson

Jan 11 1871 William A. Koonz, Hamptonburgh, Mary A. Hallock, Goshen, witnesses, George Conning, H. V. D. Hoyt

Jan 24 1871 Joseph C. Wickam, Wawayada, Fannie E. Horton, Goshen, witnesses, Chauncy S. Hulse, Frances C. Hulse

Feb 28 1871 John L. Drake, Patterson, N. Jersey, Uphila J. Christman, do, witnesses, Charlotte H. Snodgrass, Margaret Dundy

March 23 1871 Charles H. Samuel, Goshen, Julia L. Moore, do, witnesses, Hezekiah Ludlum, John E. Moore

July 26 1871 Henry Sinsabaugh, Goshen, Clara E. Valentine, do, witnesses, Charles E. Merriam, Rev. O. M. Johnston

Sep 30 1871 George Whittington, Goshen, Ann Maria Fowler, do, witness, Colored Maria Smith

Feb 28 1872 James Tuthill, Goshen, Sarah A. Doughty, do, witnesses, James S. Hopkins, Chas. B. Tuthill

March 3 1872 Charles N. Jervis, Goshen, Emma Lowe, do, witnesses, A. Alex. Snodgrass, Mrs. C. H. Snodgrass

March 21 1872 Ely S. Conkling, Goshen, Phoebe A. Durland, do, witnesses, Nathanl. Conkling, Andrew J. Jessup

June 6 1872 Rev. Marcus Burr, L. Island, Cornelia W. Payne, Goshen, witnesses, Robt. Young, Jonah K. Payne

July 5 1872 William H. Martine, Calafornia, Emma LaForge, Orange Co. N. Y., witness, Mrs. C. H. Snodgrass

July 9 1872 John De Frees, Ringwood, N. J., Sarah E. Vandyke, Gooshen, Colored witnesses, Mrs. C. H. Snodgrass, A. Alex. Snodgrass

March 5 1873 Dr. J. Irving Marclay, Plainfield, N. J., M. Frank Webb, Elmira, N. Y., witnesses, Charles C. Babbitt, Jason W. Corwin

April 13 1873 Stephen Morris, Goshen, Elizabeth J. Lowe, do, witnesses, Colored Eliza Lowe, Eliza Farrell

May 13 1873 Saml. Wickam Slaughter, Waverly, N. Y., Charlotte Wells, Goshen, witnesses, James E. Wells, Nathaniel Ackerly

June 26 1873 James H. Garner, Goshen, Mary Jane Green, do, witnesses, Colored John Green, Rosanna Green

July 31 1873 Charles Bank, Goshen, Harriet Gardner, do, witnesses, Morris Bayard, Sarah Bayard.

Sep 9 1873 Isaac R. Oakley, Salisbury, N. Y., Sarah E. Oakley, Goshen, Witnesses, Jason W. Corwin, Chas. Millspaugh

Oct 2 1873 William Brown, Goshen, Joanna Cullen, do, witnesses, Mrs. C. H. Snodgrass, Mrs. E. K. Snodgrass

Oct 15 1873 Henry D. Hopkins, Goshen, Julia E. Ayers, do, witnesses, Gilbert H. Hopkins, Horace Thompson

Nov 28 1873 Jerome Green, Goshen, Eliza Lowe, do, witnesses, George A. Colored Brown, Saml S. Snodgrass

Dec 10 1873 Alfred Carling, Pine Island, Mary Kniffin, Goshen, Nathaniel Vansickle, Carpenter Howell

May 5 1874 S. Logan Kniffin, Goshen, Sarah J. Bennet, do, witnesses, J. Wells Corwin, Gabriel B. Jones

James M. Haggery, Goshen, Fannie L. Coleman, do, witnesses, J. Edward Wells, Adrian Holbert

RECORD OF MARRIAGES 45

June 22, 1874 James M. Lathroop, Connecticut, Kattie Lawrence, do, witness, Mattie A. Lathrop

Sep 21 1874 Phillip Graham, Piermont, Sarah Wilcox, Goshen, witness, Robt. D. Snodgrass

Oct 7 1874 Sylvanus J. Howell, Goshen, Mary K. Tuthill, do, witnesses, John Tuthill, Carpenter Howell

Nov 5 1874 Gunning B. Ostrom, Goshen, Susan C. Howell, do, witnesses, Gilbert H. Hopkins, Willm. Jackson

Nov 13 1874 Robert C. Thurston, Middletown, Mary A. Hawley, do, witness, Phillip Graham

Nov 25 1874 Horace D. Thompson, Goshen, Sallie Millspaugh, Walden, witnesses, J. Harvey Goodale, Virgil Thompson, Jr.

Dec 2 1874 Daniel Carpenter, Goshen, Mary Ryerson, do, witnesses, John Wallace, John Cooper

March 13 1875 William P. Clarke, Waywayanda, Sarah A. De Hart, Goshen, William Judson, Bertha Judson

May 29 1875 DeWitt C Hallock, P. Jervis, Jennie Lateer, Wantage, N. J., witnesses, Charlotte H. Snodgrass, Emma Snodgrass

July 3 1875 Frank N. Brown, Goshen, Allie M. Jackson, do, witnesses, D. O. Wetmon, Augusta J. Wetmon

Augt 2 1875 Stephen B. Russell, Goshen, Sarah Bowman, Washington, D. C., Colored witnesses, Robt. D. Snodgrass, Caroline Green

Augt 28 1875 Richard Cook, Vernon, N. J., Mary Brown, do, witnesses, Sarah C. Searles, C. H. Snodgrass

Augt 30 1875 Rufus Forchee, Warwick, Fannie Christie, do, witnesses, James L. Vanbraner, Mary Vanbraner

Sep 23 1875 Thomas Nelson, Circleville, Mary E. Ogden, New Vernon, witness, Robert D. Snodgrass

Sept 25 1875 John Maurice, Hamptonburgh, Ellen Stuart, do, witnesses, Solomon T. Smith, Mrs. S. T. Smith

Oct 14 1875 Arthur M. Woodruff, Goshen, Fannie C. Wallace, do, witnesses, John Cooper, John C. Wallace

Jan 26 1876 Andrew J. Moore, Goshen, Sarah A. Woodruff, do, witnesses, Henry Hill, Jane A. Hill

June 22, 1876 Robert Carr, Florida, N. Y., Jennie Mc Glouchlin, do, witness, Mrs. W. D. Snodgrass

Augt 3 1876 John Fitzgerald, Warwick, N. Y., Mary Neely, do, witness, Mrs. C. H. Snodgrass

Oct 23 1876 David B. Myers, Walkill, Ann Eliza Gabby, do, witnesses, James Gabby, George Mc Ewen

Oct 24 1876 Wm. H. Stanton, New York, Laura E. Kinsey, do, witnesses, James Wilson, Bridget Cox

Oct 31 1876 Hiram W. Bull, Mt. Hope, Alice J. Vernon, do, witnesses, Sarah A. Wright, Mrs. C. H. Snodgrass

Feb 13 1877 Arthur M. Dutcher, Middletown, Marietta A. Puffer, do, witnesses, Danl. Van Sickel, J. E. Wickham

March 14 1877 Daniel Howell, New York, Ann M. Howell, Goshen, witnesses, J. W. Corwin, Levi L. Lockwood

May 1 1877 John Dansler, Goshen, Lidia Waters, do, witnesses, Robert Colored Garrison, Margt. Freeman

May 8 1877 Newton K. Delavan, Pittsburgh, Pa., Jennie V. D. Heard, Goshen, witnesses, John J. Heard, Dubois Staats

May 9 1877 Augustus T. Cuddeback, Port Jervis, Mary B. Sanford, Goshen, witnesses, N. C. Sanford, Benjamin S. Smith

July 12 1877 Wellington Mc Bride, Goshen, Belle M. Post, do, witnesses, Ed. Dykeman, Willm. H. Wyker

RECORD OF MARRIAGES

Nov 13 1877 John J. Healy, Goshen, Gussie M. Bishop, do, witnesses, Willm. H. Wyker, George Dennistion

Feb 27 1878 Malvin Hotalen, Warwick, Mrs. T. J. Bradner, Goshen, witnesses, David Redfield, Dr. Woodruff

April 4 1878 James Conklin, Southfield, OC., Hanna E. Lewis, Central Valley, witnesses, C. H. Snodgrass, R. D. Snodgrass

July 31 1878 Niall Milburn, Chester, Maggie Farrell, do, witness, Mrs. C. H. Snodgrass

Augt 5 1878 A. H. Lyan, Middletown, Jennie E. Fletcher, Goshen, J. B. Crosby, Emma Fletcher

Oct 30 1878 Henry C. Payne, Goshen, Hattie S. Scott, do, witnesses, Harrison S. Nanny, Geo. Dennistown

March 25 1879 Jewet M. Ashman, Goshen, Sarah F. Tuthill, do, witnesses Chas. B. Tuthill, Wickham Smith

Dec 18 1879 Leman Hemman, Goshen, Libby Coyle, do, witnesses, Robt. D. Snodgrass

Dec 23 1879 Frank G. Everrett, Goshen, Mary T. Jackson, do, witnesses, Arthur Newman, James B. Tuthill

April 20 1880 Sidney Reid, Marlborough, N. Y., Mrs. Sarah Denton, Goshen, witnesses, Wellington Mc Bride, Mrs. Belle McBride

Nov 3 1880 William B. Oldfield, Blooming Grove, Ella Rysdyke, Goshen, witnesses, Rev. Arthur Newman, Danl. Banker

Nov 11 1880 Elias Mann, Florida, N. Y., Sarah J. Decker, Florida, witnesses, Robt. D. Snodgrass, Lizzie Nolan

Nov 17 1880 John B. Slawson, Jersey City, N. J., Annie Ryerson, Goshen, witnesses, Rev. Arthur Newman, Adrian Holbert

Jan 5 1881 James H. Reed, Goshen, Katie Dalton, Goshen, witness, Robt. D. Snodgrass

Feb 16 1881 Francis J. Herrick, Middletown, Ella J. Armstrong, Middlletown, witnesses, Francis J. Meehan, Mrs. C. E. O'Neill

March 2 1881 William A. Rumsey, Goshen, Alice C. Young, Goshen, witnesses, Dr. J. H. Thompson, Theodore Smith

June 1 1881 Hiram P. Tuthill, Washingtonville, Josie Taylor, Washingtonville, R. D. Snodgrass

Sep 13 1881 Frank O. Parson, Middletown, Jennie Connell, Middletown, R. D. Snodgrass

Sep 21 1881 Oliver O. Hulse, City of New York, Carrie M. Dikeman, Goshen, witnesses, E. Dikeman, B. R. Champion.

Oct 5 1881 James R. Eschelman, Brooklyn, L. I., Hanna G. Newman, Goshen, witnesses, Hez C. Newman, H. C. Newman

Oct 12 1881 Edgar P. Redfield, Goshen, Melissa J. Crane, Goshen, witnesses, Rev. Floyd A. Crane, Mrs. F. A. Crane

Oct 18 1881 Edward H. Ray, Goshen, Annie E. Owen, Goshen, witnesses, William V. Ray, William H. Owen

Oct 24 1881 Noah Brown, Goshen, Sarah E. Miller, Goshen, witness, R. D. Snodgrass

Jan 14 1882 Harry J. E. Condon, Stockton, California, Annie J. Post, Goshen, witnesses, Wellington McBride, Belle McBride

Jan 25 1882 Alfred Wells Coleman, New York City, Sarah Thurston, Goshen, witnesses, Edward P. Shaw, Kittie Sweet

April 12 1882 Isaac T. Earl, Munroe, Carrie Babcook, Southfield, witness R. D. Snodgrass

April 17 1882 J. W. Welch, Middletown, Addie L. Eckert, Middletown, witnesses, R. D. Snodgrass, S. S. Snodgrass

Apl 22 1882 Philip Hendricks, New Paltz, Margaret A. Townsend, Clintondale, witness, S. S. Snodgrass

RECORD OF MARRIAGES

Sep 6 1882   George W. Holman, Jr., Brooklyn, L. I., Jennie L. **Rawline**, Goshen, witnesses, Horton Smith, W. H. Bennet, **Thomas Mathews**, Robt. Wallace
Oct 25 1882   Geo. M. Wilkes, Centreville, Mary J. Gardiner, **Goshen**, witnesses, Charles B. Wilkes, Mary Wilkinson
Dec 19 1882   David A. Sease, Middletown, Emma Hallock, Middletown, witnesses, W. H. Wyker, R. C. Snodgrass
Feb 21 1883   Charles G. Elliott, Goshen, Frances L. Strong, Goshen, witnesses, John Wallace, M. B. Stafford
April 4 1883   Charles E. Barkman, Port Jervis, Marrietta Cassady, Goshen, witnesses, Rosilla A. Tuthill, Cornelia Weymer
Oct 3 1883   T. D. Schoonmaker, Goshen, Julia A. Poppino, Goshen, witnesses, Alex. J. Hardine, Susie A. Homan
Oct 6 1883   Wm. T. Wallace, Philadelphia, Emma Wallace, Goshen, witnesses, Mary M. Vail, F. H. Steel
Oct 18 1883   James Demarest, City of New York, Minnie A. Ackley, Goshen, witnesses, John T. Ackley, Sarah J. Ackley
Nov 28 1883   George A. Denniston, Goshen, Jennie H. Bishop, Goshen, witnesses, Mrs. John J. Healey, Emma C. Griffin
Jan 5 1884   Chancey E. Morse, Florida, Mary E. DeWitt, Florida, witness, R. D. Snodgrass
Feb 20 1884   Asher Johnson, Goshen, Kate Hawkins, Hamptonburgh, witnesses, Floyd Hawkins, Jothan C. Johnson
April 9 1884   Charles W. Faulkner, Wallkill, Lena R. Briggs, Wallkill, witnesses, Ida Reynolds, R. D. Snodgrass
June 18 1884   Frank B. Ayers, Middletown, Dolly S. Jackson, Hamptonburgh, witnesses, F. H. Bertholf, H. B. Hill
Oct 1 1884   John B. Wickham, Deckertown, N. Y., Anna Thurston, Goshen, witnesses, John D. Thurston, Annie Coleman
Oct 8 1884   Robert Wallace, Brooklyn, N. Y., Mary F. Smiley, **Rochester**, N. Y., witnesses, J. W. Corwin, Nathl. J. Kelsey
Dec 23 1884   Robert H. Andruss, N. Y. City, Nellie J. Sinsabaugh, **Goshen**, witnesses, Charles Andruss, Kate H. Andrus
May 28 1885   Charles C. Luckey, Middletown, Sadie R. Russell, Middletown, witnesses, Mrs. A. S. Brink, A. J. Brink
June 10 1885   Wesley Wait, Goshen, Emily S. Rawlins, Goshen, witnesses, Sarah J. Smith, Fredk. W. Seward.

Register of Members

REGISTER OF THE MEMBERS OF THE PRESBYTERIAN CHURCH IN GOSHEN

Beginning May 30, 1767
Those marked x are dead.
Those marked * never before in communion.
Those marked I received on certificate.
Those marked z dismissed or removed away.
Those marked s suspended.
All those on the first 8 pages are now dead or removed away.

                                                         Jany. 1st, 1817.

x		Elizabeth Everett, wife of Danl. Everett
x		Patience Corey
x	*	John Finch
x	I	Benjamin Coleman
x	*	Martha Coleman
x	I	Mary Tusten
x	I	Lois Booth
x	*	Israel Rickey
x	I	Nathaniel Webb &
x	I	Sarah Webb his wife
x	I	Samuel Wickham
x	I	Jane Butler, wife of James Butler, Senr.
x	z	Eleanor Thompson
x	I	Abijah Wells
x	z	Mary Robinson
x	I	Mary Carpenter
x	*	Isaiah Vail
z	*	Hannah Davis
x	*	Martha Jackson
z	*	Mary Smith
z	*	Ephriam Everett
x	*	William Stringham
x	*	John Allison
x	I	Hannah Gale
x	*	Parshall Terry
x	*	Hannah Smith
x	I	Elisha Hulse &
x	I	Elizabeth Hulse his wife
x	I	William Stubbs
x	I	Catherine Ludlum
x	I	Benjamin Tusten
z	I	Mary Vail

October 1767
| x | * | Abigail Drake |
| z | * | William Paul |

June 1768
| z | * | Susannah Rhoades |
| x | * | Ann Ellison |

REGISTER OF MEMBERS

October 1768
    x * Henry Wisner, Esq.
    x * Samuel Carpenter—an Elder
    z * Alexander Thompson
    x * Mary Booth
June 1769
    x * Rebecka Rickey
    x * Jane Butterfield
October 1769
    x * Elizabeth Smith
    x * Nathaniel Owens
June 1770
    x * Thomas Neely &
    x * Margaret Neely his wife
    x * Mary Oldfield
    x * Kezia Oldfield
    x * Ruth Mc Nish
September 1771
    z * Robert Thompson
    z * Abigail Moore
1772
    x * Phebe Jackson
1774
    x * David Moore, Junr.
    x I Hannah Pettitt
    z I Hannah Vail
1775
    z * Amy Case
1777
    x I Ephriam Mastin
    x I Nehemiah Carpenter
1779
    x * Eliud Tryon—Elder
1781
    x z Jonathan Bailey
    x I Priscilla Carpenter
    x * James Little
    x * Phebe Vail
    x * Abigail Carpenter
    x I Isaac Smith
June 2nd 1782
    x * Elizabeth Sawyer, Wid. of Capt. Jas. Sawyer
    x * Isaac Smith Son of
    z * Isaac Witter
    x * Hannah Jones, Wid. of Capt. Saml. Jones
    x * Rebecka Gale wife of Thos. Gale
    x * Sarah Gale
    z * Josiah Vail
    x * Matthew Smith
    x * Gilbert Carpenter
    x * William Mc Mullen
October 1782
    x * John Smith—Elder
    z * Richard Carpenter—Dec. 9, 1798

REGISTER OF MEMBERS

  x * Richard Wood
  z * Millicent Knapp
  x * Sarah Smith
  x * Martha Allison
x z * Abigail Tuthill
  z * Mehitable Tuthill, now Boyd, Deer Park.
  x * Ruth Mosier
  x * Sarah Carpenter

July 19, 1783
  z * John Hulse
  x * Peter Arnout
  z * Mary Vail

July 19, 1783
  x * Hannah Owen, wife of Gershom Owen
  x * Susannah Roe, wife of Capt. Nathl. Roe.

June 1784
x z * Lucretia Tusten, married Alex. Wood.

November 7, 1784
  z * James Howell—April 22, 1795
  x * Hannah Gale, wife of Coe Gale
  x * Susannah Carpenter

June 12, 1785
  x * Doctr. Jonathan Swezy (Elder) &
  x * Elizabeth Swezy his wife
  x * Samuel Moffatt &
  x * Solomon Smith, suspended May 24, 1804
  z * Daniel Conkling
  z * Archibald Armstrong
  x * David Arnold &
  x * Mary Arnold his wife
  z * Rebecka Borland wife of Chas. Borland
  x * Lydia Carpenter, wife of Benj. Carpenter
  z * Kezia Wells wife of Wm. Wells—Westtown
  z I Jacob Wright &
  z I Margaret Wright his wife

October 4, 1785
  x * Peter Gale—Elder
  x * Abigail Carpenter
  x * Henry Jackson
  z * William Stubbs &
  z * Mary Stubbs his wife

June 1786
  x * Uriah Terry &
  x * Bethiah Terry his wife
  z * James Horton (Elder in Deerpark)

January 21, 1787
  z * James Keeler
  z * Margaret Mc Nish
  x * Jonathan Smith Esq.

January 21, 1787
  z * Ezra Howell (Blooming Grove)
  x * Catherine Smith
  x I Archibald Hall

May 27, 1787
  z * Abel Woodhull   (Deerpark)

REGISTER OF MEMBERS 51

    z * Doctr. Jesse Woodhull (Long Island)
    z * Revd. Simon Hosack, DD, Johnstown
    z * John Gale, Senr—Son of Coe Gale (New York)
October 14, 1787
    z * Charles Tooker (Deerpark)
    x * Nathaniel Bailey
    z * George Owen
    x * Sybile Cooley
    x * Susanna Carpenter
    x * Mehitable Corwin
June 29, 1788
    x * David Crawford &
    x * Jane Crawford his wife
    x * Sarah Phillips wife Col. Moses Phillips
October 1788
    x I Solomon Carpenter
    z I Benjamin Codington
    z * Edward Mc Henry
June 7, 1789
    x * Phebe Smith wife of Solomon Smith
    z * Juliana Smith wife of Henry C. Smith
October 4, 1789
    z I Sarah Townsend
    x * Benjamin Gale—Elder &
    x * Mary Gale his wife
November 28, 1790
    z * Mary Roe—Scotchtown
    z * Samuel Tooker—Octr. 1795
    x I Deborah Smith
June 1, 1791
    x * Benjamin Conkling
x z * Abiel Frye, Esq.
    z * Silas Pierson (Scotchtown)
September 25, 1792
    z I Ann Moffat recommend here from a Church in Ireland, now Richd. Graham wife
    z * Isaiah Vail, Junr.
September 30 1792
    x * Henry Wisner, Esq.
    z * Samuel Boughton (Deerpark)
        * Letitia Crans wife Wilhelmus Crans Decr. 9 1798
June 2nd 1793
    z * William Thompson, Esq.
    x * Asa Smith
    z * Margaret Clark Ker, now Mrs. Freeman
    z * Elizabeth Ker, now Mrs. Mc Carthy
November 13, 1793
    x * Jeremiah Jessup
    z * Abigail Mc Cane
    z * Benjamin B. Hopkins
    z * Thomas Cooper
    x * Sarah Smith
    x * Mary Scoit
    z * George Corwin
    x * Beulah Moore

REGISTER OF MEMBERS

June 22, 1794
- x * Thomas Curtice
- z * Terry Owens—Feby. 19, 1809
- x * John Smith, Junr.
- z * John Vail (Middletown)
- x * Elizabeth Carpenter
- x * Anna Tusten

November 16, 1794
- x * Joshua Davis, Esq.
- z * Susanna Bradner, wife of Jno. Bradner

June 14, 1795
- x * Anna Wisner, wid. of John Wisner, decd.
- x * Kezia Townsend, wid. of Roger Townsend
- x * Sarah Howell, wife of Benj. Howell
- x * William Townsend. Suspended June 28, 1798
- z I James Mitchell, from Rahway N. Jersey June 15, 1799
- x I Jeheil Ross, from Rahway N. Jersey June 15, 1799
- x I Calvin Ross, from Rahway N. Jersey June 15, 1799
- z I Joanna Ross, from Rahway N. Jersey June 15, 1799

October 11, 1795
- x * Anne Bradner
- z I Simeon Wood

June 5, 1796
- x I Margaret Caldwell wife Jas. Caldwell, from Wallkilll
- x I Elizabeth Caldwell wife Thos. Cadwell, from Wallkill
- z I Amy Fairchild
- z I Hannah Smith
- x z * Samuel Tucker
- z I Mary Ketcham
- z * Frances Munnell—Sept. 20, 1800

October 8, 1796
- z I Joseph Doolittle &   from Crompond
- z I Abigail his wife   from Crompond
- z * John Jarvis, Free man of Color
- z I ″ Smith

October 7, 1797
- x * Elizabeth Bull wife of Crisse Bull
- x I James Caldwell from Wallkill, July 14th 1798

June 15, 1799
- z * Mary Sayre wife of Jonathan Sayre

October 5, 1799
- z I Matthew Adams

June 21, 1800
- x * Esther Munson
- z * John White (Elder at Scotchtown)
- z I Gilbert Roberts &   admitted
- z I Elizabeth Roberts   admitted
- z * Adam Millspaugh (Elder at Scotchtown)
- x * Hannah Bull wife of John Bull   Oct. 6, 1804
- x * Doctr. William Elmer   Oct. 6, 1804
- x * Sarah Tuthill wife of Jonathn. Tuthill   May 3, 1806
- x * Mary Brewster wife of John Brewster   May 1 1808
- x * Benjamin Robinson   May 1 1808
- x * Mary Brown wid of John Brown, Sept 30
- z * Dorcas wife of John Jarvis,   May 6 1809
- x * Hannah Brown wife of Joshua Brown, Oct 1

REGISTER OF MEMBERS 53

x	*	Anna wife of Barna Horton, Oct 14, 1810
x z	*	Phebe Bodle August 9 1811
x	*	Robert Wood Esq. August 9 1811
x	*	Julia Budd, November 14, 1812
z	*	Christiana Hawkins—Aug 3, 1814
z	*	Sally Smith wife of Gab. Smith, Nov 3, 1814
x	*	Mary Servt. of Thos. Waters Aug. 3, 1814
x	*	Nathaniel Conkling, Nov 3, 1814
z	*	Mary wife Col. John Seward, Novr. 6, 1815
x	*	John G. Jessup Nov. 6, 1815
x I		Deborah Green wife of James Green May 11 1809
x	*	Abigail wife of John A. Smith, Aug 3, 1814
z	*	George Evertson Arnout, May 6, 1816

The following persons were living and Members of the Church Jany. 1, 1817.

x	*	Deborah, wid. of Solomon Finch June 1770
x	*	Elsa Wood, wife of Joseph Wood — 1774
x z I		Hannah, wife of Reuben Hopkins 1781
x	*	Thomas Gale & June 7 1782
x	*	Juliana Gale (late Moore) his wife 1790

Feb. 25, 1814

x	*	Asa Steward & (Elder) October 1782
x	*	Elizabeth his wife October 1782
x	*	Annanias Valentine (Elder) July 19 1783
x	*	Abigail, wid. of Daniel Hall Esq. July 19 1783
x	*	Coe Gale Novr. 7 1784
x	*	Anna Kinner Nov. 7 1784
x z	*	William Bodle (Elder) June 12 1785
x	*	Martha Conkling wid. of Nat. Conkling June 12 1785
x	*	Thomas Borland June 12 1785
x	*	Benjamin Carpenter June 12 1785
x	*	Sarah, wife of Wm Bodle June 12 1785
x	*	Elizabeth, wife of Thos. Borland June 12 1785
x z	*	Reuben Hopkins, (Elder) Oct. 4, 1785
x	*	Sarah wife of Saml. Moffat Oct. 4, 1785
x	*	Dolly, wid. of Mich. Carpenter June 1786
x	*	Mary, wife of David Case, June 1786
x z	*	Doctr. Eusebius Austin June 1786
	*	Elisha Reeves—(Middletown) Jany 21 1787
x	*	Daniel Bailey (Elder) Jany 21 1787
x z	*	Esther, wid. of Elder P. Gale Jany 21 1787
	*	Eleanor Smith Jany 21 1787
x	*	Eleanor Carpenter Jany 21 1787
	*	Gone off Juliana wife of Jas. Everett Jany 21 1787
x	*	Margaret, wid. of Capt. S. Smith Jany 21 1787
x	*	Mary, wid. of Dr. Wm. Elmer June 29 1788
x	*	Stephen Smith & Oct 4 1789

April 27 1818

x	*	Sarah Smith his wife June 7 1789
x	*	Abigail wife of Wm. Jackson Nov 28 1790
z	*	Stephen Crane Nov 28 1790
x	*	Bethiah, wid. of Nathn. Bailey, Nov 7 1784
x	*	Bethiah, wid. of Benj. Conkling, June 19 1791
x	*	Albert Foster Sept 30 1792
x	*	Hannah wife of Danl. Corwin June 2 1793
x	*	Elizabeth wid. of Henry Jackson June 2 1793

REGISTER OF MEMBERS

   x * William Phillips, (Elder)—On account of disorderly & unchristian conduct, Session resolved that his name be struck from the records, Dec. 14th 1839
   x * John Steward Esq   Nov 13 1793
   x * Hannah wid of Jer. Jessup   Nov 13 1793, his uncle states that Mr. Jessup died in 1816 & Joined the church with his wife.
   x * John Bradner Esq. &   Nov 13 1793
   x * Margaret his wife   Nov 13 1793
   x * Elizabeth wife of Coe Gale   Nov 13 1793
   x * Sarah wife of Jas. Dunning,   Nov 13 1793
      * Sarah Coleman   May 27 1787
   x * Miriam, wife of Benjn. Howell, Ridgebury   May 27 1787
   x * James Carpenter &   died April 1, 1817   June 22 1794
   x * Mary Carpenter his wife   June 22 1794
      * Sarah, wife of Dav. Hawkins   June 22 1794
   x * Ann, wife of Michl. Jackson   June 22 1794
   x * Deziah Case, Wid   June 22 1794
z x * Luther Steward &   June 22 1794
   x * Kezia Steward, his wife   June 22 1794
   x * Doctr. David Reeve Arnell (Elder)   June 22 1794
   x * Azubah Davis widow   June 22 1794
   x * Mary wife of Timothy Dunning
   x * Mary, wife Benjn. Bradner, Nov. 16, 1794
   x * Wid. Abigail Smith   June 14 1795
   x * Lucy Billson (free woman) June 14 1795
   x * Kezia, wife of D. M. Westcott   June 4 1797
      * Gone off   Phebe, wife of Saml. Harlow   June 4 1797
   x * Phebe, wid. of Abel Gale, Esq.   October 7 1797
   x * Daniel Corwin   October 7 1797
   x * Isaac Hallock &   Nov. 6 1815
  z * Tamar his wife
   x * Mary wife of Nathl. Tuthill   Oct. 6 1798
   x * Eunice Brown wife of Jo. Brown   Oct 1798
   x * James Dunning   Oct 1798
   x * Sarah Hall, wid. of Timothy Hall   Oct 1798
   z * Christian, wid. of Richard Wood   Oct 1798
   x * Martha wid. of Eben. Dunning   June 21 1800
   x * Abigail, wife of David Swezy   June 21 1800
      * Widow of Daniel Burnett,   June 21 1800
x s * Alexander Corey   June 21 1800
   x I Richard Jackson from Hopewelll   Oct 4 1800
      * Martha, wid. of Isaac Vanduzer Hopewell   June 19, 1802
   x I Margaret, wid. of Joseph Martin from a Presbyterian Church in Ireland   June 25 1803
x z * Martha, wid. of Nathan Coleman   Oct 5 1803
   x * Hannah, wife of Abel B. Watkins   May 26 1804
x z * Hannah Arnell   May 26 1804
x z * Noah Carpenter, from Newark   May 26 1804
   x * Mary wife of Robert Boak   Oct 6 1804
   x * Margaret, wid of Nathl. Conkling, Junr.   May 31 1806
      * Gone off   John Gale, son of Thos. Gale   May 31 1806
      * Ditto   Seth L. Poppino &   May 31 1806
      * Ditto   Sarah Poppino, his wife   May 31 1806
   x * Mary wife of Thos Carmer   May 31 1806
   z * Catharine Lewis wife of the Revd. Isaac Lewis of Cooperstown May 31 1806

REGISTER OF MEMBERS 55

x	z	*	Wid. Deborah Ross May 31 1806
	x	*	Mary, wid. of Aaron Hetfield, Oct 1 1806
		*	Gone Sarah wife of Jared Mosier May 24 1807
	x	*	Hannah, Servt. of Col. Phillips May 24 1807
	x	I	Samuel Harlow from Chester Oct 11, 1807
	x	*	Benjamin Strong (Elder) Oct 11, 1807
	x	*	Hannah wife of Benj. Coleman Oct 11, 1807
	x	*	Col. Moses Phillips Sept 30, 1808
	x	*	Mary wife of Benjn. Robinson Sept 30, 1808
x	I	*	John Steward (Ridgebury) May 6 1809
z	x	*	Sally wife of Wm. Phillips May 6 1809
	x	*	Phebe wife of James Egbert May 6 1809
	x	*	Mary wife of John Steward, Esq., Oct 1 1809
	x	I	Mary M Arnell (Neelytown wife of Dr. Arnell) Oct 1 1809
	x	*	David Webb Oct 1 1809
	x	*	Deborah wife of Joshua Goldsmith Oct 1 1809
	x	*	Susannah wife of Benj. Strong June 10 1810
	x	*	Eliza P. wife of Dr. Phillip June 10 1810
	x	*	Hannah wife of Genl. Wilkin June 10 1810
	x	*	Samuel Vail & June 10 1810
	x	*	Hannah his wife June 10 1810
	z	*	Michael Carpenter, Ordained to the Gospel Ministrey April 22, 1830 June 10 1810
	z	*	Clarissa Gale (now Otis) June 10 1810
	z	I	James Clason & Abigail June 10 1810
	z	I	his wife from Stanwich June 10 1810
	x	*	Mary wife of Daniel Bailey Octr. 14 1810
	x	*	Margaret wife of Fredk. Dolson Octr. 14 1810
	x	*	Gone off Elsa wife of James Gale Octr. 14 1810
x	z	*	Mary Hopkins Octr. 14 1810
		*	Hannibal Mason Hopkins Elder Octr. 14 1810
	x	*	Julia, wife of John Gale April 28 1811
x	z	*	Mary, wife of Samuel Clason from Stamford Connet. Aug. 9 1811
	x	*	Eunice, wid. of Benj. Carpenter Aug 9 1811
	x	*	Abigail, wife of John Crane Nov. 3 1811
	x	*	James Butler June 19 1812
	x	*	Margaret, wid. of Phins. Rumsey June 19 1812
	x	*	Sarah, wife of Jno. Taylor June 19 1812
	x	*	Hannah Newman Nov. 14 1812
	z	*	Sarah, wife of Saml. Butler Oct. 10 1813
	x	*	Jennet Giles, from Neely Town
	x	*	Jane Butler wife of James May 2 1814
	x	*	Julia, wife of Henry W. Denton May 2 1814
	x	*	Hannah wife of Danrl. Tooker May 2 1814
	s	*	restored Sally Hathaway widow of Dan. Hathaway, Suspended, January 20th 1817, gone off May 2 1814
	x	*	Widow Hannah Kelsey died Jany. 11 May 2 1814
	z	*	Charlotte, wife of Jas. Wood May 2 1814
	x	*	Elizabeth wife of Paul Masters May 2 1814
	x	*	Solomon Carpenter and May 2 1814
	z	*	Phebe his wife May 2 1814
		*	Eleanor, wife of Andrew Noble, abandoned the church in 1845 May 2, 1814
		*	Eleanor Carpenter May 2, 1814
		*	Eleanor Vail, now Coleman May 2, 1814

REGISTER OF MEMBERS

x	*	Abigail, Wid. of Jonathan Smith	May 2, 1814
x	*	Elizabeth, wife of Jesse Smith	May 7 1814
	*	Letitia Boak, abandoned the Church 1845	May 7 1814
z	I	Sally wife of Gilbert Williams from Newburgh	August 3, 1814
x	*	Jane, wife Thos Booth	August 3, 1814
	*	Gone off, Mary Brown	August 3, 1814
z	*	Abigail Borland, dismissed 1847	August 7 1814
z	*	Leana, wife of Theoph. Dolsen	August 7 1814
x	I	Nancy, wife of Joshua Conkling from Florida	August 7 1814
z	*	Samuel Clason	Nov 3 1814
x	*	Sally, wife of Josiah Kitchell	Nov 3 1814
z	*	Fanny, wife of David Webb,	Nov 3 1814
I z	*	Nehemiah Carpenter gone to Chester	Nov 3 1814
z	*	John A Smith	Nov 3 1814
x	*	Joseph Wood, Junr &	Nov 5 1814
x	*	Abigail Wood, his wife	Nov 5 1814
x	*	Luther Harris & Elder	Nov 5 1814
x	*	Mary Harris, his wife	Nov 5 1814
x	*	Joshua Goldsmith	Nov 5 1814
x	*	Timothy Wood &	Nov 5 1814
x	*	Dolly Wood his wife	Nov 5 1814
x s	*	William Noble	Nov 5 1814
z	*	John Herod Tuthill	Nov 5 1814
	*	Charles Smith	Nov 5 1814
x	*	Abigail wid. of Stephen Smith	Nov 5 1814
x	*	Mary, wife of Willm. Edsall	Nov 5 1814
z	*	Mary, wife of Gilbt. Hawkins	Nov 5 1814
z	*	Wid. Amy Morgan	Nov 5 1814
s	*	Maria Ingraham	Nov 5 1814
z	*	Azuba Cory, now Austin Tery wife	Nov 5 1814
	*	Catharine Corey	Nov 5 1814
x	*	Phebe, wife of Wm. Foster	Nov 5 1814
z	*	Mary, wid. of Geo. Smith	May 6 1815
	*	Lois, wid. of Nehemiah Denton	May 6 1815
	*	John Jay Thompson	May 6 1815
z	*	Samuel Butler	May 6 1815
z	*	John Amon Carpenter	May 6 1815
	I	Esther Fisk wife of Rev. Ezra Fisk	May 6 1815
x	*	Dinah Hubbard (free woman)	Nov. 3 1814
x	*	Juda wife of Joshua Whitman	July 31 1815
x	*	Sarah wife of Wm. Corning	July 31 1815
x	*	Martha wife of Jno. Dunning	July 31 1815
z	*	Timothy B. Crowell & Elder	July 31 1815
x	*	Maria his wife	July 31 1815
	*	Hannah Corey	July 31 1815
z	*	William Howe &	July 31 1815
x	*	Elizabeth Howe, his wife	July 31 1815
z	*	Benjamin C. Smith Elder	July 31 1815
z	*	Benjamin Corey	July 31 1815
z	*	Sally Maria Brewster, now Woodhull	July 31 1815
x	*	Josiah Kitchell	July 31 1815
x	*	Lydia Vail	July 31 1815
z	*	Mary wife of Daniel Sloan, dismissed Nov. 1817,	August 5, 1815
z	*	Mary Brewster	August 5, 1815
x z	*	Anna Fisk, July 7, 1817, Dis.	August 5, 1815
z	*	Susanna Horton	August 5, 1815

REGISTER OF MEMBERS 57

z	I	Tabitha wife of Benj. Wade, from N. York	August 5, 1815
z	I	Orange Green & from Neelytown	August 5, 1815
z	I	Mary Green his wife from Neelytown	August 5, 1815
z	I	Eliza L'Hommidieu, now Ostrander	August 5, 1815
z	*	Henry Wisner Nov. 6 1815	
	*	went off James Gale, Abandoned the church 1845	August 5, 1815
x	I *	Peter Gale & Nov 6 1815	
z	*	Julia Gale, his wife Nov. 6 1815	
	*	Rebecka Brown Nov. 6 1815	
z	*	John L'Hommidieu & Nov. 6 1815	
z	*	Dolly L'Hommidieu his wife Nov. 6 1815	
x	*	Frederick Horton Nov. 6 1815	
	*	Joshua Smith & Nov. 6 1815	
x	*	Sarah Smith, his wife Nov. 6 1815	
z	*	Hester Smith Nov. 6 1815	
	*	Sarah Denton now Bradner Nov 6 1815	
x	*	Daniel Foster & Nov. 6 1815	
z	*	Sally Foster, his wife Nov. 6 1815	
z	*	Olivia Brewster, now Marvin Nov. 6 1815	
x z	*	Delinda Hopkins, married Dr. Wm. Johnston, Georgia, since died Nov. 6 1815	
x	*	Fanny Bodle Nov. 6 1815	
z	*	William Mc Koy & Nov. 6 1815	
z	*	Abigail Mc Koy, his wife Nov. 6 1815	
	*	Abigail wife of Harry Smith Nov. 6 1815	
z	*	Widow Jane Turner Nov. 6 1815	
x	*	Hannah Budd, now Mrs. Jessup Nov. 6 1815	
z	*	Elizabeth Maria Hawkins Nov. 6 1815	
z	*	Hannah Jane Hawkins (now Carpenter) Nov. 6 1815	
z	*	Hudson Goldsmith Nov. 6 1815	
	*	Selah Goldsmith Nov. 6 1815	
z	*	James W. Dekay, Junr. Nov. 6 1815	
z	*	gone off William Stephens & Nov. 6 1815	
x	*	Fanny Stephens, his wife gone away disorderly, Nov. 6 1815	
	*	Elizabeth Smith, now Denton Nov. 6 1815	
	*	Dolly Smith now Dolly Jones Nov. 6 1815	
z	*	Hilah Holley now Goldsmith Nov. 6 1815	
z	*	Juliann Jessup, now Miller Nov. 6 1815	
	*	Fanny Owens Nov. 6 1815	
z	*	Hannah Valentine, now Sawyer, gone to Methodist Nov. 6 1815	
z	*	Gabriel Dunning Nov. 6 1815	
z	*	gone off William H. Jessup Nov. 6 1815	
x	*	William Vail Nov. 6 1815	
s	*	Stephen Smith, Junr. Restored Nov. 6 1815	
z	*	Gilbert B. Gale Nov. 6 1815	
z	*	Samuel Borthwick, dismissed Oct. 6, 1817 Nov. 6 1815	
x	*	Ebenezer Bowens off Nov. 6 1815	
z	*	Patience Smith Nov. 6 1815	
z	*	Joanna Smith Nov. 6 1815	
	*	Sally Maria Smith absent Nov. 6 1815	
x	I	Mary Jackson from Chester Nov. 6 1815	
z	I	Gilbert King from Monroe Nov. 6 1815	
z	*	Aden Gibbs, an Indian Nov. 6 1815	
z	*	Letitia Hill, a freewoman, March 29, 1817 Nov. 6 1815	
z	*	Nathaniel Bailey Nov. 6 1815	
	*	**Maria Corey Nov. 6, 1815**	

REGISTER OF MEMBERS

x	*	Elizabeth Moore, now Smith	Nov. 6, 1815
x	*	Casar Servt. of Dr. G. N. Phillips	Nov. 6, 1815
x	*	Jane Servt of Daniel Bailey	Nov. 6, 1815
x	*	Rachel Servt of Stephen Smith	Nov. 6, 1815
x z	*	Sophronia G. Arnell, now Borland	Nov. 11th 1815
x	*	Juliann Sawyer	Nov. 11th 1815
x	*	Nancy Horton, now, King	Nov. 11th 1815
	*	Christian Vail	Nov. 11th 1815
x	*	James W. Wilkin now Elder	Nov. 11th 1815
x	*	Thomas W. Bradner now Elder Left the Church dearranged Nov. 11th 1815	
	*	Off Sally Jessup	Nov. 11th 1815
z	*	William R. Gale	Nov. 11th 1815
x z	*	Jeptha Marsh	Nov. 11th 1815
z	*	Katy Forman Serv. of Moses Phillips Jr. Dismissed 9, Oct. 1848 Nov. 11 1815	
x	*	Phana Servt. of Dr. Phillips	Nov. 11 1815
z	*	Mary Dunning	Nov. 12 1815
z	*	John T. Wood &	Nov. 12 1815
z	*	Catharine Wood his wife	Nov 12 1815
s	*	Jacob A. Vail	Nov 12 1815
x	*	Mary Harrison	Nov 12 1815
z	*	John A. Morrison Preacher	May 6 1816
	*	Benjamin Slaughter	May 6 1816
z	*	Gone off, William Arnout	May 6 1816
	*	Hannah Oakley	May 6 1816
z	*	Matilda Brown	May 6 1816
x	*	Benjamin Sawyer &	May 6 1816
x	*	Hannah Sawyer, his wife	May 6 1816
x	*	Wid. Abigail Gale	May 6 1816
z	*	James Sawyer & dis. Feb. 18, 1818	May 6 1816
z	*	Catharine Sawyer, his wife, dis. Feb. 18, 1818 May 6 1816	
z	*	Mary Gale now Smith	May 6 1816
z	*	Mary wife of Jno. Denton, E. D.	May 6 1816
	*	Hilah Gale, restored, Now Osborune	May 6 1816
x z	*	Jane wife of John Vail	May 6 1816
z	*	Sally Maria Brewster	May 6 1816
x	*	Susan wife of Thos. W. Bradner	May 6 1816
z	*	Jeremiah Terbell	May 6 1816
x	*	Coe Smith &	May 6 1816
x	*	Susan Smith his wife	May 6 1816
	x	Eunice Corey May 6 1816	
x	*	John Brewster, April 30 1817	May 6 1816
z	*	Gilbert Crawford	May 6 1816
x s	*	Nero Hunting & restored May 1831	May 6 1816
z	*	Mary Hunting his wife,	May 6 1816
x	*	George Hubbard freeman of color	May 6 1816
s	*	Francis Darby Freeman of color	May 6 1816
s	*	Ralph Servt. of Dr. Phillips	May 6 1816

May 11, 1816

x	*	Rachel Tooker
x	*	Catharine Lewis now Wiggins
x	*	Mary Conkling
x	*	Sally Taylor
x	*	Deborah wife of Jason Gay
x	*	Deborah wife of Stephen G. Smith

REGISTER OF MEMBERS

```
z  x  *  Sarah Elliott now Gildersleeve
   z  *  Phebe Dunning
   z  *  Susanna wife of Jon. Fisk, March 29, 1817
   x  *  John Gregg &
   x  *  Martha Gregg, his wife
   z  *  Francis Emily Wood, now Bradner
   z  *  Mary Allison Wood, now Willis
x  s  *  Israel Hendershot
   z  *  Theophilus L. Houghton
   z  *  Calvin Gardner Sawyer
   z  *  York, Servt. of Thos. Booth
   z  *  Betsey, Servt. of Wm Stephens
   s  *  Jeffrey Servt. of N. Phillips, Junr.
   x  *  Mehitable Jessup    May 12 1816    Noble
   z  *  Jane wife of Amzi L. Bale from Bloomfield, N. Jersey.
   z  I  James Green from Wallkill    May 12 1816
```

August 5, 1816
```
   x  *  Mehitable wife of Benj. Conkling
   x  *  George Whitman &    Nov 10 1818
   x  *  Bethiah Whitman, his wife
   x  *  Isaac Bowers, Jun.
```

August 10, 1816
```
   z  *  gone off George Phillips, Elder, Disorderly left the church &
          gone off to another body
I  z  *  Sarah wife of Colvin Corey
      *  Mary Ann Phillips    now Arnout
   x  *  Richard Smith Denton
      x  Elenor wife of Joseph Conkling
      *  Hannah Vail
   x  *  Hannah Moore    now Smith
   z  *  Mary Ann Eldred
   z  *  Elijah D. Wells
   z  *  Cornelia Denton    now L'Hommidieu
   x  *  Susan wife of Charles Howell
   x  *  Wid Mary Thorne
   x  *  Juda, Servt. of Judge Steward
   x  *  Juda Servt. of Wm Phillips
   x  *  Prime Wisner free man
   x  *  Wid. Jane Van Horn, free woman
```

Nov 5 1816
```
   z  *  Rainsford A. Ferris &    dismissed April 28, 1817
   z  *  Lydia Ferris, his wife
   z  *  Phebe Loisa Corwin
   z  *  William Holland Arnell
```

Nov 10 1816
```
      *  Jacob Peppard
   z  *  Henry Smith Youngs
      *  Chiliam Stephens
   z  *  Selah Horton
      *  Deborah wife of Nath. Conkling now Oneal
   x  *  Joanna Salmon    Feb. 10 1817
x  z  *  Mary Harris now Little    free woman
   z  *  Maria Smith    free woman
   z  *  Margaret wife of Jacob Decker
```

April 28 1817
```
x  s  *  Morris Lockyer
```

REGISTER OF MEMBERS

```
 x  s  *  John Halsey free man of color
    x  *  Silvia, wife of John Halsey free
May 3 1817
    z  *  Raymond Mather
 x  s  *  Richard Smith
    z  *  Elizabeth Baldwin
    z  *  Jesse Marvin
    z  *  William Bradner
    x  *  Sally Jones—Wid.
    x  *  Elizabeth Hudson  wife of Ebenezer Hudson
July 28 1817
    x  *  Ethelinda wife of William Elliott
    z  *  Maria wife of Thomas W. Goble
    z  *  Almira wife of Benjn. Van Duzer
 I  z  *  Dolly Maria wife of Gilbert B. Gale
August 2 1817
 x  I  *  Rufus Horton
    x  *  Elilzabeth wife of Rufus Horton
    x  *  Hannah wife of William Poppino
    z  *  Charlotte Elliott
    x  *  Jane Westcott
    z  *  Ann wife of Joseph Tolman
    s  *  Ecom. Morris Green Servt. of Joseph Wood, Jr.
    x  *  Lois Gardner free woman of color
    x  *  Rachel Bags free woman of color
    x  *  Malinda servt. of Gilbert B. Gale
    x  *  Jane, Servt. of James W. Wilkin
    z  I  Sally Mather wife of Raymond Mather from Warwick, May 3, 1817
    x  I  Maria Cruttendon from So. Hampton, Long Island
Nov 8 1817
    z  *  Joseph Tolman
    z  *  Benjamin Van Duzer
    z  *  Stauts Furgurson
    z  *  Mowbray Millspaugh
    x  *  Mary Howell wid. of Philetus Howell
       *  Jane P. Strong   now Marvin
    s  *  restored  Peter, Servt. of John Seward
Jany. 5 1818
    z  *  John Moir   —D. C. Bloomingdale
    z  I  Isabel Moir wife of J. Moir
Feb. 2 1818
    s  I  Hugh Gregg &    From Bethlehem
    z  I  Jane his wife
    z  I  Ann Doughei y From Hopewell
April 6
    z  I  Archibald Bogue Fr. Ceder St. Church N. Y.
May 2
    z  I  Deborah Mills wife of Thomas Mills, from Hanover, N Jersey
May 2 1818
    z  *  Elizabeth Elliott now Hoffman
Augt 1
    x  *  Ellizabeth wife of Charles Bradner
    x  I  Sarah Drake wife of Jeremiah Drake
Novr 2 1818
    x  *  Jason Wilkin
    x  *  Abigail Wickham, widow of Isreal Wickham
    z  *  Mary Carpenter
```

REGISTER OF MEMBERS

Feb. 1, 1819
- z * John C. Green
- x * Nathaniel Tuthill
- x * Elizabeth Rumsey, widow of Samuel Rumsey

April 5 1819
- z * Benjamin Ayers
- z * Christian Ayers

May 3 1819
- x * Jennet B. Moir
- x * Letitia Boak, the younger
- z * Daniel Whitman
- z * Hannah Whitman

May 8 1819
- x * Charity Smith, widow of Abel Smith
-    * Harriet Vail
- x * Mary Dunning

Jany 4 1819
- z * Ferdinand Bailey

July 19 1819
- z * Nathan Stark

July 31
- x I Adelaide Hull, died April 6, 1846
- x I Ellen Joline
- z * Olivia Jackson wife G. B. Jackson
- x * Tabitha Smith wid. of Danl. Smith
- z * Priscilla Barker wife of Jno. Barker
- x * Jane Lewis wife of Jas. Lewis
- z * Kitty D. Case
- z * Pamela Curtice

Nov. 2
- x * Elizabeth Tuthill widow

Nov 6
- z * John Boak
-    * John B. Booth

May 6 1820
- z * Sarah Rowley—wife of Haines Rowley
- z I Richard I. Thorne
-   I Hannah, wife of Stephen Smith
- z * Lewis H. Hobby
- x I Abigail Hobby, his wife
- z I Mercy Williams wife of Samuel Williams

July 22, 1820
- x * Mary wife of Silas Hawkins
- z * John Egbert
- z * Daniel Baldwin
-    * Alfred Harris dead
-    * Oscar Harris, Licensed to Preach
- x * Jane, wife of John R. Smith
-    * off Sevia Gibson
- z * Silvester M. Gregg
- x z * James Wood, 2nd
-    * James Foster
- x s * Horace Smith
- z * Rachel Egbert, now Smith
- s   Sarah Carpenter
-    * Adeline Wells, now wife of Jas. C. Reeve

REGISTER OF MEMBERS

	*	Matilda Wood, now Smith
z	*	Lucy Ayres—now Gregory
x	*	Hannah Ayers
x	*	Melinda Goldsmith
z	*	1847 Elizabeth Goldsmith, now Owen
x	*	Eliza Jane Gardner
x	*	Emeline Carpenter
x	*	Dolly Denton

July 29, 1820

	*	Beriah Cooley
s	*	Samuel Hawkins
z	*	George Milton Newman
x	*	Isaac Mapes
z	*	Hilah wife of Jesse Booth, Junr.
	*	Joshuah Goldsmith, Junr
x	*	Prudence Goldsmith
	*	Emeline Tusten now Smith
z	*	Harriet, wife of John B. Booth, dismissed 18th May, 1852
z	*	James Morrison Arnell, Preacher

Augt. 4 1820

x	*	William Jackson
x	*	Frances, wife of Geo. W. Howell
x	*	Phebe, wife of Moses Hawkins
z	*	Daniel Howell
z	*	Jane, wife William Case
x	*	gone off Julia Rumsey, now Newman
x	*	Widow Mary Newman
	*	Miriam wife of Grant Smith
x	*	Fanny wife of John Budd, Junr.
z	*	Hilinda Hawkins (now Wickham)
s	*	Maria Luckey, note, now Vail
s z	*	Restored Harriet Fisk, now Gillespie
z	*	gone off Horace Vail
z	*	Isaac Lewis Wood

Aug 5 1820

x	*	Hannah Goldsmith people of color
x s	*	Oliver Richardson people of Color
z	*	Phillip Thomas people of Color
x	*	Henietta wife of Wm. Goldsmith
	*	Elizabeth Moon
x	*	Deborah wife of Jno. Seward
x	*	Joshua Wells

Oct 28 1820

z	*	Jesse Rhoads
x	*	James Lewis
z s	*	Sarah Luckey, restored
z	*	Maria Rhoads, wife Jesse R.
z	*	Sarah Jane Hall
		Ruth Smith, gone to another
z	*	Moses Sawyer
x z	*	Thomas Boak
	*	Henry Conkling
z	*	Laura Youngs

Nov 4 1820

x s	*	John Webster
z	*	Calvin Corey

REGISTER OF MEMBERS 63

    x * Julia Dekay wife of James W D.
    z * Hiram Phillips
x z * Harriet Barker
    z * Catherine Barker now Robinson
    z * Rhoda Ross now Howell
    x * George W. Howell
    z * Carpenter Coleman
        * gone off   Maria R. Whitman
        * gone off Mehitable Whitman
    x * Katy, Servt. of Andrew Wilson Jr.
    x I Noah Carpenter
    z I Jean Boak, widow Ireland

May 5 1821
    x I Avis Wood, wife of Benj. Wood
    z * Maria Bradner now Seely
        * Sarah Loisa Conklin   now Wilson
    x * Frances Satterly   wid.

Nov 3 1821
    z * William I. Norris
    x * Betsey wife of Peter Bogue, free

April 29 1822
    x * Eliza Waters wife of Henry E. Waters
        * Sally Gale
        I Diana Killis—Amity

May 4 1822
    x * Abigail Case
    x I Eunice Case wife of David Case, Junr.
        * Eliza Hawkins
    z I Mary Stark wife of Nathan Stark, Esq. fr. County, Conn.

Nov. 2, 1822
    x * Alfred Mills
    x * Lydia Horton wife of Squire Horton

April 30, 1823
    x * Sarah Wilkin wife of Sam. J. Wilkin, died 23d March 1854
    z * Jane Harriet Potter

May 3, 1823
    z I Jane Badger, County, Conn.
    z I Juliann Loomis, now Bush

August 2, 1823
    x * Frances Jansen, wife of Dr. Egbert Jansen
    x * Maria Bradner, wife of Dr. James Bradner
    x * Mary Birdsley wid. of Zina Birdsley
    x * Joshua Conkling   (Died Oct. 1851)
    x * Nancy Reeve wife of Daniel Reeve

October 8 1823
    z I Rhoda James wife of Thomas James

October 29, 1823
    z * Mary Burns (now Mc Laughlin)
    z * Julia Ann Butler

November 1, 1823
    z * Clarissa Clark
I z * Gabriel Owens
        * left the Church Mary Jackson   (now Black)

March 2, 1824
        I Henry Scofield—Chester

May 1, 1824
    x * Mary Jane Wells
       * Frances Wells
July 31, 1824
    z I Jacob C. Tooker Westown
    z * Frances Elmira Potter
    z * Elizabeth Lusk, wife of Francis Lusk
    x * Catherine Wells wife of Joshua Wells
    x * Joseph Wood
Nov 6, 1824
    z * John Knapp, Jr.
    z * Elizabeth Sawyer, wife of Moses S. gone off to another body
January 24, 1825
    x * James Cooper Reeve
Jany. 29, 1825
    z * Abigail Cook
    z * Amanda Hudson
    z * Eliza Bailey
       * Julia Pain, abandoned the Church
       I Mary Taylor wife of Morrison Taylor
July 25, 1825
    z * Horace Milton Crane
    z * Clarissa Horton
August 6, 1825
    x * Abigail Jackson wife of Stephen Jackson, Jr.
    z I Fanny Vail   now Jackson
       I Phebe Vail
    z I Adelaide Little   now Denton
       I Eliza Pierson
November 5, 1825
    z I Charles McCorn   Bloomingburgh
    z I Margaret McCorn   Blolomingburgh
Feb 4 1826
    z I Jonathan Sweezy White &
    z I Dolly White, his wife
    x I Mary Smith wife of Horace Smith
March 30 1826
    x * Abigail Bailey wife of Nathaniel Bailey
May 6, 1826
    x * Usher H. Case
June 13, 1826
    z I Daniel Odle—Chester
Augt. 5, 1826
       I Anna Harrison wife of Wm. H.
Nov. 4, 1826
  x z * James A. Wilkin
        * Robert W. Sawyer   from Scotchtown
        I James H. Genung &   from Scotchtown
        I Maria Genung his wife   from Scotchtown
          (These three names are crossed out.)
May 5, 1827
    z * Francis Little now Scudder
August 4, 1827
    z * Morris Ostrander
  x z * Flemming H. Valentine
    x * Rhoda Halsey, free woman of color
    x I Preacher   John J. Thompson, Licensed to preach, Middletown

REGISTER OF MEMBERS. 65

Nov. 3, 1827
  x z * Robert W. Sawyer, dead, Minister & Missionary
         I away James H. Genung &   from Scotchtown
         I Maria Genung his wife   From Scotchtown
May 3, 1828
  x z * Eleanor Jackson
      z I Mary Smith wife of John A. Smith, Goodwill
         I gone off Hiram Vail &   Chester
         I gone off Phebe Vail his wife,   Chester
August 2, 1828
  x z I Charles Monell &   dead   Westtown
      z I Jane Monell, his wife,   Westtown
         I Sarah D. Little, wife of John Little, Chester, name crossed out
Nov. 1, 1828
      x I Sarah D. Little, wife of John Little, Chester
         * Naomiette Moore
         * Mary Dodge
      z * Amanda Darby, colored woman
Jan. 31, 1829
      x * David Case
      z * Sarah Thompson wife T. D. Thompson
May 2, 1829
      z * Nancy Merriam wife of Saml. G. Merrian fr. Cicero
         * Frances Gifford Denton
Augt. 1,
      x * Jane Wells, now Wallace
      z I Daniel Wells, Elder fr. Wall St. New York, now minister
      z I Eliza Smyley, fr. Strabem Inland
Nov.
         * Mary Evans, wid. of Doct. Thomas G. Evans
           Gone to another denomination is dismissed Agnes Bull, wife
           James Bull
      x * Ila Watkins wife of James Watkins
      z * Mary Caroline Watkins, (now Hendrie)
Feb. 6, 1830
      z * Caroline Phillips
      x * Deborah Goldsmith
         * Melinda Owen
         * Increase Stoddart Goldsmith
May 1, 1830
         * Christiana Smiley, wife of Wm. R. Smiley
      z * Elsa Terry, wife of Nathl N. Terry
July 3, Nov. 6, 1830. 1830
      z * Elizabeth Mc Crea from Piney Cink, May 1828
Nov. 6, 1830
         I gone off Adelaide Denton, from Amity
      x I Eliza Rumsey wife of Phineas Rumsey from Bloomingrove
      z I Elimra Tuthill wife of Oliver Tuthill from Bloomingrove
         * Catherine Cox, wid. Hezekiah G. Cox
         * gone off Mary Fink wife of Alexander H. Fink
      z * Nancy Gourlay
Feb. 5, 1831
      z * Beulah Ann Seward, wife of Henry Seward
         * Mrs Julia Ann Seward, now Van Invegin
      z * Eliza C. Little, now Brown

REGISTER OF MEMBERS

April 25, 1831
- z * Sally Conner now Newton
- x * Abraham Purdy & Elder
- x * Charity Purdy, his wife
-   * Maria Cheeve, wife of Jas. A. Cheeve, Gone off to another church disorderly
- z * Frances Garahan, wid. Bryan Garahan
- z * Sarah Ann Jackson wid. Andrew M. Jackson
-   * gone off Hannah Jackson
-   * Melinda Jackson
- z * Mary Jones now Beyea
-   * Hannah Waters Jones
-   * Julia Ann Jackson
-   * Doct. John Sears Crane, Elder
-   * gone off Samuel W. Classon
-   * gone off Hiram Halstead
-   * John Howell

April 30, 1831
- I Nehemiah Carpenter &
- I Elizabeth Carpenter, his wife, Deer Park
-   * Nancy Maria Lusk
- x * Sally Jackson
-   * Sarah Elizabeth Jones
-   * Ann Payne wid Rosswell Payne
- z * Christian Denton, wid. of Hezekiah Denton
- z * James Horton &
- z * Mary Horton, his wife
-   * Rebecca Ann Howell, wife of John Howell
- x * Emeline Phillips, now Condit
-   * Ann Susan Wilson wife of John Wilson
- x * Julia Ford Wells
- x * Mary Young wife of Colvin Young
- z * David Harris
- x * Mary Jane Harris now Little
-   * Solomon Denton
-   * Abba Tupper now Smith

June 13, 1831
- x * Amira Cory

Augt. 6, 1831
- x I Benjamin C. Smith, & Elder from Monroe
- x I Mary Smith, his wife
-   I Emily Hammond widow of David Hammond, from Salem, Mass.
- x I Sarah Ellis wife of Wm. Ellis, From West Milford, N. Jersey
- z * Edward Steward
- x * 1856 John Wilson,—"Elected Elder."
-   * Almina Vail
- z * Silas Rose
- z * Jane Vail Clark
- z * Sarah Jane Savage
-   * Cynthia Martin
- x * Clarissa Wilkin wife of Jas. D. Wilkin
- x * Julia Ann Seward, wife of Doct. David Seward
- z * Sarah Smith wife of Lemuel B. Smith
-   * gone off Kezia Wood, now Stepperfield
- z * Eunice Mapes
-     Ellen Mapes

REGISTER OF MEMBERS 67

    z * Elizabeth Reeve wife of Chapman S. Reeve, and now Horton
       * Mary Elizabeth Owen
       * Mary Ann Moffatt
    z * Virgil Sweezy Seward
    z * Lucas Decker
    z * Horace Elmer Dunning
       * gone off Sarah Bowers widow of Isaac Bowers
    z * Elizabeth Ann wife of George D. Dunning
    x * Juliette Wood, now wife of Wm. Wood
       * Elizabeth Eunice Wells, (May 1st 1855)

Augt. 7, 1831
    z * George Davis Dunning
    z * David Arnell Wood

Oct. 29, 1831
    z I Jonathan Fisk & his wife
    z I Susanna Fisk
    x * Mary Edsall
       * Esther Vail, now Denton
       * Mary Vail
    x * Eve Crane wid. of Benjm Crane
    x * William Poppino
    x * Huldah Bedford wife of Benjn. Bedford
    z * Jane Myers
       * Abigail Payne
         Maria De Camp wid of John De Camp
       * Adeline Augusta Sweezy (now Corwin)
       * Harriet Elizabeth Sweezy
    x * Susanna Mapes
    x * Abraham Smith
    s * Samuel Rumsey
       * Fanelia Corry

January 18, 1832
       * Robert Emmete Potter
       * Margaret Watkins
    z * Milicent Strong Jackson, now Watkins

Feb. 1,
    z I Christiana Bradner
    z * Ira Hawkins

Feb. 2,
    x * Elizabeth Rumsey

Feb. 4
       * Emy Adams wife of Loudon Adams
       * gone off Eliza Ann Oakly wid. of Ichabod S. Oakley, now Halstead
    s * Daniel Case & his wife
       * Julia Case
       * Eliza Houston
       * Horace Ball
       * Mary Elizabeth Case
    z * Esther Susanna Fisk

Feb. 11,
    x I Gabriel Owen & his wife
    x I Sarah Owen
  x z * William Barker
    x * Sarah Helms wife of Reuben Helms
       * Nancy Johnson wife of John H. Johnson
       * Eliza Bodle

REGISTER OF MEMBERS

    s * Jane Cabrey wife of John Cabrey
    x * Julia Case wid. of David Case
    z * Ira Coleman &
    z * Emily Coleman, his wife
       * Al—i— Helms

May 5, 1832
    s * Henry I. Smith, "Suspended"
    x * Mary Corey wife of Lemuel Corey
       * Sally Jane McCarter

Augt 4,
    I   Maria Steward, now Davidson
    I   Clarrissa Miller, wife John D. Miller
      * Sarah Steward
    x * Elizabeth Steward, died 12th April 1847
      * Elizabeth Ann Lusk
      * Ecommunicated George Washington Connor
      * Jane Taylor, colored woman

Oct. 20
      * Eliza Margaret Strong now Denton
      * gone off Elizabeth Wood wife of Anthony Wood.

Feby. 3, 1833
      * Elizabeth P. Phillips
    x * Charlotte wife of Wm. I. Norris

May 5th
    z * Julia Phillips
    z * Maria Phillips
    x * Louisa, wife of Joseph Sayre
      * gone off Agnes Eager—Widow

Augt 10
    z * Harriet Phillips wife of Moses Phillips
  x s * Phineas Rumsey
    x * Harriet Valentine wife of Flemming Valentine
    x * Anna Wood wife of Isaac Lois Wood
    I   John C. Wallace, from Scotchtown.

Oct. 26,
    x * William Robinson
    x I Sarah Seward wife of Virgil S. Seward

May 3, 1834
    x * James Wood

Feby. 1st, 1835
      * Mary, wife of Hiram Phillips
      * Latitia, wife of John J. Lusk
        gone off Julia Ann Teed.

May 2d
    z I Dr. Jas. S. Horton
      * Austin Terry
    z I Jas. G. Thompson & Hannah his wife, Elder

July 31, 1849
        Nancy Thompson, (now Duryea)
    I   Margaret Stewart, formerly members of the Bloomingrove Church
    x * William Wood
        Sarah Strong—on examination
        Elder Thompson & wife dismissed to Pres. Ch. Washingtonville Nov. 23, 1864 & received again on certificate (& daughter) Oct. 12th, 1869

REGISTER OF MEMBERS 69

Augst 1st. 1835 on examination
x z * Henry A. Van Dyck
x * Horace Sweezy
* gone off Elizabeth Valentine wife of Stephen Valentine
x * Rachel Connelly wife of Constant Connelly, since deceased.

Oct. 3
x z * Abigail Denton on examination & public profession.

Febry 6th 1836
x I Mrs. Mary Howell—widow of Joshua Howell from Bloomingrove Church

April 30
* Scudder Newman &
* Ila his wife—on examination
z * James Holbert—by certificate

August 6
No admissions

Nov 5
I Nathan Stark & Mary his wife, by certificate
z * Mary Giles, widow of John Giles & on examination
* Sarah Jane Smith on examination

1837
Lord's Supper dispensed

Feby 4th
I Nathaniel Webb on certificate

May 6th
z Adrian Holbert & Hannah his wife on certificate, gone off
I Maxwell Bigart & Rebecca his wife, on certificate
z * Susan Gregg, on examination, now Topping

Augst 6th
Sacrament dispensed, no admissions

Nov. 5
Sacrament dispensed, no admissions

Febry 3d, 1838
Sacrament dispensed, no admissions

May 12
z gone off Mary Ann Wells, on profession, abandoned the church

August 5
x * gone off Elizabeth Walace wife of Robert Wallace on certificate

Feb 1st. 1839
Elizabeth Denton wife of Theodorus B. Denton & Horace Denton admitted on personal examination, gone off

May 4th
John Wallace & Elizabeth his wife
Corlinda Malvince Newman now Harlow
Adam G. Cross, admitted in examination now Elder
x I John Little from Church at Centerville &
Margaret Phillips from Scotch Presbytern Church, New York on certificate.

August 3d
z Sarah Ann Phillips admitted on examination &
z I Mary P. Horton, wife of Dr. Jas. J. Horton on certificate from church at Florida.

Nov 2d
* Antionette Barker widow of Henry Barker
x * Belinda Gale wife David Gale
gone off Nancy Romaine—all on examination & unbaptised

REGISTER OF MEMBERS

Jany 25th 1840
        Solomon T. Smith   unbaptised
Augt 1st
  z * Harriet Elizabeth Phillips, do
  z x * Adaline L. Phillips
  z x * Widow Diannah Fisk
Oct 31st
        Dr. William A. Westcott, Preacher
  z x * William B. Tuthill
  z x * Widow Catharine Robinson &
      x I Betsy Ann Satterly on certificate   from Hamptonburg
1841 Feby 6th
        Charlott Elliott, wife of H. W. Elliott
  z * Harriet Randolph Kitchel do of Saml. B. Kitchel   unbaptised
  z * Charlott Wells, widow of Dr. Jerome Wells, unbaptised
  z * Mary Ann Smith, unbaptised
April 28th
      * Margaret Bryson Mc Cartee admitted on certificate from Leight Church New York, & Nelson Newman & May, his wife from Centerville Church
      x * & Sarah Carpenter wife of Daniel Carpenter unbaptised was admitted an examination
1841 Nov 1st   admitted
      s * gone off John Romine gone to the Methodist
          * Lavinia Elizabeth Drake &
          * Solomon G. Carpenter on examination
          I Geo H Crans, name is erased
      x I Clarissa Wilkin (widow of Jas Wilkin)
            Mrs Maria Thompson wife of A. W. Thompson,
      z I & Ann Eliza Thompson   on certificate
Sept 19th
          I Catharine A. Hammond   on certificate
Nov 6th
          I Maria Thompson wife of Abjah W. Thompson on certificate
          I Widow Clarissa Wilkin, certificate
          I Geo. H. Crans, certificate
Feby 5
         * Harriot Banker wife of Philander Banker   on confession
         * Sarah Rose   on confession
         * Synthia Crans wife of Adam I. Cary   on confession
April 26
  z * Samuel Beyea & Sarah his wife, May 1, 1850   profession
  z * Phebe Beyea   profession
  z * Mary Frances Terry   profession
  z I Harriot Harrington wife of Jubel Harrington   Certificate
  z I Susan Carpenter wife Robt. Carpenter   & Examination
Do 30th
  x * John Little   ditto
  z * Eliza Vail now Hawkins, dismissed 1857 Nov.
      * Sally Ann Vail   ditto
              unbaptised
Augt 3rd
  x * Esther Hulse wife of Andrew Hulse   Examination
      * Louisa Webb   do   Natl. Webb   Examination
  z * James J Reeve   Examination
      s   restored   Jas. T. Tuthill   suspended 15 Sep 1851

REGISTER OF MEMBERS

			unbaptised all above
	z	*	Wm A Smith Examination
	z	*	Sarah Ann Goudy now Mc Carty Examination
		*	Frances Elvina Crane Examination
		*	Maria L. Strong Examination
	x	*	Isabella Graham McCartee Examination
	z	*	Eliza Anderson Bradner Examination
	z	*	Mary M Mc Cartee, now Reeve Examination
	x	*	Harriot Newel Bradner Examination
		*	Sarah E. Smith Examination
s	z	*	gone off John D Monell, gone off to Episcopal Church
	z	*	Ira S. Bradner
	z	*	Thos. Scott Bradner Preacher
	x	*	Mary Ellis wife of Joseph Ellis
	z	I	Charlotte M Cory now Reeve certificate
	z	I	Sarah Corey, widow of Calvin Cory do
	z	I	Davis Bathune Mc Cartee, Missionary in China do
	z	I	William A. Corey

Aug 6th
* Caroline Johnson   examination
x * Julia Schofield wife of Henry Schofield   do   unbaptised
* Bernard M. Clark, unbaptized
z * Elizabeth Waters widow of H. W. Waters
z * Catharine Water   certificate   do
z I R. S. C. Hendrie   do
x * Mary Hendrie   his wife
z I Jas Brown   do
z I Margaret Brown his wife   do

Nov 5
z * Alpheus Gillet (colored) unbaptized   exam
x * Clarrissa Smith wife Joshua Smith   unbaptized

1842 Nov 5th
x I Nathl. Jenning   Certificate
z I Frances do his wife   do
 I Lydea N. Wells wife of Alfred Wells   do

" 8
z * Abigail Terry unbaptized   Examination
z * Wilmot C. Terry   do   Dismissed to Centerville
z * Cornelia Hawkins   do   Certificate of Christian Character
z * Mary Howell   do   Now Green, dismissed
x * Eusibius Austin Gale   do
z I Dr. Eusibius Austin Webb   Certificate
z I Sarah Webb his wife   do
z * John B. Ackerman   do
z I Eliza G, his wife   do
x I Hannah H. Howell   do
 I Sylevester A. Jervis (Colored)   do

1843 Feby 4th
* Henry J. Duryea   Examination
* Harriot Tuthill wife of Jas. S. Tuthill   do
x I John F. Marvin &   Certificate
x I Amelia his wife   Certificate
z x I Obediah Crance, dead & wife   do

May 3rd
* Frances Jane Tuthill unbaptized   Examination
z * Oliver B. Tuthill unbaptized   do

REGISTER OF MEMBERS

          Gone off to Methodists 1847
      *   Ann Romeyne unbaptized wife of John Romeyne, examination
" 4th
      *   Jane Kelsey wife of J. D. Kelsey, examination
Aug. 5
      I   Jerusha Harris wife of A. Harris   certificate
  z   I   Cornelia B. wife of Isaac L. Wood   do
      I   Ann C. Bodel, wife of Wm W Bodle   do
  z   I   ran off S. D. Bross, (Ran away) ditto
  z   *   Mary Bradner   one examination
      *   Wm W Bodle   do
  z   *   Jas M Steward, unbaptized, (colored) do
Oct 1st,
  z   *   Dr. Stephen S. Comstock,   certificate   gone away
Nov 4th
  z   *   Sarah G Reeve, now Talmadge   examination
1844, Feby 3rd
  x   *   Phebe Pierson (Colored)   certificate
Jany 25
     .I   Moses B. Crans   do
Augt 3
  s   I   Daniel O Neal   do
  x   *   Mary Steward (colored), unbaptized, examination, Banks
1845, Feby 1st
      *   Temperence W Owen wife of
          Samuel R. Owen unbaptized   do
      *   John Clawson   do
May 1st
      *   John Jorden unbaptized   do
  x   *   Phebe A Case   do
      *   Margaret E. Case   do
      *   Mary Smith   do
Augt 2nd
      *   Caroline Smith   do
      *   Ann Eliza Merriman wife of H Meriman   do   unbaptised
  z   *   George R. Mapes "Unbaptized" Examination
  o   I   Sarah Elliott, wife H. W Elliott, Certificate
1846 .
  z   I   Sarah Maria   do Chas Ross   do
May 3rd
  z   I   Margaret S Lickner now wife of David A. Wood, certificate
Augt 3d
  x   *   Stephen Howell Strong, Unbaptized, examination
Oct 31
      *   Sarah E Vail   do
  x   *   Jane Hammond Storm   do
  z   I   Robt. Wallace, Jr.   certificate
      I   wife of Peter Storm   do
1847, Feby 1st
      *   Agness Wilson, now Bradner, examination
  z   *   Jesse B Mc Cater   do
  z   *   Catharine B. Case   do
      *   Mary wife of Richard Montgomery Vail   do
May 1st
      *   Catherine Tuthill (widow)   examination
  x   *   Mary G wife of Isaac Andrews   do

REGISTER OF MEMBERS

 x * Mary P wife " Gabriel Goldsmith unbaptized
 x * Martha Maria " of Horace Tuthill   do
  * Susan Emily Vanduzer   confession
  * Mary Caroline Wilkin   Do
 x * Mary, wife of H. M. Hopkins   do
  * Mary Lewis   do
 z * Christianna Schofield   do
  * gone off Mary Ann Green, (Col) (gone off)   do

Aug 1
 z * Charolotte Elliott   now Stafford   do
 z * Harriet E. Goldsmith unbaptized   do

Nov 7
  * Francis Wood   do
 z * Harriot Elizabeth Carpenter, unbaptized   do
  * Adeline Goldsmith   do   do
  * Julia Ann Goldsmith   do   do
  * Elizabeth Goldsmith   do   do

1848, Feby 5
  * Jane Clancy, dismissed   do
  * Bridget W. Cox   do
  * Ann M. Howell   do
  I Christianna Vanduzer, wife of Aaron Vanduzer, Certificate

Augt 5
  * David Redfield

Nov 4
  * John E. Watkins,   dismissed
  * Mary E. Jennings

1849, Feby 3
  I Jane Howell, wife of Ira Howell
 x * Ann Eliza Redfield wife of David Redfield
  * Ann Eliza Schofield
  * Sarah Jane Wood

May 5
  * Sarah Jane Booth, now Wycough, June 26, 1850
  * Harriet Booth

1849, May 6
 z * Ellen Booth   18th May 1852
 z * Mary Ellen Gillespie
 z * Caroline Wilson, now Taylor
  * off Mary Louisa Vanriper

Nov 3
  * Caroline A. Case, unbaptized
 z * Mary Booth, 18th May 1852
 z I Elizabeth S. Thompson wife of Dr. Benj. Thompson Dismissed Sept. 15, 1854
  I Charlotte Brewster wife of Joseph Brewster
  I Gabriel P Reeve   on certificate,   Elder

1850, Feby 3
  * Ann Eliza, wife of George A Crans
 z * Mary Jane Gregory, now Stage
  * Margaret Lander
  * Hector C. Moore
  * Govenier M Smith
  * John Fitzgerald
  * Hezekiah C. Newman
  * James T Reeve, The above unbaptized

REGISTER OF MEMBERS

* Coe H Clark
* Daniel S. Jackson
* Gabriel S Owen, Feb 30 1820
* George H Newman
* Melissa A. Jennings, now Crane

The Following Members Dismissed

The following members dismissed since 1817

1840, Augt 1
 Harriet E Phillips

Jany 29th
 Ann Eliza Thompson
 Harriet Harrington
 Wm A Smith
 Eliza Waters &
 Catharine Waters
 Jas Brown & wife Margaret
 Altheas Gillet (colored)
 Dr. E. A. Webb & wife Sarah
 Cornelia B Wood wife of J. L. Wood
 Jas. M. Steward (colored)
 Dr. Stephen S Comstock
 Sarah T Reeve (now Talmage)
 Sarah Maria wife of Chas Ross
 Robt Wallace, Jr (to Phileda-)
 Dr. Jas. S Horton & wife Sarah G.
 Nancy Thompson (now Duryea)
 Julia Phillips &
 Maria Phillips
 Harriet Phillips wife of Moses Phillips
 Ira Coleman & wife Elmira
 Esther S Fisk
 Christian Bradner & Ira Hawkins
 Melicient Strong Jackson (now Watkins)
 Jonathan Fisk & wife
 Geo. D Dunning & wife
 Lucas Decker
 Sarah Smith wife of L. B. Smith
 Edward Steward
 Jas Horton & Mary his wife
x Mary Jane Harris (now Little)
 Christiana Denton (now Vanduzer) returned
 Frances Grahan
 Sarah Ann Jackson wife A M Jackson
 Oliver B Tuthill & wife
 Sally Corwin (now Newton)
 Eliza C. Little (now Brown)
 Beulah Ann Seward wife of Henry
 Nancy Gourley
 Eliza Ann Terry wife N. N. Terry
 Caroline Phillips
 Eliza Smiley (Long Island)
 Nancy Merriam wife S. G. Merriam
 Sarah Thompson wife of John J Thompson
 Ann Darby (colored)
 Mary Smith wife of John A Smith

REGISTER OF MEMBERS

    Eleanor Jackson
x Flemming Valentine
x Rob W Sawyer
    Morris Ostrander
    Francis Little   now Scudder
x Jas. A. Wilkin
    Daniel Odle
    Jonathan S White & wife Dolly
    Chas Mc Corn & wife
    Adeline Little (now Denton)
    Fanny Vail (now Jackson)
    Clarissa Horton
    Horace M Crane
    Amanda Hudson
    Elizabeth Lusk wife of Frances Lusk
    Frances E. Potter
    Jacob C Tooker
    Julia Ann Butler
    Rhoda James wife of Thos James
    Julia Ann Lommis (now Bush)
    Jane Bogart
    Mary Stark wife of Nathan Stark
    Dinah Killis
    Sally Gale
    Wm. I Norris
    Maria Bradner (now Seely) Divorsed
x Avis Wood (wife of Benj. Wood)
    Jean Boak (from Ireland)
    Carpenter Coleman
    Rhoda Ross now (Howell)
    Catherine Barker   now Robinson
x Harriet Barker
x Calvin Cory
    Lura Youngs
    Henry Conkling
x Thos Boak
    Moses Sawyer (gone to New School)
    Sarah Jane Hall
    Maria Rhoads wife of Jesse
    Sarah Lucky
    Jesse Rhoads
    Phillips Thomas (colored)
    Isaac L. Wood
    Daniel Howell
    Jane wife of Wm Case
    Hilinda Hawkins now Wickham
    Jas. M. Arnell (now Preacher)
    let off Ap 1820 Hilah wife of Jesse Booth, Junr.
    Geoge M. Newman   dismissed
    Elizabeth Goldsmith (now Owen)
    Lucy Ayers (now Gregory)
    Jas. Wood 3rd   dead
    Rachael Egbert (now Smith)
    Sylvester M. Gregg
    Danl. Baldwin
    John Egbert

Lewis H. Holly
May Williams wife of Saml. Williams
John C. Green
Benj. Ayers
Christian Ayers
Letitia Boak
Danl. Whitman
Hannah Whitman
Ferdinand Baely
Nathan Slack
Ellen Joline
Olivia Jackson, wife of G. B. Jackson
Pricilla Barker wife of John
Kitty D. Case
Pamelia Curtice
John Boak
Sarah Rowley wife of Harris Rowly
Richd. I Thorne
Raymond Mathew
Elizabeth Baldwin
Jesse Marvin
Wm. Bradner
Maria wife of T. W. Goble
Charlotte Elliott
Amelia wife of Benj. Vanduzer
Dolly M. Wife of G. B. Goble
Ann wife of Jos Tallman
Sally Mather wife Benj. Mather
Joseph Talman
Benj. Vanduzer
Stewart Ferguson
Mabey Millspaugh
John Moir
Isabel wife of John Moir
Jane Gregg wife of Hugh
Ann Dougherty
Archd. Basure
Elizabeth Elliott
Jas. Green
Sarah wife of Calvin Corey
Mary Ann Eldred
Elijah D. Wells
Cornelia Denton   now L'Homedieu
Reynsford A Ferris & Lydia his wife
Wm. H Arnell
Selah Horton
Mariah Smith
Sally M. Brewster
Mary Hunting wife of New ——
Phebe Dunning
Francis E Wood (now Bradner)
S. L. Houghton
Yerk, Servt. of Thos Both
Jane wife of Amzi L. Ball
Saphronia G. Arnell, now Borland
Jephtha Marsh

REGISTER OF MEMBERS

Mary Dunning
Catharine Wood wife of J. T. W.
John A. Morrison (Preacher)
Mary Gale (now Smith)
Gilbert King
Lelitia Hill (woman of color)
Patience Smith
Gilbert B. Gale
Gabriel Dunning
Hilah Holly (now Goldsmith)
Jas. W. Dekay, Jr.
Hannah Jane Hawkins (now Carpenter)
Jane Tunn (widow)
Delinder Hopkins (now Johnson)
Hester Smith
Julia Gale, wife of Peter Gale
Eliza H. L'Hommedieu now Ostrand
Tabitha Wade wife of Benjn. Wade
Anna Fisk
Phebe L. Corwin
Henry Smith Youngs
Mary Harris, now Little (dead)
Margaret wife of John Decker
Jeremiah Terbell
Sarah Elliott, now Gildersleve
Susan wife of Jonathan Fisk
Mary A Wood (now Wells)
C. G. Sawyer
Betsey Servt. of Wm. Stephens
Nathaniel Bailey
Wm. R. Gale
Katy Ferman (woman of color)
John T. Wood
Matilda Brown
Jas. Sawyer & wife Catharine
Mary wife of John Denton
Aden Gibbs (An Indian)
Joannah Smith
Saml. Bostwick
Wm. H. Jessup
Juliann Jessup (now
Wm. Stephens
Hudson Goldsmith
Elizabeth M. Hawkins
Wm. M. Cory & Abigail his wife
Olivia Brewster (now Marvin)
John L'Hommidieu & wife
Henry B. Wisner
Orange Green & Mary his wife
Susannah Herton
Mary Brewster
Mary, wife of Danl. Sloan
Benj. Corey
William How
John A. Carpenter
John Jay Thompson, Preacher 1849

REGISTER OF MEMBERS

Amy Morgan (widow)
John H. Tuthill
Fanny wife of David Webb
Lina wife of Theophilus Dolson
Abigail Borland
Sally, wife of Gilbt. Williams
Phebe, wife of Solomon Carpenter
Sarah, wife of Saml. Butler
Mary Hawkins (crossed out)
Jas. Clawson & wife Abigail
Michael Carpenter
Widow Deborah Ross *
Noah Carpenter * returned
Martha widow of Nathan Coleman
Luther Steward
Esther widow of Peter Gale, Elder
Reubin Hopkins Elder *
Hannah wife of Reuben Hopkins *
Sally M. Brewster (now Woodhull)
Benj. C. Smith, now Elder 1849
T. B. Crowell & wife
Saml. Butler
Mary, widow of Geo. Smith
Mary, wife of Gilbt. Hawkins
John A Smith
Saml. Clawson
Jane wife of Thos. Booth
Jane, wife of Thos. Booth
Charlotte Wood, wife of James Wood
Mary, wife of Saml. Clawson
Mary Hopkins, in Cincinatti
Clarrisa Gale, (now Otis)
Sally, wife of Wm. Phillips
Catherine Lewis wife of Parson Lewis
Hannah Arnell
Christian (wid. of Richd. Wood)
Stephen Crane
Dr. Eusebius Austin *
Wm Bodle, Elder

The above and foregoing names have been Dismissed since the year 1817

Phebe Beyea on the 1st Oct. 1849
Sally Foster, dismissed 3rd Nov 1849
Sarah Elliott, wife of Henry W. Elliott, do 19th 1849
David A Wood & Margaret S his wife, do 19th 1849
Sarah Jane Booth (now Wyncoop, June 26, 1850
Samuel Beyea (to Methodists) May 1st, 1850
Jane Hetfield wife of Thos. T. Hetfield 1851
William A Corey   1851
John E Watkins   1851
Hiram C Newman & wife, to New York
Mrs. Sarah Corey
Jas. I Reeve
Eliza Vail, Oct 1851
Mary Howell, now Green 1851
Wm Lewis Allison   Nov. 4, do
Sarah Ann Goudy, 6 Sept. 1852

Record of Deaths

Record of Deaths in the Congregation of Goshen since the 5th day of November, 1805. No record as we can discover having been kept before that time.

1805
Nov   9   Molly Hughes
1806
Jany   12   Child of Stephen Jackson Esq. 3 w, Fits.
        29   Capt. Benoi Bradner—Chester, 50, Pleurisy
Feb   7   Ruliff Van Brunt—Florida, 57, do
March   8   A stranger
         9   Hannah Conkling, 14, Consumption
        16   Silsbee, 38, Pleurisy
        16   Jude, a free woman of color, 63, do
        21   James Caldwell, 70, do
        26   John Minthorn, Warwick, 20, Typhus
April   7   David Crawford, 70, Pleurisy
June   16   Puah, wife of Dr. Arnell, 36, Consumption
        16   William Tremble, Neelytown, 47, Apoplexy
        16   Child of Daniel E. Ludlum, 1 yr., Dysentery
Aug   3   Child of Jno Brewster, N. York, 2, do
Sept   1   Mrs. Mary Allison, 70, Old age
         4   Sarah Bull, 85, do
         8   Gilbert Brown—Scotchtown, 47, Colic
        14   Joshua Davis, 73, Fever
        21   Doctr. John Gale, 75, Old age
        23   Ellsworth Beekman, 26, Fever
Oct   2   Abiel Frye, Esq. of Tioga, 67, do
1807
Jany   A child of   , 1
              A child of James Egbert, 3, Croup
Feby   8   Charles Brannon, 53, Rheumatism
        19   Ichabod Lewis, 58, Pleurisy
March   11   Mrs.   Paine, 80, do
        15   Wife of Benjamin Gale, 50, Colic
April   1   Mahala Hawkins, 9, Consumption
May   23   Zechariah Baldwin, 36, do
June   4   Abigail Randall, 51, do
July   28   Hannah Carpenter, 23, Phrenitis
Aug   5   Mary Holbert, 66, do
        12   Joseph Drake, 87, Old age
Sept   2   Sally Jane Gourlay, 4, Hooping Cough
         2   Child of Nat. G. Minthorn, 1½, do
        10   Wid of Doct. John Gale, 82, Old age
Oct   9   John Ludlum, 63, Stranguary
        11   Child of Dan Hathaway, 5 w, Influenza
        13   Child of Joseph Wood, Junr., 4 yr, Hooping Cough
        15   Child of Thomas Carmen, 1½, do

Decr		O. Horton son of Fred, 14, Fall
Oct	26	Child of William Phillips, 1 yr, Pneumonia

1808
Feby	6	William Crawford, 33, Pleurisy
	24	John Gale, 45, do
March	3	William Kelsey, 51, Consumption
	5	Wid Phebe Dolson, 68, Old age
April	8	Benjamin Conkling, 64, do
May	3	Wife of Benjamin Crane, 28, Apoplexy
	22	Albert Watkins, 14 mo., Chorela Infantum
Aug	6	Samuel Moffat, 69, Tumor
	10	Isaac Smith, 65, do
	12	Bridget Mc Donald, 18, Fever
Dec	16	Wid. Amy Strong, 72, Old age

1809
Jany	6	Child of William Phillips, 3, Pneumonia
	7	Child of Timothy Wood, 3 w, Sprue
	18	Child of Seth L. Poppino, 3 w, do
	25	Child of Henry W Denton, 4 mo., Pneumonia
	26	Child of John Duer, Esq., 3 w, do
Feby	18	Elisha Goldsmith, 79, Old age
	19	Eliza Deborah Phillips, 22, fever Puerperal
March	3	Wid. Susan Carpenter, 65, Fever
	4	Lois wife of John Denton, 37, Asthma
April	15	Charles Phillips, 7, Fall
June	8	Elizabeth wife of Crisse Bull, 41, Consumpt.
	22	Sevia Springsted, 22, Dropsy
	22	Jabez Nobles, 60, Intemper-
Aug	25	James Pierson, 45, Phrenitis
	9	Child of John Knapp, 2 yr. 11 mo., Burn
Nov	4	Child of Major James Tusten, 3 mo, Sprue
	16	Widow Clark, 54, Apoplexy
	18	Sheba Boak, 40, Spotted fever
	28	Col. Jacobus De Kay, 82, Consumption
Decr	8	Loisa Catharine Lewis, 6 yr 10 mo, Typhus
	9	Child of John Wood Junr., 1½, Croup
	18	Sally Conner, 8 yr 1 mo, Typhus
	29	Grandchild of Benjamin Carpenter, 1½, Croup

1810
Jany	5	Sally daughter of Saml. Vail, 10, Spotted fever
	21	Jacob Vanderhoof, 50, Consumption
Feby	5	John Herod Bailey, 27, do
	14	Richard Wood, 77, Dropsey
March	3	Schuyler Bennett, 9, Spotted fever
	20	Anna Pierson, 44, Pleurisy
	22	Matilda Youngs, 15, Typhus
	23	Abner Smith, 28, Pleurisy
	30	Mary Elmer, 40, Spotted fever
April	4	Phebe Vail, 19, do
		Capt. Daniel Gale, 45, Phrenitis
	4	Child of Lucy Billson, 6, Consumption
May	5	Wife of Capt. David Webb, 35, Spotted fever
April		Son of Michael Jackson, 17, do
		Polly Reed, 21, Consumption
July	26	Wife of Isaac J. Beekwith, 26, Typhus

RECORD OF DEATHS

Aug	4	Major John Wood, 67, Apoplexy
	8	Mrs. Hannah Brown, 51, Consumption
	15	Thomas Mickens, 20, Lock jaw
	25	Daniel Smith, 47, Pleurisy
Sept	2	Genl. Moses Hetfield, 78, Old age
	6	Isaac Jessup, 57, Consumption
	13	Elsa Owens, 27, Cholera Morbus
	21	Mrs. Randall, 61, do
	24	Child of Joel C. Jackson, 1½, do
	24	Child of Genl. J. W. Wilkin, 1½
	26	Mrs. Denton, 41, Liver Complaint
	29	Elsa Ludlum, 15, Pneumonia
Octr	1	Anna Kinner, 84, Old age
		Anthony Y. Denton, 27 Hemorrhage
	14	Wife of Col. Moses Phillips, 64, Typhus
Decr	31	Wife of Thomas Cleves, 49, Consump
1811		
Jany	3	Daniel Bailey, Junr., 25, Consumption
	7	Huldah Fox, 26, Phrenitis
March	15	Child of Joshua Roe, 1, Pneumonia
	27	Mrs. Abigail Austin, 45, Phrenitis
June	1	Mrs Mary Vail, 70, Pleurisy
	5	Rachel Millspaugh, 45, Fever
July	5	Child of Elliott Hopkins, 3 mo, Pneumonia
	31	Child of Joseph W. Mc Collough, 11 mo, do
Aug	2	Hannah DuBois, 27, Consumption
	17	Henry son of Saml. G Lewis, 26, Cholera infant
Septr	9	Child of James Smith, 2 w, Sprue
	11	Robert Wood Esq., 32, Consumption
		Child of John Wood, 2, Burn
Octr	4	Wife of James Horton, 31, Consumption
		Child of James Horton, 5 w, do
	7	Child of Andrew Noble, 1¾, Scrophula
	8	Deborah wife of Jonat. Smith Esq., 88, Old age
		Rebecka, wife of Thos Gale, 56, Pleurisy
Decr	10	Christian wid. of Saml. Gale, 79, Asthma
1812		
Jany	27	Wife of Joshua Wells, Junr., 36, Pneumonia
April	15	Catharine Tusten, 19, Phrenitis
June	20	Betsey Bodle, 38, Consumption
Octr	26	Mary Brown, widow, 57, Dropsey
		Milicent Bull
		Benjamin Harlow, Junr.
		Gideon Coleman & wife
		Benjamin Gale (Elder)
		Dr. Jonathan Swezey, (Elder)

(These died of a prevalent complaint called Pneumonia Typhus)
No regular record kept untill August 22, 1813

Dec		George Carr, 70, Pleurisy
1813		
Jany		Child of Dan Hathway, 3 w, opium
Jany		Captn. Dan Hathway, 36, Typhus Pneumonia
Feby	6	Bridget Water, 52, do
March	20	Maj. John Antill, 62, Liver Dise.
		Nathaniel Conkling, Junr., 56, Consumption
		Lydia Carpenter, 59, do

RECORD OF DEATHS

Aug	22	Child of Nehemiah Denton, 7 mo, Cholera infant
Sept	7	Child of Thomas Hawkins, 14 mo, do
	16	Wid Elsa Gale * 86, Old age
Oct	17	Wickham Vail, 10, Fall
	18	Sarah Webb, 88 2-3, Old age
Nov	4	Jonathan Smith, Esq. * 95, Cancer
	9	Margaret, wife of Phillip Miller, 32, Consumption
	11	David Conkling, 9, Fever
		Ethelinda Webster, 6 mo, Pneumonia
	21	Child of James Bull, 4 mos, Fits
	25	Child of Mrs Lynch, Twins, 14 mos, Hooping cough
	27	Child of Mrs Lynch, Twins, 14 mos, do
Dec	4	Child of Henry G Wisner, Esq., 9 mos., do
	30	Joshua Watkins, 33, Intemperance
1814		
Jany	9	Hannah Bull, 21, Consumption
	10	Huldah Crabtree, 57, do
	25	William E. Smith, 9 mos, Hooping cough
	28	Charles Servt. of Danl. Carpenter, 60, Old age
Feby	3	William Clark, 20, Consumption
	7	Fanny Knapp, 15, do
	13	Joseph, Son of Benj. Strong, 1½, Measles
	24	William, Son of Benj. Strong, 6, Measles
	20	Child of Andrew Noble, 9 mos, Scrophula
	28	Johannis Weeks, 30, Hemopthosis
March	8	Sally Maria Thompson, 2, Worms
April	6	William Wickham Esq., 82, Gout
	10	James Brasted, 10, Typhus
May	6	Jesse Arnell (Physican), 27, Consumption
July	12	Rosanna Kinner, 61, Old age
	31	Dick Hetfield, 85, Old age
Aug	6	Elizabeth Hulse, 47, Fit
	10	Child of Elliott Hopkins, 4 mos, Herpes
	11	Joseph Smith, 64 Typhus
Sept	6	Dennis Clark, 7, Killed in a cyder Mill
	26	Child of Joel C Jackson, 15 mo, Typhus
Oct	18	Isaac Van Duzer, 60, Cholic
Novr	27	Mary wife of John Budd * 49, Consumption
Dec	2	Child of Timothy B. Crowell, 1 yr 8 mo, Hydrocephalis
	17	Child of Charles Howell, 1 yr 8 mo, do
	25	Morris Swezy, 21, Typhus
	29	William Crowell, 4, Hydrocephelus
1815		
Jany	3	Child of Timothy B. Crowell, 5 mo, do
	12	Gideon Salmon, 67, Intemperance
	15	Stephen Smith, Junr., 22, Typhus
Feby	1	Child of Jack Wallace, 3, Hooping cough
	3	John Vail, 70, Palsy
	6	Phinehas Case, 74, do
	19	Thomas Eager, 50, Typhus
March	1	Abraham Dunlap, 50, Intoxication
	12	Child of Miss Clark, 6 mo, Croup
	23	Charles C Case, 2 3-4, do
	26	James L. Dunning, 4, Hooping cough
	26	Hannah Banker, 41, Apoplexy
	28	John Conner, 47, do

RECORD OF DEATHS

	28	Child of David Conkling, 1, Pneumonia
	28	Black child of Richard Jackson, 7, Worms
April	3	Adam Douglas, 65, Intemperance
	4	Sally Tustin, 39, Consumption
May	14	Polly Knapp, 17, do
	27	Anna Tuthill, 20, Child bed fever
June	28	Tabitha Borland, widow, 91, old age
July	20	Mary wife of Thos. Edsall, 40, Child bed
	21	Abigail Mc Donald, 25, do
Aug	15	Harriett wife of Geo Smith, 20, Typhus
	18	Aaron Hetfield, 47, do
	20	Child of Richard A. Holley, 2 mo, Fits
Septr	7	Patty wife of Harry Gale, 23, Spotted fever
	7	Child of Henry Thompson, 19 mo, Dysentry
Oct	3	Child of Isaac Reeves, 3 yrs., Burn
	4	Julia Budde, 23, Consumption
	11	Child of Harry Smith, 14 mo, Pneumonia
Nov	14	Lucy a black woman, 85, Fever, old age
Dec	8	Daniel Thorne, 48, Consumption
	8	Nathaniel Conkling * 77, Palsey
	8	Child of Birdsey Case, 3 mo, Croup
	18	Child of Francis Lusk, 3 yrs, Burn
1816		
Jany	6	Dianah Servt. of Anthony Dobbins, 60, Phrenitis
	16	Widow Sarah Tuthill, 80, Old age
	16	Rebeckah, wife of Saml. Gale, 40, lock jaw
	19	Child of Colville B Ludlum, 10 mo, Pneumonia
	20	Besty Falls, 42, Consumption
	27	Child of Jack Decker, 9, Fever
	20	Child of Horace Hudson, 3, Burn
Feby	19	Rebecka wife of Thos. M. Clark, 45, Consumption
	23	William Holly, 15, Dysuria
	24	Abigail Hudson, 33, Plurisy
	—	Tamer, Servt of Jas. Everett, Esq., 60, Dropsy
	28	Capt. Stephen Smith, 59, Plurisy
March	1	Mary Servt. of Thos. Waters * 29, Typhus
	13	Morris do do, 22, do
	14	child of Joseph Wood Junr., 5 days, fits
	16	Patty Colley, 30, Child bed
	19	Hannah Maria Stephens, 1 ½, Croup
	27	Christopher Telleball, 67, Intemperance
	27	Child of Nelly Phillips, 10 mo, cold croup
April	1	Ann Board, 88, old age
	2	Archibald Theophilus Howell, 10 mo, Hydrocephilis
	3	Jeremiah Jessup * 66, Pleurisy
	4	Nehemiah Denton, 46, Plurisy
	—	Joshua Case, 60, do
	5	Child of Joshua Reeves, 3 mo, Fits
	7	Child of Peter & Peggy, 9 mo, Consumption
	9	Child of Harry Gale, 2 yrs, Worms
	17	Edward Ely Tuthill, 6 mos, Inflam-fever
	20	Thomas B Noble, 9 yr, Worms
	23	John G. Jessup, * 20, Plurisy
	26	Neal Brown, 58, Intemperance
	27	William Phillips Child, 1, Pneumonia

RECORD OF DEATHS

May	2	Daughter of Joseph Conkling, 12, Phrenitis
	6	Mrs Sally Dillon, 50, Hernia
	9	Child of Thomas Mills, 2, Fits
		Wife of James Ellis, 40, Hemoptisis
	17	Phebe Rumsey, 4½, Enterity
	26	Doctor William Elmer * 59, Typhus
June	2	Josh'ia Smith, 34, Consumption
	16	Child of Timothy Wood, 20 days, Sprue
	17	Lucretia Conkling, 33 yrs, Consumption
	24	Phinehas Rumsey, 47, Palsey
	25	Wid. Phebe Smith, 58, Consumption
Sept	19	Child of Richard S. Horton, 6 mo, Hydrocep
Oct	3	Abigail wife of John A Smith * 32 Consumption
	9	Anna wife of Smith Bendict, 22, Cholic
	28	William Gorham, 34, Typhus
Nov	23	Mary wife of John Brewster * 48, Insanity
Dec	14	John son of John Duer Esq., 5 mo, Enteritis
	15	Benjamin Robinson * 70, Old age
	29	Deborah wife of James Green, 28, Consumption
	30	Platt Newman, 25, do
1817		
Jany	21	Sarah wife of Horace Hudson, 23, do
Feby	10	Joanna Salmon, 54, do
	18	Wid. Anna Ludlum, 34, Child bed
	19	Child of Richard S. Denton, 9 mo, Inflam. of Lungs
	21	William Sidway, 35, Consumption
March	26	Susan Webb, 3 yr. 6 mo, Worms
April	1	James Carpenter * 69, Inflamation of lungs
	8	Child of Colvin Ludlum
	23	Gabriel Webb, 3 Debility
	28	Mary Newman, 20, Consumption
	30	John Brewster * 62, Inflam. of lungs
May	4	Nathaniel J. Drake, 33, Plurisy
	5	Hannah Smith, 86, Old age
	7	Robert Brewster, 22, Consumption
	19	Child of James Ellis, 5, Burnt in house
	30	Child of R. L. Wilkes, 2, Fits
June	4	Scudder Newman, 64, Plurisy
	11	Philetus Howell, 50, Fever
	12	Hannah Lusk, 27, Consumption
	22	George Silsby, 39, Fall from a Building
	24	Child of David Barnum, 8 weeks, Inflam. lungs
	28	Flora Sans free black woman, 27, Cossump
July	9	Elizabeth Foster * 62, Anasarchis Pulmonia
	10	Braddock L'Hommedieu, 1, Burn
	26	Betsey Rumsey, 2 yr. 9 mo, Fall
Sep	11	Child of Timothy Wood, 2 weeks, Fits
	17	Mercy Carpenter * 83, Old age
Oct	20	Rufus Crist, 2, Fits
Nov	1	Daniel Everett, 72, Cancer
1818		
Jany	10	Abigail Jackson * 76, Old age
	13	Hannah Kelsey * 48, Consumption
Feb	3	Rachael Bago, 73, Fit
	24	Asa Steward, Elder * 70, Kidney Complaint
March	14	James B. Tooker, 27, Consumption

RECORD OF DEATHS 85

	29	Child of John Duer, 5 mo, Fits
	30	Child of Joseph Tolman, 11 mo, Compression on Brain
	—	Child of Thomas Sodon, 2 y, Infl Lungs
April	6	Child of Samuel Rumsey, 1, Infl lungs
	12	Deborah Finch, 89, Old age
	27	Elizabeth Bull, 53, Consump.
	28	Sarah Smith * 53, Apoplexy
May	5	Cornelia Mandeville, 63, Infl. lungs
	11	Elizabeth Everett, 83, Old age
	22	Charity Thompson, 78, Old age
June	16	Martha Lewis, 66, Liver Compl.
	29	Margaret Horton, 84, Old age
July	3	Abijah Middlebrook, 31, Typhus fever
	13	Hiram Weller, 40, Liver com.
	25	Martha Conkling * 82, Old age Dropsey
	26	Samuel Rumsey, 45, Consumption
	28	Abel Smith, 44, Plurisy
	29	William Foster, 41, Consumption
Augt	20	Linson Servt Dr. Phillips, 24, Dropsy
	26	Samuel Dunning, 25, Consumption
	27	Dolly Carpenter, 64, Typhus
Sep	18	David Reeves Arnell, 6 mos, Fits
Oct	14	Child of Henry Gale, 10 mos
	16	Hannah Corwin, 65, Consup.
Nov	28	George Newman, 25, Consumption
Dec	21	Child of Samuel Reynolds, 3 weeks, Hives
	25	Anthony Dobbins, 64, Consumption
	30	Col. Moses Phillips * 76, Old age
1819		
Jan	3	Matthew Mc Kinney, 70, Old age
	16	Margaret Horton, 21, Consump
Feb	7	William Bennet, 11, Cholera morbus
	9	Joseph Brown, 68, Asthma
	13	John Case, 77, Old age
	14	Samuel Hulse, 51, Consump.
March	9	Child of James Wilkin, 10 weeks, Inflm. lungs
	13	Child of Joshua Wells Jur., 3 mo, do
	19	Child of Henry Gale, 2 mo, do. debility
	20	David Case, 37, Fall
	24	Child of Nathan Cooley, 10 days, Fits
April	21	Silas Pierson, 55, Intemperance
	30	Child of Jarvis Valentine, 5 weeks, Fits
May	8	Elizabeth Masters, Child bed
	19	Child of Daniel Case, 18 mo, Hydrocephalis
June	15	Joshua Wells, 73, Dropsy
	27	Elizabeth Smith, 54, do
July	7	Isaac Reeve, 35, Liver complaint
June	4	Elizabeth Bradner, 29, Mania
Augt	1	Elsa Wood * 74, Liver complaint
	3	Edward Boyle, 24, Heat
	15	Samuel Hull, 52, Consump
	20	John Wilkham, 12, Inflm. brain
Oct	12	Freegift Tuthill, 44, Intemp.
	16	Mary Dunning * 28, Consumption
	26	Mary Booth, 88, Old age
	28	Joshua Whitman, 76, Apoplexy

RECORD OF DEATHS

Nov	12	Elijah Wheeler, 55, Intemp
	14	Moses Gale, 70, old age
	19	Susan Decker, 14, Inflam fever
	25	Rebeckah Decker, 21, Consump.
	—	Jenet B. Moir, 21, Inflam. fever
	28	Mary Budd, 100 yrs & 8 mos., old age
Dec	2	John Dougherty, 19, Inflm. head
	3	Child of Robt. Blakely, 8, Lock jaw
	6	Keziah Westcott, 49, Consumption
	23	Sarah Wickham, 76, Old age

1820

Jany	1	Child of Saml. Reynolds, 3 weeks, Inflm. lungs
	3	Henry Shaw, 32, Consumption
	9	James Everett, Esq., 74, Palsey
	12	Ebenezer Stephens, 32, Injury
	30	Hester Howell, 29, Consump
Feby	28	Stephen Valentine's child, 3 w, Sprue
		Silas Horton, 90, Old age
	6	Abigail Swezy (wife of David Swezy), 71, Dropsey
March		William Barker Junr., 23 Hemoptisis
	23	Maria Hudson, 4½, Ulcer
April	14	John Taylor, 74, Burn
	12	Charles Paul, 26, Dropsey
May	7	Mary Bailey * 56, Liver Comp.
	15	Margaret Rumsey * 40, Disease of heart
June	11	Samuel O. Wood, 24, Diarrhoea
July	1	Lois Gardner, 22, Consump.
	13	Daniel Mc Laughlin, 9, Typhus
	23	Widow Willoughby, 69, Hernia
Augt	7	Margt Dunning, 36, mortification
	20	Margaret Conkling wid. of Nathl Conkling Junr., 61, Consumption
		Theophilus Dolsen, 36, Marasmus
Oct	26	Martha Steward, 33, Child bed
Nov	22	Jason Gay, 72, Old age
Dec	25	Child of Phillip Crane, 3, Fever
	30	Mary Ann Horton, 14, Lock jaw

1821

Jan	14	Child of Sukey Webb, 6 mo, Consup.
	18	Mary Steward, 67, Old age
Feb	3	Abijah Wells, 68, Dropsy chest.
	9	Child of David Dean, 4 mos, Casualty
	14	Thomas Gale * 70, Dropsey in Chest
	16	Samuel Webb, 70, Typhus
	—	Thomas E. Webb, 2, Fits
	21	Joseph Jackson, 38, Consump.
	24	Betsey Crane, 22, Consump.
March	11	Child of William Hultse, 10 mo, Inflm. Lungs
	—	Henry, Servat of Judge Bodle, 60, Dropsy
	26	Benjamin Crane, Consump
	29	Abigail Tuthill, 79, Old age
April	5	Child of Richard Holley, 3 mo, Inf'm. Lungs
		Aaron Springstead, 37, Consumption
	6	Hannah Dean, 27, do
	7	Charles, Servt. of Judge Steward, 17, do
	12	Thomas Goble, 6, Dropsy
		Child of John Steward, 6 mos, Inflm lungs

RECORD OF DEATHS

	20	Deborah Gay * 58, Fever
	22	Phebe Banker, 3, Burn
	—	Mary Elmer * 57, Fits
May	7	Phineas Salmon, 69, Apoplexy
June	8	Dinah Bounty, 27, Dropsy
	21	Cornelia Everett, 23, Consump.
	22	Elizabeth Case, 65, Consump
	26	John Johnson, 55, Typhus
	30	Nathan Colley, 56, Consump
July	8	Grace Ann Lockyear, 2, Fits
	26	John Seward, 54, Paralysis
Augt	1	James Findley, 74, Old age
	11	Elsa Phillips, 46, Dropsy
	16	Mary Ann Tolman, 6 mos, Inflm. Lungs
Sep	5	Quinton Dougherty, 35, Drowned
	9	Jane Butler * 78, Old age
	29	Robert T. Jackson, 18, Consump.
Oct	13	Child of John Wilson, 2, Cholera Infant.
	25	Sarah Everett, 81, Old age
Nov	15	Nancy Mc Laughlin, 30, Consump.
	18	Child of Timothy Wood, 2 weeks, Sprue
Dec	1	Child of John Banker, 6 do, Chol Inf.
	3	Child of Dener, 17, Hooping C.
	19	Emeline Vail, 17, Hydrocephalis
	30	Child of Richard Wickham, 2 days, Fits
1822		
Jan	12	Zacheus Case, 81, Old age
	26	Child of Isaac Brown, 1, Hooping cough
	27	Sarah Smith, 19, Burn
Feb	8	Bethiah Conkling * 77, Old age
		Child of Jonas Smith, 2 mo, Fits
March	10	Coe Gale * 77, Palsey
	14	Ruth Davis, 36, Dropsy
	19	Hannah Watkins, 41, Infln. Lungs
	26	Robt. M. Potter, 55, Intemperance
April	7	Child of Isaac Brown, 4, Debility
	17	Sarah Taylor, 60, consump.
	21	Child of Nathan Vail, 9 mos
	24	Sarah Austin of Chester, 60, Apoplexy
	26	Bethiah Whitman * 48, Dropsy
May	10	Sarah Bodle * 71, Colic
	28	Child of Catherine Horton, 2, Hooping cough
	30	Child of John Gale, 1, do
June	6	Emeline Carpenter * 14, Infl. lungs
	15	Abagail Tusten, 52, Fits
July	14	Mary Carpenter * 72, Old age
	23	Julia Ann Sawyer, 24, Typhus fever
	25	Lois Seely colored woman 19, Consump
	26	Nancy Bodle, 19, Fit
	27	John C Jackson, 45, Intemp.
Augt	4	William Valentine, 8, Palsy
	8	Elisha Goldsmith, 11, Wound by scyth
	27	Frances Jansen, 16 mo, Fit
	28	Joseph Wickham, 51, Typhus
	29	Child of James Horton, 10 weeks, Infln. lungs
	31	Child of Hannah Seely, 3 do, Fits

RECORD OF DEATHS

Sept	5	Dr. Thomas Wickham, 54, Palsey
	9	Child of Mr. Egerton from Conn., 2, Dysentery
	20	Child of Birdseye Case, 3 mo, Whooping cough
	22	Colored child of Morrison Taylor, 18 mo, Dysentery
	23	Child of Jonathan Bodle, 18 do, do
	25	John Borland, 85, old age
	29	Child of Daniel Carpenter, 2, Worms
Oct	3	Child of Garritt Duryea, 14 mo, Dysentery
	8	Alexander Corey, 60, Apoplexy
	8	Child of Jesse Odle, 9, Dysentery
	31	Child of Samuel Crowell, 2, do
Nov	13	Charity Shaw, 56, Typhus
Dec	10	Child of Caesar Wickham, 4 mo, Fits
	16	Tamer Wickham, 25, Typhus
	18	John Delancy, 44, Apoplexy
	26	Mary Shaw, 26, Consump.
	30	Elizabeth Rumsey * 38, Do
1823		
Jan	14	Hannah Jessup * 60, Consumption
	19	Gabriel Smith, 41, Intemp.
	25	Child of John Gale, 4 mo, Cholera Inf.
Feb	1	Lois Noble, 74, Old age
	12	George W Case, 4, Dropsey head
March	8	Child of Wm. E. Thorne, 8 mo, Infln. lungs
	23	Julia A. Denton Noble, 5 yr, Dropsey head
April	18	Zebina Beardsley, 48
	21	Child of Widow Payne, 6 weeks, croup
	22	Enos Conkling, 58, Consump.
	23	William E. Gildersleeve, 4, Croup
	23	Michael Jackson, 48, Apoplexy
May	11	Lydia Vail, 46, Debility
	12	Wilmot Case, 12, Fall from a horse
	15	Child of Archibald Bogue, 3 mo, Fits
	20	Francis, 80, Old age
	26	James Robinson, 60, Intemp.
June	26	Charles Servt. of Joshua Conkling, 13, Consump.
July	18	Hannah Jessup, 28, Child bed
	31	Doct. James Bradner, 62, Liver Compl.
Augt	4	Mary Conkline, colored woman, 34, Gravel
	9	Mary Dunning * 80, Asthma
	24	Deborah Seward, 56, Dropsy
	29	Alexander Mc Gregor, 62, Diarrhoea
Sep	13	Hannah Case, 77, Typhus fever
	16	Adeline Halsey, 15 Consump
	19	William Brown, 62, Typhus
	19	Child of Timothy Wood, 2 mo, Cholera Inf.
	25	Child of John Odle, 5 mo, Infim. head
Oct	1	Child of Joseph Smith, 1 year, Croup
	5	Eleazer Hudson, 50, Intemperance
	10	Letitia Brown, 61, Typhus
	31	Child of Benjamin Elliott, 7 weeks
Nov	5	Henry Smith, 90, Old age
Dec	9	Martha Brewster, 64, Pneumonia
	17	Abigail Hobby * 27, Consumption
1824		
Jan	13	Patience Titus, 70, Old age

RECORD OF DEATHS

	19	Child of Andrew Tuthill, 4 weeks, Fit
	22	Child of Henry Thompson, 3 yrs., Burn
	31	James N. Halsey, 4, Hydrocephalis
Feb	16	Child of Andrew Webb, 6 weeks, Fits
	16	Child of Caesar Wickham, 4 yr.
	18	Child of Thomas O. Kelsey, 2 yr. 6 mo., Worms
	22	Timothy Dunning, 73, Dropsy
	24	William McBride, 40, Consump
March	8	Elianor Wood, 36, Consump
April	3	Child of Maria Smith, 2
	17	William Seward, 25, Intermp.
May	1	Child of Wid. Mc Bride, 7 mo, Dropsy in brain
	21	Nathan Smith, 27, Consump
	30	Mary Horton, 74, Old age
June	2	Stephen Smith, 59, Diarrhoea
	3	Lydia Vail, 74, Old age
	30	Burnitt Tallman, 7, Measles
July	9	Christian Ludlum, 71, Typhus
	16	Mary Jackson, 7, Measles
Sep	6	Jason Wilkin, 55, Apoplexy
	7	Thomas James, 41, Consump
	10	Elizabeth Valentine, 63, Dropsy
	12	Benjamin Harlow, 83, Liver Com.
	12	Child of Reuben Shaw, 6 mo., Laudanum
	16	Hector Seward, 26, Kick of horse
	27	Mary Conkling * 65, Dysentery
Oct	3	John Crane, 59, Entiric mania
	12	Daniel Reeves, 62, Suicide
Nov	21	Rebecca Budd, 73, age
	29	William Wilkin, 33, Diarrhoea
Dec	21	William W. Shaw, 2 yr 7 mo, Burn
1825		
Jan	9	Christian Owen, 33, Fever
	15	Child of Morrison Taylor, 7 mo, Dropsy in head
	17	Juda Serv't of Rob't Seely—18, Typhus
	17	Ananias Valentine, Elder * 65, Consump
	17	Child of Hanibald M. Hopkins, 2 days
	26	James Vail, 9 yr, infim head
Feb	10	Caesar Serv't of Benjm. Strong, 56, Rheumatism
	14	Charles T. Seward, 8, Typhus
March	1	Jane Smith * 37, Child bed
	8	Child of Herman Fink, 3 mo, Malformation of heart
	13	Child of Thomas O. Kelsey, 9 do, Cosump
	26	Child of John Wallace, 3 days, Cholera
	28	Child of Horace Bennett, 13 mo, Influenza
	29	Mary Thorne, 53, Consump
April	3	Child of John Budd, 8 mo, Hydrocephalus
	18	Robert Kizer, 12 yr, Supperative Rheumatism
	30	Child of Hector Tuthill, 2 weeks, Infim.
May	11	Mary M. Arnell * 44, Consump
June	12	Child of Moses Sawyer, 15 mo, Fits
	14	Julia Denton * 47, affection of laranyx
	4	Child of Albert S Benton, 9 mo, Measles
July	22	Nancy Wilson, 82, Old age
	24	Hugh Gallagher, 40, Intemperance

RECORD OF DEATHS

	25	Child of Jack Wallace, 1½ yr, Measles
	29	Christian Wood, 86, Old age
Augt	5	Alexander McVey, 80, Fit
	9	David Hawkins, 75, Consump.
	23	Child of John Budd, 2½, Dysentery
	26	Pierre Griffen, Stranger about 37, Found dead in road
Sep	13	Joseph Wood * 81, age
	15	Bow Ludum, colored man, 25, Typhus
		Child of Timothy Wood, 2 mos., Sprue
Oct	15	Helen Conkling, 48, Consump
	17	Edward Ely, Esq., 49, Infm. Bowels
Nov	11	Thomas O. Kelsey, 34, Cosumption
	16	Child of Edward Hulse, 2, Croup
	29	Charity Simmons, 76, Old age
	30	William Jackson, 6, Enlargement of heart
Dec	23	Child of Horace Smith, 3 weeks
	23	Rhoda Wells, 87, Palsy

1826

Jan	5	Child of Elizabeth at J. Strong's, 4 mo., Infm. lungs
	7	Child of Widow Mapes, 16 mos, Hooping cough
	31	Child of George Sp——, 4 years, Influenza
Feb	10	Sarah Moffatt *, 77, Apoplexy
	15	Isaac Bowers, 78, Old age
	11	Elizabeth Howe, died below West Point, 40, Influenza
	23	Sally Taylor * 31, Consump.
	26	Solomon Serv't of Thos. Waters, 50, Delirium tremans
	28	James Butler * 86, Asthma
March	16	Alfred Mills * 23, Pleruisy
April	12	Child of Joseph Impson, 5 mo, Hooping cough
	28	Abigail Bailey * 62, Consump
	28	Child of Colvin B. Ludlum, 15 mo, Infm lungs
May	6	Josiah Kitchel * 57, Bilious Rem.
	7	James Lusk, 78, Old age
	10	Child of Wm. Lewis, 1, Infm. lungs
	12	Benjamin Strong, Esq., Elder * 56, Hernia
	23	Child of Andrew Webb, 6 weeks, Infm. lungs
	22	Juda Whitman * 77, Old age
June	6	Eli Corwin, 60, Infm lungs
	12	Child of John T. Wood, 10 days, Croup
July	14	John Beardsley, 15 yrs., Black vomit
	21	John Denton, 65, Dropsy in chest
	22	Child of Isaac Bowers, 2, Croup
	22	Adam Guellish, 60
	25	Child of Gabriel Thompson, 3 weeks, Infm. lungs
	26	Silvia Halsey * 40, Child bed
Augt	10	Daniel Seward, 86, Dropsy
	10	Azuleah Titus, 61, Consump.
	11	Fanny Bodle * 36, Do
	20	Anna Wilson, 57, Consump
	27	Mary Hulse, 17, Dysentery
	28	George Hubbard * 72, Old age
Sept	4	David R. Arnell, M. D., Elder * 51, Consump
	7	Juda Brinson, 33, Dropsy
Oct	19	Mary Higson, 59, Suffocation
	27	Child of James A Cheeve, 2 mo., Infm. lungs
Nov	2	Child of Doct. John S Crane, 17 mo, Burns

RECORD OF DEATHS

	6	Mary Ann Phillips, 27 y, Phihsis
Dec	25	Abigail Smith * 70, Consump.
1827		
Jan	3	John Scantling, 45, Intemperance
	4	Child of Horace Ball, 3, Croup
	10	Chloe, Servant of Dr. Phillips, 68
	10	Mary Ann Case, near 27, Consump.
	13	Richard Wade, 25, Pneumo-Typ.
	23	Child of Horace T. Ball, 18 mo., Blister
	23	Cyrus Servt of A. Wells, more than 100, old age
Feb	2	Child of Henry Phillips, 2, Croup
	9	Hannah Howell, 63, Palsy
	15	Jonathan Owen, 60, Pneumonia
	23	Sophronia Odle, 38, Consump
March	6	Peter Randol, 75, Old age
	6	Henry, colored child, 8, Consump.
April	8	Bryan Garrahan, 50, Typhus
	21	Child of Joseph Aspell, 2 weeks, Fits
	27	Peggy Jessup, 62, Dropsy
May	7	John Owen, 45, Intemp.
	26	Juliana Gale * 68, Consump.
June	16	Child of Austin Terry, 14 mo, Croup
	20	Albert Foster * near 77, Asthma
July	6	Thomas Sodon, 60, Consump
Augt	7	Thomas W. Denton, 35, Delerium Tremens
	20	Mrs. Thompson, 83, Cholera Mor.
	23	Harriet Hurtin, 28, Inward bleeding
	26	Frederick Horton * 75, Gangrene
Sep	10	Patience Case, 58, Dysentery
Oct	17	Benjamin Bradner, 57
	18	William Crane, 63, Dysentery
	18	Mary Crane, 62, Dysentery
		(Husband and wife; burried in one grave)
Nov	18	Child of John Vail, 5 mo, Bowel comp.
	19	Silas H. Hawkins, 31, Intemp.
Dec	4	James Mc Laughlin, 32, Intemp.
	8	Mary Boak * 53, Liver comp.
	16	Alexander Martin, 68, Debility
1828		
Jan	3	Lydia Horton * 77, Palsey
Feb	27	Rufus Drake, 52, Intemp
March	25	Anthony I. Ross, 56, Do.
April	1	Daniel Smith, 36, Cosump.
	18	Joanna Owen, Wid., 56, Billious int.
	20	Jane Lusk, Wid., 76, Old age
May		Child of Widow Mc Laughlin, 7, Drunkenness
	24	Roswell Lewis, 26, Intemp.
	26	John Budd, 75, Intemp.
June	19	Martha Dunning * 44, Bleeding (from) liver
July	2	Child of John Boak, M. D., 3 weeks, Sprue
	3	Henry Wheeler, Middletown, 25, Affection of spine
	22	Samuel Jones Wilkin, 5 days, Jaundice
Augt	25	Rachel Tooker * 64, Lunacy
Sep	3	Maria Coleman, 22
	8	George Babcock, 32, Apoplexy

RECORD OF DEATHS

	19	John Bradner, Esq., * 70, Palsey
	21	Mary Barker, 69, Do
	30	Benjamin Carpenter * 75, Obstruction in urethra
Oct	13	Renselaer Green, colored stranger, 35, Intemp.
	18	John Webster, 56, Intemp.
	25	Child of David Dillon, 16 mo, Worms
Nov	12	Nancy White, 28 yrs, Typhus
	14	Child of Dr. J. Warner, 4, Typhus
	14	Evelina Case, 25, Conusmp.
	23	John Sodon, 24, Intemp.
	25	Jane Ann Decker, 14, Ulcers
	25	Phebe Ann Wallace, 19, Consump.
Dec	9	Child of Henry E. Waters, 8 weeks, Infim. lungs
	15	Letitia Smith, Wid., 85 yr., Old age
	22	Child of James A. Cheeve, 2 weeks, Bowel comp.
	28	James Denton, 74, Fit
1829		
Jany	8	Jesse Smith, 71, Fall
	8	William Thurston, 45, Intemp.
	11	Child of Benjm. Denton, Cold., 8 mo, Hydrocephalis
	27	Roswell Payne, 50, Intemp.
Feb	5	David H. Ellis, 22, Consumption
	13	John Halsey, 55, Dropsey by intemperance
March	14	Joseph Hunt, 16, Hydrocephalis
	23	Benjamin Wade, 65, Intemp.
April	4	Eleanor Sawyer, wid. of Moses, 58, Consump.
	8	Abigail Wells, 56, Engorgement of heart
	17	John Wilson, Junr., 5 mo, Infim. lungs
	23	Abigail Jackson, 76, Hydro thorax
	28	John Hudson, 72, Inflam. of Bladder
	29	Child of Thomas C. Waters, 4, Fit
May	30	A female stranger in jail, about 45
June	5	Child of Stephen Valentine, 3 mo, Defective organization
	28	Mary Thorne * 53, Abcess
July	17	Tinah Taylor, 56, Intemp.
	23	Daniel Corwin * 71, Inflamation of liver & lungs
	25	Eleanor Carpenter * 70, Dropsy
Augt	1	Benjamin, Twin son of Benjamin Strong died in New York 10 mo, Infim. of Bowels
	5	Child of Timothy Wood, 3 week, Bowel comp.
	5	Child of Joseph R. Smith, 4 mo, Croup
	9	Child of J. J. Poppino, 2 yrs., Hydrocephalis
	12	Child of James Horton, 2 yrs, Hydrocephalis
	13	John Steward * 83, Palsey
	15	Ethelinda Elliott * 63, Diarrhoea
	16	Doct. Thomas G. Evans, 41, Bil. Remittant
Sep	3	Doct. William Elliott, 74, Diarrhoea
	11	John Potter, 17, Dysentery
	12	Child of Wm. Wooden, 20 mo, Do
	13	Margaret Arnott, 70, Do
	18	William Westbrook, 30, Intemp.
	30	Child of Saml. G Merriam, Sore throat
Oct	1	Grant Smith, 39, Consump.
	8	Joshua Mc Nish, Middletown, 50, Consump
	9	Ann Jackson * 72, Old age
	20	Joanna Stuart Reeve, 28, Consump

RECORD OF DEATHS

Nov	19	James Irwin, Stranger, 22, Killed by the fall of bank.
	30	Daniel Dougherty, 35, Intemp.
Dec	5	Phillis Elmer, 84, Old age
	9	Theophilus Howell, 70, Fever
	15	Child of William Goldsmith, 2, Fever
	25	Edward Campbell, Stranger, 35, Disease heart
	31	Amanda Dean (burried Jan 4), 33, Consump.
1830		
Jan	9	Jane Denton, 25, Typhus
	11	Sarah Crabtree, 35, Consump.
	13	Child of Wheeler Case, 2 weeks, Mal-form-
	20	Newman Gilbert, 38, Mania Potu.
Feb	7	William Stewart, 44, Mania Potu
	14	William A. Howell, 13, Disease Bowels
March	24	Isaac Bowers * 49, Kick of horse
	26	Daniel S. Sutton, 26, Constipation
April	5	Hannah Wilkin * 64, Calt-Debility
	24	John Monell, 85, Old age
	28	Susan Metcalf, 51, Inflam. Rheumatism
May	7	Edward Kelley—Colored—80, Old age
July	10	Dorothy Bull, 28, Consumption
Augt	14	Susannah Gourlay, 55, Cancer
	16	Child of John Wallace, 3 days, Bleeding
	21	Child of Widow Sutton, 7 weeks, Intero Sus-
Sep	5	Lewis Denton, Died in Monmouth Co N. J, 29, Bil. Ret.
	7	Child of Tice, 11 days, Jaundice
	24	Egbert J. Horton, 1 yr, Hydrocephalis
		Isaac Mapes * 60
	25	Hannah Sawyer * 59, Palsy
Oct	7	Child of George Dunning, 2 mo, Dysentery
	21	Sarah Dunning * 72, Enlargement of heart
	23	William Lusk, 33, Intemp.
Nov	4	David Case * 75, Old age
	26	John Waters, 55, Consump. by intemp.
	27	Andrew Noble, 46, Consump. by intemp.
Dec	2	Christian Hurtin (Esiscop.) 87, Pneumonia Nothus
	11	Thurston Corey, 12, Rheumatism
	23	James Pearson, 46, Intemp.
	29	Experience Bull, 66, Fever
	30	Sarah Ann Hammond, 12, Croup
1831		
Jan	3	Child of Hubbard Smith, 11 mo, Infm. lungs
	5	Hezekiah Denton, 27, Apoplexy by intemp.
	5	Mary Beardsly * 55, Consump.
	16	Solomon Carpenter * 60, Apoplexy
Feb	3	Egbert Strong, 27, Typhus
	20	Child of Benjamin Strong, Twin daughter died in New York 2 yr. 6 mo, Scarlet fever
	25	Deborah Goldsmith * 18, Rem. Fever
March	11	Andrew M. Jackson, 38, Delerium Tremens
	28	Matthias K. Murray, 35, Do
April	29	Child of Mr. Parson of Scotchtown, 2, Infim. Lungs
May	5	Sarah Saxton, Poor house, 6, Croup
		Mehitable Conkling * 51, Infmy. Rheumatism
		Martha Corey * 69, Derangement
June	21	Child of James D. Wilkin, 2, Scald

RECORD OF DEATHS

	22	Child of Edward Hulse, 2, Hydrocephalis
	23	Amira Jane Corey * 22, Consump.
July	5	Elizabeth Gale, died in N. York, 78, Inflm lungs
	9	Child of John Carpenter, 17 mo., Croup
	17	Child of Henry Barker, 21 mo, Hooping cough
	25	Anthony Jackson, 45, Inflm. Fever
Augt	2	Child of Jeremiah Kelsey, 2, Hydrocephalis
	5	John Gregg, Junr., 14, Scarlet fever
	18	Stephen Cooper, Chester, 40, Intemperance
Sept	17	James Edsall, 27, Typhus
Oct	2	Child of Doct. John S. Crane, 5 days, Mal-conformation
	2	Child of James R. Van Duzer, 1 year, Fit
	21	Child of William Barker, 1
Nov	24	Charles F. Monell, 6 years, Bilious Rem
	24	William F. Gale, 26, Injuried spine
	27	William Thompson, 86, Old age
	29	Daniel H. Tuthill, Consumption
Dec	1	Haven Terry, 42, Liver comp.
	4	Wheeler Case, Esq., 40, Intemp.
	1	Harry Wade, 28, Intemp.
	10	Child of Constantine Connely, 2, Malformation
	14	Child of Horace Bennet, 1
	14	Child of Dublin Gardner, 2
	23	Charles Howell, 45, Inflm. lungs
	26	James Kerr, 36, Consump.
1832		
Jan	10	Virgil R. Case, 24, Consump.
	18	Margaret Gregg, 13, Inflm. lungs
	21	Ichabod Smith Oakley, 32, Intemp.
		Phineas Rumsey, Consumption
Feb	2	Agnes Wilson, 85, Influenza
	7	Elizabeth Rumsey * 19, Consump.
	8	Rebecca Borland, 79, Paralysis
	14	Child of J. Lewis Wood, 4 weeks, Cholera
	14	Mary Watkins, 22, Consump.
	15	Elizabeth P. Phillips * 52, Internal cancer
	17	James D. Wilkin, 41, Intemp.
	19	Jane Carpenter, 27, Consump.
	24	Child of John Carpenter, 5 mo, Cholera
March	2	Jane Wescott * 32, Consump.
	3	Child of James S. Banker, 5 weeks, Sprue
	4	Child of Samuel Dunning, 11 mo, Dysentery
	12	Juliann, Child of Anthony Wood, 5 yr, Scarlet fever
	17	Child of Andrew Hulse, 1 year, Hydrocephalis
	18	Child of George W. Connor, 13 mo, Closing of rectum
	23	Catherine Carpenter, 9 years, Scarletina
	26	Child of Hiram Smith, 3, Scarletina
April	8	Emily Smith, 25, Fits
	16	Gilbert Garahan, 11, Scarletine
	27	Sally Ann Wilkin, 38, Consump.
May	1	Child of Henry Smith, 5 w, Malformation
	1	Child of Randolph, 1, Burn
	2	Child of William Jackson, 5, Measles
June	13	Beyea Horton, 19, Killed by a horse
	11	Child of Horace W Elliott, 9 mo, Hydrocephalis
	17	Frances Maria Bradner, 5 yr, Scarletina

RECORD OF DEATHS

June	26	Nathaniel H. Dunning, 5, Dropsy
	27	Deborah Goldsmith, 65, Nervous Deb.
July	5	Horace Howard Bradner, 3, Scarletina
	29	Charles Hull, 22, Drowned
Augt	6	Benjamin Coleman * 77, Fall
	10	Joseph Denton, 73, Fever
Sep	24	Child of Freegift Tuthill, 11 mo, Fit
Novr	2	Mary Oakley, 5 yrs, Consumption
Dec	3	Abigail Smith, 78, Palsy
	23	Mary Dillen, daughter of David Dillen, 4, Scarletina

1833

Jany	3	Frances Amelia, daughter of Joseph Sayre, 2½, Croup
Feb	4	David W. Hoyt, 31, Delirium Tremenes
	15	Mary Isaabella—wife of John Steward—of N. Y. (Died in New York, whence the corpse was brought) 30, Consumption
	28	Mary Jane Wells, 25, Fever
March	8	Joseph Conkling, 59, Unknown
	9	Charlotte—wife of Wm. J. Norris, 27, Consumption
	25	Phineas A—son of Phineas Rumsey, 4 mo, Croup
	29	Ila Watkins, 48, Inflamation of the lungs
April	7	Prime Wisner, 43, Consumption
	9	Harriet Jane—daughter of James H. Genung, 12, Inflamation lungs
May	10	James S. Reeves, 32, Consumption
June	15	Charles C. Moore, 6, Scarlet fever
	17	Child of James Moore, 2, Do
	17	Child of John B. Booth, 1 day, Mal. Form
	20	Child of Horace Ball, 5, Scarletina
	23	Emily Scofield, Scarletina
July	27	Frances Satterly * 48, Consump.
Sep	14	Hannah Tooker * 65, Rupture of a Blood vessel
	17	Daniel Westervelt, 29, Intemperance
	21	Mary Robinson * 88, Dysentery
Oct	6	William Horton, 62, Fever
	24	Child of Dublin Gardner, 18 mo
	26	James Steward, 22 yrs., Consump.
Nov	28	Maria Bradner, Wid. of Dr. Bradner, 45, Fever
Decr	5	Dr. Ezra Fisk, Late Pastor, 48, Inflm. lungs with fever
Feby	20	Jeremiah Drake, 72, Typhus fever
	21	John Brentnel, 67, Fever
	25	Jane An Bond, 12, Scarlet fever
	28	Martha Christ, wife of P Crist, 42, Consumption
March	12	Jane Gilis, widow, 80, Consumption
	15	Abraham Smith, 30, Consumption
	25	Mary Wallace, 8, Scarletine
	26	Rachel Quarters, colored woman, 80, Drowned
	31	Frances Jansen, 49, Pneumonia
Apr	5	Lavinia Winne, 35, Consumption
	11	Nathaniel Conkling, 43, Intemperance
	21	William Robinson, 36, Inflm. of lungs
May	12	Richard Owen, Consumption
		Child of Widow Tuthill
Augt	31	Nathaniel Kelsey
	10	Mary Newman, 75, Dysentery
Sept	26	Edward, child of Widow Hoyt, 4, Dropsy in head

RECORD OF DEATHS

Octr	10	Catherine Wells, Consumption
	11	Frances McLaughlin, 18, Consumption
	16	Elizabeth Case, 8, Fever
	26	Dr. Egbert Jansen, 58, Fever
	28	Hannah Sawyer, 39, Consumption
Dec	11	Child of John Lusk, Accident
	19	Mrs. Terry, wife of Austin Terry, Consumption

1835

Jany	26	Abigail Gale, widow, 58, Consumption
Feby	14	Child of Mrs. Banker, 6 weeks
	21	Henry Mandeville, Old age
March	19	Samuel Smith, Exposure
	21	Infant of John Wilson, 6 weeks
	26	David Sweezy, Cpt., Rev. Ar., 89, Old age
	28	Mrs. Mary Thompson, Old age
April	19	Mrs. Mary Hatfield, Memb., Paral.
May	1	Child of William T. Barker, Hydrocephalis
	15	Child of Noah Carpenter, Croup
July	10	Child of David Wood, 5 yrs., Scarlet fever
	19	Wm. Edsall
Aug	10	Horatio Howell, son of Widw Ho., 20, Consumption
Sept	20	Rachel Connely, wife Constant Connely
	26	Twin children of Dr. Wells
	28	Child of Mr. Crawford
Nov	20	Mary Edsall, aged 11, Bilious fever
Dec	10	Benjamin Sawyer, 68, Dropsy

1836

Jany	25	Virgil Bennett, Nephritis
Feby	28	Child of Jas. Foster, 5 months
March	15	Mrs. Gale, wife of Henry Gale, Consumption
April	7	Child of Stephen Valentine, 10 years
	14	Child of John Ross, 10 months
	14	Garrett, Rysdick, 66 years
	14	William Noble
	26	Child of Aaron Van Duzer, 10 months
May	1	Elizabeth Smith, daughter of Henry Smith, 17 years
	4	Charles Burrell, 75
	6	Theophilus Howell, 38
	7	Infant of John Willson, 1 week
	9	Sarah Newman & wife of George M. Newman, 27
	31	Child of George Grier, 2½ years
July	30	Mrs. Randolph, wife of Newton F. Randolph
Aug	2	John Giles—Consumption, 45
	4	Oliver Richerson, colored man
	17	Joshua Tuthill, 65, Bilious Colick
Oct	6	William Gale, 28, Do

1837

Jany	2	Hannah Denton, widow, 74, Pulmonia
Feby	3	Mary Garahan, 20, Inflm. lungs
	16	William Henry Denton, 15, Fever
March	3	Margarett—wife of John Gregg
	9	Infant of Gabriel Bennett
June	29	Child of James Conner, 4 years
July	22	Thomas Boarland, 82, Old age

RECORD OF DEATHS

Aug	7	Elkanah Mills, 39, Consumption
Sept	6	Infant of Gabriel Smith
	14	Daughter of Hector Smith, 1 year
	15	Child of John Budd
Oct	16	Frances, wife of John I. Thompson

1838
Jany	16	Richard Jackson, 70
	19	Charles Tuthill, Consumption
Feby	6	John Budd, 49, Consumption
	17	James Dunning, 85, Dropsy
March	5	Mary Hudson, widow, 77
	8	Edward Phillips, Consumption
April	6	Henry Barker, 45
	8	Hannah, wife of Cooper Reeve, Consumption
Sept	8	Simon Fisk, 77
	10	Louisa Sayer wife of Joseph Sayre, 32, Consumption
	15	Child of George & Julia Van Inwigin

1839
May	31	Emily Howell, 17, Hydrocephalis
June	29	Widow—Mary Case, 81, Conspt.
	14	Mrs Bedford, 73
Aug	1	Saml Vail
	9	Robert Wallace, 27, Conspt
	22	Charles Wilkin, 17, Accident
Sept	6	Child of Mrs. Wallace, widow of Robert Wallace, 1 year 8 days
	7	Moses Smith, 62, Fever
	22	Child of Noah Gregory, 6 mos
	26	Joshua Goldsmith, 72 yrs., Old age

During the interval between the time Rev. Jas. R. Johnston left and the settlement of Rev. Dr. McCarty the following persons died this Congregation, viz

1839
Oct	13	Doctor Jerome Wells, Consumption, 35 years

1840
Jany	12	William C Wood, do, 27
		Child of Asa Dunning, Dysentery, 8 months
		James Harvey Carpenter, Fever, 35
		Sarah Fall (widow), Old age, 79
April	22	Elizabeth Jackson (widow), Palsy, 69
	3	Colvill Bradner, Consumption
		wife of Joshua Smith, do
Oct	19	Widow Mehetable Jackson, 87 yrs., old age

1841
Feby	6	Infant of Hamilton Jackson
April		Widow Henry Smith, Old age
		Miss Romine, daughter of Benjm. Romaine, Consumption
		do Hopkins, do of Gilbert Hopkins
		do, Reeve do of Jas. C. Reeve, 14
	27	Col. David M. Westcott, Gravel, 72
	16	Danl. Bailey (Elder) about 50 years, aged 84, Old age

1851
Oct	30	Joshua Conkling, 78, do
Nov	3	Foster, Brain fever

Register of Baptisms

A Register of the 1st Presbyterian Church at Goshen began by Nathan Ker, A. D. 1773, then Pastor of sd Church.

William, son of David & Mary More, born Feb. 28, 1766, baptized Decemr. 23, 1773.
*David, son of Ditt. born Jany. 21, 1768, baptized Decemr. 23, 1773.
Wilmut, son of ditt born Decemr. 2, 1769, baptized Decemr. 23, 1773.
Eunice, Daughter of ditt. born Novr. 20, 1771, baptized Decemr. 23, 1773.
Mary Daughter of ditt. born Augt. 31, 1773, baptized Novr. 1773.
*Levi, Son of George Smith born Septr. 1, 1772, baptized Decemr. 23, 1773.
Nancy, Daughter of Robert Forguson baptized Decemr. 23, 1773.
David, Son of David Curren & Ruth Mc Nish his wife born Octr. 25, 1772 Baptized Decemr. 23, 1773.
John Son of Joshua Wells & Rhoda Booth his wife, born Mar. 10, 1773 Baptized Jany 2, 1774.
Sarah Smith Daughter of Hezekiah Howell baptized Jany 9-1774, of Bloomingrove.
*Robert Allexander Son of Robert Thomson born Decemr. 27, 1773, baptized Feb. 13, 1774.
Jemimah, Daughtr. of Phillip Ketcham born Mar. 13, 1773, baptized Jany. 16, 1774.
Jonathan, Son of Stephen Sayre Baptized Jany 16, 1774.
Thomas Son of Joseph Sayre born Novr. 10, 1773 Baptized Jany 30, 1774.
John, Son of Bazaleel Tyler & Abigail Calkin his wife, born June 30-1767. of Kashetonck.
Phebe Daugtr of ditt born Augt. 30, 1767.
Elam Son of ditt born Apl 5 1771
Oliver, Son of ditt born Septr. 4, 1773.
*Martha Daughtr of Derrick Smith & Hannah Gale his wife born Jany 5, 1757.
*Allexander son of ditt born Mar 3, 1759
*Alletta Daugtr of ditt born July 9, 1761.
*Danl son of ditt born Novr. 1-1763.
Abel son of ditt born Jany 20, 1766.
*James son of ditt born Octr 20-1768.
Mary Daughtr of ditt born Mar: 30, 1771.
John son Edward Mc Neal & Hannah Colt his wife born Feby 8, 1774 baptized Mar 13, 1774.
*Hannah, Daugtr of Israel & Elizabeth Wells, born   baptized Mar 13, 1774.
*Joseph Son of Joseph Coleman, Junr. Baptized Apl 10, 1774.
Keziah, Daughtr of Joseph & Keziah Oldfield Born Jany 12, 1774 Baptized Apl 10 1774.
Anna Gale Daught of Abel Gale born July 25, 1771, Baptized
*Nathaniel Son of Abel Gale born Septr. 4, 1773, baptd. Apl 17 1774.
*Oliver Livermor Son of the Rev. Nathan & Ann Ker born Mar:5-1766 Baptized
*Catharine Daughtr of ditt born Augt 9 1767, Baptized same day.
Hannah Daugtr of ditt born Jany 20 1769. Baptized
Margaret Clark Daugtr ditt born Mar 7 1770. Baptized

*Mary Daugtr of ditt born May 30 1772. Baptized Elizabeth Daugtr of ditt born Mar:14, 1774. Baptd. Apl 17 1774.
Reuben son of Charles & Elizabeth Tucker born Septr 29-1772 Baptized Apl 18 1774.
*Jacob son of Peter & Esther Gale born Apl 9 1772 baptd May 11, 1774.
James Son of Benj. & Ann Brown Tusten born Feb 18 1770. Bapt. Mar.-1770.
*Thomas Son of ditt born Novr. 22, 1771 Baptd Decemr 1771.
*Catharine Daugtr of ditt born Feb 8 1774. Baptd May 15, 1774.
Elizabeth, Daughtr of Samuel & Elizabeth Carpenter Baptd May 15, 1774.
Allin Son of John Mc Carter born Novr. 18, 1773, Baptd. May 29 1774.
*Keziah Daugtr of Henry Mapes Baptized June 8 1774.
Hannah Daughtr of ditt Baptd. same day.
Katarena Daugtr of John Saibolt & Mary Criszer, his wife Baptd. June 8 1774.
Isaac son of Isaac Cooly Junr. & Ann Kinner his wife born Novr. 6, 1773 Baptd. June 26, 1774.
Osman Son of James Ensign & Ruth Finch his wife born June 1, 1764 Bapt June 26, 1774.
Rebeckah Daught of Peter & Esther Gale born May 30 1769 Baptd July 10, 1774.
*Daniel Son of ditt born Septr 22, 1773, Baptd July 10, 1774.
Margaret Daugtr of John Carpenter born Apl 30 1774 Baptd July 10, 1774.
Mary Daugtr of Samuel & Mary Wilson born Mar. 14, 1774 Baptd July 17 1774.
Charles Whittelsey Son of William & Lydia Booth born Feb. 4, 1772, Baptd. Septr. 1772.
*George Son of John & Mary Ludlum, Bapt. Augt. 14, 1774.
*Mary Daughtr. of Wm. & Phebe Vail born Baptd. Augt. 14, 1774.
Colvill Son of Collvill & Sarah Carpenter born Septr. 15, 1771 Baptd.—
Elizabeth Daughtr of Collvill & Sarah Carpenter born Jany. 28, 1774 Baptd Septr. 11, 1774.
*Charity, Daughtr of Noah & Keziah Curtice, born May 16, 1774 Baptd. Octr. 9 1774.
Eleanor Daughtr of John & Mary Vail born Septr. 6, 1774, Baptd. Oct. 16, 1774.
John son of Thomas & Mary Peck Born Augt. 13, 1774, Baptd Oct. 30, 1774.
Mary Decker Daughtr of Abraham & Rachel Smith born July 30 1774.
John, son of James & Jane Butler Born Octr. 1, 1774 Baptd. Decm. 11, 1774.
*David son of David Crawford Born Nov. 21, 1774, baptd Jany 1, 1775.
*Elizabeth Daughtr of Ebenezer & Nancy Keeler Born July 16, 1767 Baptd. Jany 13, 1775.
*Jane Daughtr of ditt. born Decemr. 28 1769, Baptd Jany 13, 1775.
*Thomas Son born June 8, 1772 Baptd Jany 13, 1775.
James Son of ditt. Born Octr 18 1774 Baptd. Jany 13, 1775.
Elizabeth Runyen, Daughtr of Moses & Elizabeth Carpenter, Born Octr. 2, 1774, Baptd Feb 6, 1775.
Gabriel son of John & Mary Stewart born Decembr. 19 1774, Baptd. Feb 19 1775.
Phebe, daughtr of William & Margarett Stringham born Feb. 13, 1775 Baptd Feb 26, 1775.
*John Pain, Son of Joseph & Mary Conkling Born Augt. 2, 1774, Baptd Apl 30, 1775.
*Mary, Daughtr of Jonathan & Mary Sayre, Born Mar. 11, 1775 Baptd May 7, 1775.

REGISTER OF BAPTISMS

Lydia More Daughtr of David More Junr. & Mary his wife Born Apl 7 1775 Baptd May 28, 1775.

Elias Son of Samuel & Mary Baily Born Octr 14, 1774 Baptd June 4, 1775.

Patience Daughtr of Stephen & Abigail Smith born Feby 8 1775 Baptd June 18 1775.

*Sarah Daughtr of Coe & Hannah Gale born   Baptd July 16, 1775.

John son of John Wood Baptd July 16, 1775.

John Son of John McCarter Born Mar 26, 1775, Baptd July 20, 1775.

Sylvester son of John & Abigail Hulse born Octr. 27, 1774, Baptd. July 23, 1775.

Christian daughtr of Wm. & Mary Thomson born Mar 13 1775. Baptd. July 30, 1775.

Moses, son of Archibald & Rebeckah Brown, born June 29 1775, Baptd. Augt 13, 1775.

Suzana, Daugtr of Wm. & Sarah Boodel, born May 18 1775 Baptd Augt 13, 1775.

*Julia, daugtr. of Joseph & Elinor Wood, born   Baptd. Aug. 13, 1775.

*Tabitha, daugtr of Neal & Patience Mc Gloughlen, born July 26, 1775 Baptd. Augt. 20 1775.

Abigail, daughtr of Saml. & Elizabeth Carpenter, born Augt. 16, 1775, Baptd. Septr. 10 1775.

William Allison, son of Wm & Sarah Thomson, born Augt 8 1775, Baptd Septr. 17, 1775.

Lois, daugtr of James & Sarah Manny, born July 17, 1775, Baptd. Septr. 17, 1775.

Harriet, daugtr of Henry & Sarah Wisner, Born Feb 6, 1775 Baptd Septr. 24, 1775.

Moses, son of Moses & Sarah Philips, born   Baptd. Septr. 24, 1775.

*Dolly, daugtr. of David & Abigail Sweezy, Born May 29 1775, Baptd Septr. 24, 1775.

Michael, son of John & Phebe Jackson, Baptd. Septr 24, 1775.

Jane, daugtr. of John McGowen Born Novr. 11, 1769, Baptd Jany 7, 1776.

*James, son of ditt. born Novr 17, 1774, Baptd Jany 7, 1776.

Mary, daugtr. of ditt Born June 24, 1773, Baptd Jany 7, 1776

*Hezekiah, son of Abel Gale, born Augt 25, 1775 Baptd Jany 7, 1776.

Abijah Ketcham, son of Abijah & Margarett Yelverton Born July 15, 1775 Baptd Jany 7, 1776.

Elinor, Daugtr of John & Frances Carpenter, Born Octr 29, 1775, Baptd Jany 14, 1776.

*Abigail, Daugtr of Edward McNeal, born Octr 21, 1775 Baptd Jany 21, 1776.

Martha, daugtr. of Saml. & Mary Willson, Born   Baptd Jany 21, 1776.

Betsey, Daugtr of Samuel Dunning, Baptd Jany 21, 1776.

Abigail, Daugtr of John & Elizabeth McDowell born Jany 23, 1776, Baptd Apl 21 1776.

William, son of Benjamin & Hannah Jackson, Born Octr 24, 1775 Baptd Apl 21 1776.

Daniel, son of Oliver & Catherine Smith, Born Novr. 30, 1775 Baptd Apl 21, 1776.

Elnathan, son of Samuel & Sarah Saturly, Born Decmr. 27, 1774, Baptd Apr 21, 1776 of the Church at Blooming grove.

Sarah, Daugtr of John & Mary Chandler, Born Apl 3, 1776, Baptd June 2, 1776.

Yores, Son of George & Hannah Duryea, Born Feb. 21, 1774. Baptd same year.

REGISTER OF BAPTISMS

Hannah, daugtr of George & Hannah Duryee, Born Apl 21, 1776 Baptd June 23, 1776.
*Letty, Daugtr of John Thomson & Hannah Brooks his wife born June 28, 1773, Baptzd A D 1776.
*Hannah, daugtr of ditt Born Augt 26, 1775 Baptd A D 1776.
*Joseph, son of John & Abigail Knap, Born May 30, 1767 Baptd
Julia, Daugtr of ditt, Born Octr 30 1768 Baptd
*Sarah, daught of ditt Born Novr. 8 1770 Baptd.
Zubah, daugtr of ditt Born Decemr 11, 1772 Baptd.
*Henry, Son of Richard Wood born May 15, 1761 Baptd
Joseph, son of ditt Born Octr 13, 1764
Richard son of ditt Born July 6, 1767
Oliver son of Richard Wood Born Feb 12, 1770.
Joanna, daughtr of ditt Born Jany 12 1773.
Timothy son of ditt Born Decemr 29 1775, Baptd June 1776
Mary, daughtr of Samuel & Hannah Jones, Born   Baptd June 1776
George Washington son of Isaiah & Abigail Vail Born Apl 17th 1776 Baptd Augt 4, 1776.
Elizabeth, daughtr of John Allison, Born Octr 21, 1775 Baptd Augt 4, 1776.
Mary, Daughter of Thomas & Jane Barrans Born Augt 11, 1776 Baptd Augt 25, 1776
Eliud, son of Tryon, Born   Baptd Augt 25, 1776.
William Allison, Son of John McNeal, Born   Baptd Augt 25, 1776.
Thomas, son of ditt born   Baptd Augt 25, 1776.
*Sarah Daughtr of Benj. Tusteen Junr. Born May 18, 1776, Baptd Septr 1, 1776.
*Freegift, son of Joshua Tuthill Born Apl 29 1776 Baptd Sept 15, 1776.
*Fordine Elsworth, son of Richard Gale, Born   Baptd Septr. 16, 1776.
Lydia, daugtr of John Crane Born Novr. 29 1769, Baptd Septr 22, 1776.
Peggy, Daughtr of John Crane, Born Apl 30, 1776 Baptd Septr 22, 1776.
Hannah, Daughtr of Stephen Sayre, Born Octr 30 1775, Baptd Octr 20, 1776.
*Absalom, son of Wm Vail, Born Jany 27 1768, Baptd.
Joannah, Daughtr of ditt Born Feb 22, 1770.
Isaiah, son of ditt Born July 8 AD 1772.
Mary Daughter of ditt Born June 28 1774.
Joseph & Benjamin sons of Wm Vail Born Augt 18 1776, Baptd Octr 20 1776.
*Benjamin, son of Benj. Harlow Born Apl 19 1776, Baptd Octr 20, 1776.
Phebe, Daugtr of Colvill Carpenter, Born Apl 3, 1776 Baptd Octr 27, 1776.
*Susannah, Daugtr of Noah Curtice, Born Septr 30 1776 Baptd Octr. 27 1776.
*Jonas & *Sarah son & daugtr of Saml & Sarah Saturly, Born Augt 12, 1776 Baptd Octr 27.
*Lydia Daughter of John Vail born Novr. 1, 1776 Baptized Feby 16, 1777.
*Joseph Sayre son of Joseph Sayre & Mary Monnell Born Novr 3, 1776 Baptized May 4, 1777.
Samuel son of Henry Smith born March 4 1777 Baptized May 11, 1777.
Hannah Daughtr of David Arnold born Novr 15, 1776 Baptized May 11 1777, from Long Island.
Jesse son of Isaac Cooly & Anna Kinner his wife Born Decm 5, 1775, Baptized May 18 1777.
Samuel son of James Butler born Apl 14, 1777 Baptized June 15 1777.
*Charles son of William Thompson & Mary Decay his wife born baptized June 23, 1777.
Margarett daughtr of Wm. Willson & Agnes McCurdy his wife born June 13, 1777 Baptized June 27 1777.
Walter son of David More & Mary Mapes his wife born Apl 29 1777 Baptized June 29 1777.

REGISTER OF BAPTISMS

Mary daughter of Nathaniel Bayly & Mary Peck his wife born Novr. 8 1776, Baptized June 29 1777.
Annanias son of John McCarter born May 19 1777 Baptized July 6, 1777.
Nathaniel son of Benj. Carpenter & Lydia Chandler his wife born May 2 Baptized July 6, 1777.
*Thomas son of Archibald Brown born Mar 15 1777 Baptized July 6 1777.
Joseph Carpenter son of Joseph Carpenter born June 1st 1777 baptized July 20 1777.
Samuel son of John & Abigail Hulse born Apl 10 1777 baptized July 20 1777.
James son of David Crawford Born June 17th 1777 baptized July 27, 1777.
*Peter son of Neal McLaughlin & Patience Bourlen his wife Born May 30 1777, Baptized Augt 3 1777.
*Robert son of John Wood born   Baptized Augt 17 1777.
*Phanah daughter of Timothy Dunning & Abigail Nostran his wife born Augt 7th 1777 Baptized Septr 21, 1777.
James son of John Carpenter born   Baptized Septr 21, 1777.
Juliana Gale born Augt 8th 1777 Baptized Septr 28 1777 daughter of Abel Gale.
*Oliver son of Ichabod Lewis &   Born May 21, 1777 Baptized Septr. 28, 1777.
Sarah Arnont an adult Baptized Septr 28 1777.
Daniel Maypes son of Daniel Maypes &   born   Baptized Octr 5, 1777.
Noah son of Noah Carpenter born Augt 25, 1777 Baptized Octr 5, 1777.
*Samuel son of Joseph Conkling born Decemr 10 1776 Baptized Octr. 5 1777.
Nathaniel son of Silas Stewart & Margarett Webb his wife born May 9 1777 Baptized Octr 5, 1777.
Jerusha daughter of Samuel & Jerusha Hobart Born Septr 6, 1777 Baptd Octr. 5, 1777.
George son of Joshua Wells born Augt 15, 1777 Baptized Novr 2, 1777.
Joanna daughtr of Stephen Smith born   Baptized Novr 9 1777.
William son of John & Ann Evans born Octr 20th 1777 Baptized Decemr 14, 1777.
*Joseph McNeal son of John McNeal & Margarett Allison his wife Born Baptized Jany 1, 1778.
Johannah Daughtr of Stephen Smith & Abigail Goldsmith his wife Born June 14th 1777 Baptized
*Thomas son of John Denton & Elizabeth Wisner his wife, Born   Baptized Feby 10 1778.
Mary Daughter of Stephen Sayre Born Decemr. 21, 1777 Baptized Feby 15, 1778.
Margarett daughter of Henry Sherman & Ann Cortright his wife born Feby 19 1777 Baptized Feb 15, 1778.
Stephen son of Benjamin Jackson & Hannah Marvin his wife born Decemr 8 1777 Baptized Feby 15, 1778.
Sarah daughter of John Denton & Elizabeth his wife Born Baptized Feby 21, 1778.
*Justus son of Barnabas Horton & Rebeckah Burnett his wife born Octr 20 1777 Baptized Feby 22, 1778.
John son of Joseph Wood & Elimor Tusteen his wife born   Baptized Mar 1 AD 1778.
Esther daughter of Peter Gale Born   Baptized Mar 8 1778.
Agnes, daughter of Thomas & Jean Barran, Born Feby 25 1778, Baptzied Mar:29 1778.

REGISTER OF BAPTISMS

Joseph, son of William & Abigail Birney, born Feby 1, 1777 Baptized Apl 5, 1778.

Sarah, daughter of Henry Wisner Junr. & Sarah Barnett his wife, born Septr 17 1777, Baptized May 3, 1778.

William son of Moses Philips & Sarah Wisner his wife Born Jany 9, 1778 Baptized May 3, 1778.

Daniel, son of Israel Wells & Elizabeth Jackson his wife born Jany 9 1778, Baptized May 3, 1778.

*Gabriel son of John Jackson & Phebe Everett his wife born Mar 15 1778 Baptized May 10 1778.

Julianah daughter of Wm Thomson & Sarah Allison his wife born Feb 17 1778 Baptized May 10 1778

Isaac son of Edward McNeal born Decemr. 6, 1777 Baptized May 10, 1778.

Martha daughter of John McDowell born Feby 2d 1778, Baptized May 17 1778.

Frances daughter of William Wickham & Phebe Rose his wife Born Baptized June 21, 1778.

Phebe daughter of John Smith Born   Baptized June 21,-78.

Jacob son of John Smith born   Baptized June 21, 1778.

James & Jesse, son of Colvil Carpenter & Sarah Hall his wife born June 4, 1778, Baptized June 25, 1778.

Hannah daughter of Elisha Millard & Anna Millard born Novr. 13th 1770 Baptized June — 1778.

Martha daughter of Saml. Rackett & Rhoda Youngs Born May 8th 1777 Baptized June 1778.

Margarett daughter of Samuel Dunning born   Baptized July 19, 1778.

James Kinner son of Isaac Cooly & Ann Kinner his wife Born Apl 27 1778. Baptized July 27 1778.

Israel son of Israel Smith & Tabitha Bourlen his wife born Octobr. 16 1777 Baptized Augt 2 1778.

Fanny Daughter of Oliver Smith Born Novr 18 1777 Baptized Augt 2, 1778.

*William son of Albert Foster & Abigail Coleman his wife Born Jany 28, 1778 Baptized Augt 2, 1778.

Hannah daughter of Benj. Harlow Born June 2 Baptized Augt 9, 1778.

Azuba daughter of Joshuah Davis Born   Baptized Septr 6, 1778.

Novr 8 1778 Baptized Margaret a Negro woman of Daniel Halls.

*Decemr 2—Baptized Theophilus son of John Bateman & Christian Gale his wife Born

Ellinor, daughtr of Daniel Carpenter born Apl 17th 1761, Baptized

Suzannah, daughter of ditt, Born June 30, 1763, Baptized

Sarah, daughtr of ditt, Born Septr 27, 1765, Baptized

Ruth, daughtr of ditt, Born Mar 5th, 1771 Baptized

Daniel, son of ditt Born Augt 7 1773

*John son of ditt born Apl 6 1776.

Dolly, daughter of John More & Rebeckah Reeves his wife born June 17, 17— Baptized Mar. 7 1779.

Jesse, son of ditt, Born June 1, 1773, Baptized Mar 7, 1779.

Daniel, son of ditt, Born May 15, 1775, Baptized Mar 7 1779.

John, son of Ditt, Born June 15, 17— Baptized Mar 7 1779.

Apl 25 1779 Baptized Abigail daughter of Doctr. Benj. Tusteen who was Born Octr 23, 1778.

Hannah Vail daughter of Asa Vail & Sarah Smith his wife, Born Decemr 3, 1778 Baptized Apl 25, 1779.

*Phebe daughter of Wm Bodle born   Baptized Apl 25 1779.

Moses son of Coe Gale & Hannah Carpenter his wife born   Baptized May 16, 1779.

REGISTER OF BAPTISMS

May daughter of Silas Stewart Born Jany 31, 1779 Baptized May 16, 1779.
Elinor daughter of Allexdr. McVaugh & Hannah Maypes, his wife, born Baptized May 23, 1779.
Isaac Case Born Octr. 1 1779 son of John Case Baptized June 6 1779.
*Elisha son of David Arnold Born Apl 27th 1779 Baptized June 27, 1779.
*Jermimah daughter of Jonathan Sayre, Born Apl 27, 1779 Baptized June 27 1779.
*Robert son of Danniel Carpenter Born Jany 18 1779 Baptized June 27 1779.
Stephen Knap son of James Knap Born Mar: 18 1779 Baptized June 27 1779.
Michael Allison son of Saml. Johnes & Hannah Jackson his wife Born Apl 4 1779 Baptized June 27 1779.
Allexander Hawkins son of   Ketcham, Born   Baptized June 27, 1779.
July Daughtr of Benj. Smith & Mary his wife Born Septr 2, 1778 Baptized July 1, 1779.
Esther daughtr of Nathaniel Baily born June 9th 1779 Baptized July 1, 1779.
Margarett Daughtr of Michael Halstead Born Jany 22, 1775 Baptized July 1, 1779.
Esther daughtr of Ditt Born Jany 15, 1779 Baptized July 1, 1779.
Susannah daughter of Timothy Wood, Junr., & Nelly his wife, Born Jany 18 1772, Baptized July 1, 1779.
Abigail daughtr of Ditt Born June 6 1774 Baptized July 1, 1779.
Zephaniah, son of Zephaniah Knap & Milla his wife Born May 18 1779 Baptized July 4, 1779.
John son of Thomas Barran & Jane McCradde his wife, Born June 15th 1779, Baptized Augt 7 1779.
James son of Joseph Wood Born   Baptized Augt 29 1779.
Joshuah son of Caleb Smith Born June 4th 1779, Baptized Augt 29, 1779.
*Joseph son of Noah Carpenter Born July 16, 1779 Baptized Augt 29 1779.
Julianah daughter of John & Abigail Hulse born Apl 16 1779 Baptized Augt 29 1779.
James son of Icchabod Lewis born July 22, 1779 Baptized Augt 29 1779.
Sarah, daughter of Moses Coe & Sarah Rider his wife Born Decem 9, 1774.
Ann daugtr of ditt born Augt 10 1776.
Benjamin son of ditt born Feby 8 1774, Baptized all Septr 29 AD 1779.
Sarah daughter of John Stewart & Mary Young his wife born Augt 15 1779 Baptized Octr 2, 1779.
Mary Daughtr of Richard Allison & Amy Case his wife Born Augt 21 1779 Baptized Octr 10 1779.
Joshuah son of Saml Hobart & Jerusha King his wife born May 15 1779 Baptised Octr 17 1779.
Joshuah, son of Joshuah Wells & Rhoda Booth his wife, born Septr. 6 1779 Baptized Novr. 14 1779.
Mary daughter of Joseph Conkling born Septr 26 1779, Baptized Novr. 14 1779.
*Thomas, son of Neal McGloughlin, born Septr 5-79, Baptized Novr. 29 1779.
*William, son of David Crawford, born Septr 25, 1779, Baptized Decemr 19 1779.
Elizabeth McDowell daughter of John McDowell born Decemr 10 1779 Baptized Feby 10 1780.
Abigail, daughter of Benj. Jackson Born Novr. 15, 1779, Baptized Feby 6 1780.
Suzanna, daughter of Barnabas Horton & Rebeca Burnett his wife, born Octr 11, 1779 Baptized Feby 13 1780.
*Mary daughter of Eliud Tryon Born   Baptized Apl 23 1780.
Anna Daughter of Matthew Wickham & Ann Horton his wife born July 14 1799 Baptized May 10 1780.

REGISTER OF BAPTISMS

Saml. Wickham son of William Wickham born   Baptized May 10 1780.
Esther, daughter of Joseph Case & Esther Budd, his wife, born Feby 6 1779 Baptized May 10 1780.
*Jacob, son of Able Gale born Jany 22, 1780 Baptized May 14, 1780.
Elizabeth, daughter of James Butler, born Decemr 28 1779, Baptized May 14 1780.
Adonijah, son of Moses Hetfield born   Baptized May 21, 1780.
*Martha, daughter of Edward McNeal born Mar; 4, 1780 Baptized May 21, 1780.
Abigail, daughter of Saml Denton & Sarah Ludlum his wife born Baptized May 26 1780.
Catherine Salmon daughter of Mary Ludlum formerly wife of Nathaniel Salmon born   Baptized May 26 1780.
Mary daughter of John Denton & Elizabeth Wisner his wife Born Septr 14 1779 Baptized May 28 1780.
Anna daughter of William Vail Born Feby 3 1780 Baptized May 28 1780.

June 27 A D 1780
Baptized Mary McCarter, daughter of John McCarter born Mar: 29 1780.

July 9
Baptized William, son of Duncan McConnely & Mary Whittaker, his wife, who was born

July 16
Baptized Elizabeth, daughter of Samuel Moffatt & Sarah Wilkins his wife, who was born Jany 24, 1779.

July 23
Baptized, William Bradner Born May 12 1780 the son of Joseph Carpenter.
Baptized Milliscent born Octr 25 1779 the daughter of Jacob Arnot.

Augt 10
Baptized, James Skidmore, son of Timothy Dunning, Born June 19 1780.
Baptized Jemy born Augt 1 1780 the son of Benj Carpenter.

Septr 24
Baptized Stephen Born the Mar: 29 1780 the son of Stephen Smith.
*Baptized Thanna Born Jany 28 1780 Daughter of Israel Wells.

Octr 1
Baptized Elizabeth born Augt 5, 1780, daughter of David Arnold.
Baptized Sarah, born   daughtr of Moses Philips

Octr 15 AD 1780
Baptized Hannah Born   daughter of Hezekiah Bingham.
Also Fanny Born   daughter of Ditto.

Decemr. 31
Baptized Hannah Wood, Born Augt 23, 1780, daughter of Albert Foster & Abigail his wife.

Feby 2 1781
Baptized Priscilla & Hannah twin daughters of Henry Smith Born Septr 11 1780.

Feby 25
Baptized Sarah, born Septr 13th 1780, daughter of John Case.

Mar 23
Baptized Jonathan & Ruth born July 28 1777 son & daughter of James Mosier & Ruth Ensign his wife.
Baptized Abigail born Octr 7 1779 daughtr of ditt.
Wm Smith born Jany 24 1776 son of Wm Rowly & Margarett Smith.

May 13
Sarah Vail Born Octr 23, 1780 daughter of Asa Vail & Sarah Smith his wife.
Elizabeth Case born March 8th 1781 daughter of Joseph Case & Esther Bud his wife.

REGISTER OF BAPTISMS

May 20th A D 1781
Baptized Bethiah born—daughter of Eliud Tryon & Bethiah Aldrich his wife.
Phebe born Decemr 25 1780 daughtr of David More Junr.
*Zacheus born Augt 23 1780 son of Zacheus & Hannah Case.
Daniel born Jany 11 1781 son of David & Mary Case.
Daniel Born   son of Samuel Bodle & Catherine Vantile his wife.
May 27
William, born Apl 5th 1781 son of Samuel Carpenter.
Benjamin born son of Daniel McHenry
Jane Born   Daughtr of Daniel McHenry.
June 3
Charles, Born Jany 30th 1781, son of Neal McLaughlin.
Mary, born   daughter of Samuel Wilson.
Elizabeth born Jany 11 1781 daughter of Luther Steward.
June 10
James, born June 23 1779, son of Jacob Hulse & Rhebeckah Vantassel his wife.
Benjamin, born Feby 25 1781 son of Jacob Hulse.
June 12 AD 1781
Baptized Julianah, Born Apl 26 1769 daughter of Ephraim Everett & Beaulah More his wife.
Ephraim born Jany 11, 1771 son of ditt.
Walter born July 9 1772 son of ditt.
Lydia born Feby 4 1774 daughtr of ditt.
Hephzibah born Novr 17 1775 daughtr of ditt.
Benjamin born May 30 1779 son of ditt.
June 17
Ellenor Born Jany 18 1781 daughter of Wm Thomson & Sarah Allison his wife.
June 24
Abigail, born Apl 25 1781 daughter of Jonathan Horton & Mary his wife.
Septr 2
Margaret, born   daughter of John McCarter.
William Albertson, born Decemr. 25-80, son of Edw Howell & Clement Albertson his wife.
Septr 9
George, Born June 30 1781 son of John McDowell.
Octr 9 AD 1781
Peter born   son of Peter Gale.
Benjamin Born Augt 9 1781 son of John Smith & Elizabeth Elems his wife.
Octr 14
*Martha, born July 11 1781 daughter of Jonathan Sayer.
Christian, born Mar: 21 1781 daughter of Joshua Davies.
Octr 21
Mary, born Apl 15 1781, daughter of David Hawknis & Sarah Horton, his wife.
John, born July 26 1781, son of John Sloot & Ruth Drake his wife.
Octr 28
Mary daughter of Saml. Dunning born—
Gabriel son of James Denton & Temperance Tusteen born March 4th 1781
Novr 18
Morris, son of Icakabod Lewis, born Septr 27 1781.
Novr 25
*Coe & *Benjamin, Twin sons of Coe Gale & Hannah Carpenter his wife, born Apl 23 1781.
William, son of Silas Steward, born Septr 11, 1780.

REGISTER OF BAPTISMS

March 3 1782
Else, daughter of Joseph Wood & Else Tusteen, his wife born—.
Elizabeth, daughter of Jesse Gale & Lueretia Lee his wife, born May 30 1779.
Jane, daughter of ditt born Octr 9 1781.
March 10
*Rebeecah, daughter of Reuben Hopkins & Hannah Eliot, his wife born Jany 14 1782.
March 17
Thomas, son of Benjm. Jackson born—
Apl 7
Charity, daughter of Daniel & Suzanah Carpenter, born June 20 1781.
April 14
Mehettabel, daughter of Eliud Tryon, born
May 19
*Lueretia, daughter of Joseph Conkling, born Novr. 26, 1781.
June 2
Hannah, daughter of Saml. Rackett, born Augt 10 1781.
June 9
Thomas, son of Edward McNeal, born Mar 3, 1782
June 16
Mary, daughter of Henry Wisner, Junr born May 7 1781
Mary, daughter of Noah Carpenter Born Apl 11, 1782
Ezrah, son of Isaac Witter   born
Goshen, July 5 1782
July 7
*Baptized John, son of David & Abigail Sweezy, born
*Anna, daughtr of Barnabas Horton & Rebecca Burnet, his wife, born Feby 22, 1782.
Augt 18
John, son of John Hulse, born Novr. 26 1781.
Septr 15
Mary & Elizabeth, twin daughters of John Steward & Mary Youngs his wife, born Decemr. 30th 1781.
Sept 22
Phebe, born Mar 30 1782 daughter of Abel Gale.
Sept 29
John Thomson, born   son of William Bodle.
Octr 6
Sarah, daughtr of James Sawer, born
Benjamin, son of ditt born
Moses son of ditt born
Mary daughtr of ditt born
Matthew son of ditt born
Gilbert, son of Gilbert Carpenter, born   AD 1772.
Benjamin son of Ditt born   AD 1774
Mary daughter of ditt born
Rhoda daughter of ditt born
Nathaniel Cooly son of ditt   born AD 1780.
Octr 6 1782
Samuel son of John Finch, born
Oliver, son of Timoth Dunning born Augt 28 1782.
Novr 3
James, son of Zephaniah Knap, born Decemr. 3 1781
Decm 19
Joshua Davies, son of Clark McNish & Elizabeth Davies his wife

Mary daughter of ditt
Mary, daughter of Matthew Smith
Wait son of Ditt.
James, Son of Ditt.
Jany 19-1783
Baptized Martha, daughter of Wm. Vail, Born Augt 24, 1782.
Jany 26
Elizabeth daughter of Richard Allison, born Octr 26th 1782.
Mar 30
Elisha, son of Elisha & Temperance Reeve, born Octr 30 1782
Apl 20
Daniel, son of Daniel McHenry, born
June 5
John & * Sarah, twin children of David Crawford, born May 19 1783.
June 8 1783
Julianah born Feby 26 1783, daughtr of David Case
Amy, born   daughtr of Allexander Bodle.
June 15
Ellenor, born Mar 26 1783, daughtr of Benjm. Jackson & Hannah Marvin his wife.
Mary Born Jany 19 1783, daughtr of David Arnold
Moses Born Jany 30 1783, son of Josiah Vail.
June 22
Eunice born Septr 21, 1782, daughter of Matthew Wickham.
Octr 5
Else daughtr of Jonathan Sayre born July 21, 1783.
Hannah, daughtr of Zaccheus Case, born Novr. 22, 1782.
Octr 12
Salmon son of Hezekiah Bingham born
William, son of John Smith & Elizabeth Elms, his wife, born
Octr 26
John, son of Joseph & Esther Case, born Apl 9 1783.
William, son of Samuel & Mary Wilson, born July 28 1783.
Jany 4 AD 1784
*Baptized John Herod, son of Daniel Baily & Mary Tuthill his wife, born Octr 25 1783.
Jany 18
Catherine, daughtr of Stephen Smith & Margaret Butler, his wife, Born Decmr. 6 1783.
Jany 25
William, son of Ichabod Lewis & Martha Gale his wife, born Octr 26th 1783.
Mar 15
Coe, son of Coe Gale & Hannah Carpenter, his wife, born
Mar 21
Thomas, son of David More & Tabitha Boreland, his wife, born
May 9
*Anthony Yelverton, son of Joseph Denton & Hannah Yelverton his wife born
Jesse born Feby 15, 1784, son of Jesse Gale.
Mary daughter of John Moffatt & Mary Yelverton his wife born
*Phaneale, daughtr of Eluid Tryon, born
*William son of Benjamin Carpenter & Elinir Stewart, his wife born Apl 11, 1782.
Sarah daughtr of ditt born, Apl 10 1784.
Isaac son of Benjn Ludlum & Christian Bradner born 25 Feby 1784.
Moses, son of Gilbert Carpenter, born

May 30
James MacNeal born Jany 17th 1784 son of Edward MacNeal.
Elizabeth born March 7 1784 daugtr of Henry Smith.
Margarett, born Mar 24 1784 daughtr of Charles Borland.
June 4
*Highly, daughter of Thomas Gale, Born May 29 1777.
John, son of Ditt, born Decemr 9 1779.
Sarah, daughter of ditt born Novr 10th 1782.
Isabella, daughter of Neal McGloughlin born Feby 25 1784.
June 19
Festus Amberous, son of Cretia Tusteen.
June 20
*Gabriel William, son of Henry Wisner, Junr. Born 14th Mar 1784.
Louis born, Jany 20th 1783, son of Moses Philips.
Israel born 17th Decmr 1783 son of Israel Wells.
William Born—son of John Allison.
Gabriel Norton born 21st Feby 1769, son of Moses Philips & Sarah Wisner his wife.
George born 30th Decmr 1770 son of Ditt.
*Henry Wisner born 18th May 1773 son of Ditt.
Moses born 20th June 1775, son of Ditt.
   These four viz: Gabriel N., George, Henry W. & Moses were Baptized some years since but not registered.
Augt 1
Sarah, daughtr of William Bodle.
Augt 15
Juliana daughter of Jonathan Horton born Jany 18 1784.
Hannah daughter of Isaac Witter, born Feby 25 1784.
Augt 29
Ann daughter of Stephen Sayre born
*Juliet, daughter of Joseph Wood born
David son of John Hulse, born Feby 2 1784.
Hannah, daughter of Benjm. Conklin.
David, son of ditt. born
Abigail, daughtr of Elisha Reeves born Novm 24 1783.
Septr 12 1784
Margarett, daughtr of Samuel Carpenter, born July 25, 1784.
Octr 24
Thomas Denton son of Gilbert Denton born
Jany 9 1785
William Hector son of Reuben Hopkins born Novr 12, 1784
Feby 6
Baptized Elizabeth Seward wife of Doctr Jonathan Sweezy
Feby 13
Eleazar Owen son of Eleazar Owen & Abigail Owen born Jany 1, 1780.
Charles Frederick, son of Abiel Fry & Abigail his wife born Novr 20 1784.
Matthew son of Matthew Smith born
Catherine daughter of Samuel Dunning, ,born July 18 1784.
Mar 6
Mary Moffatt daughter of Samuel Moffatt born Septr 21, 1781.
John son of ditt. Born July 22, 1784.
Elizabeth daughter of Janathan Sweezy & Elizabeth Seward his wife, born Octr 5 1780.
Horace son of ditt born Sept 29 1782.

REGISTER OF BAPTISMS

May 22
 William, son of Israel Wells, born Feby 25th 1785.
May 29
 Matthew Howell, son of Matthew Wickham born Septr 12, 1784.
 Milla, daughter of Zephaniah Knap, born Novr. 25 1784.
June 12
 Jonathan, son of Jonathan Baily born Augt 29th 1784.
July 3
 Ephangele, daughter of Eliud Tryon, born
 Joseph, son of Danl. Conkling, born
Augt 7
 Luther son of Jonah Vail, born Jany 11 1785.
 Julia & Samuel Jones, daughter & son of Hamilton Jackson born
Septr 4
 Joshuah, son of Samuel Boyd, born March 10th 1785.
 *Margarett, daughter of David Hawkins & Sarah Horton his wife, born Apl 4th 1784.
Septr 11
 John & Gideon Twin sons of Zaccheus Case, born Decmr 31 1784.
Octr 16
 William, son of Noah Carpenter & Unice his wife born Dcemr 10th 1784.
 Birdseye, son of David Case, born Augt 1, 1785.
Novr 13
 *Mary the wife of John Budd.
 *Mary, daughtr of John Budd & Mary Hawkins his wife born Mar: 11 1784.
 Samuel, son of Gilbert Carpenter, born May 25 1785.
Novr 27
 Mary Stubs wife of William Stubs.
Jany 8 1786
 Mascy, born Octr 4 1785 daughter of John Smith & Elizabeth Elms, his wife.
Jany 15
 Julianah, daughter of Joseph Conkling.
Jany 29
 *Jesse, son of David & Mary Arnold, born July 29 1785.
 Mary, daughter of Abraham Gale.
 *Gabriel son of Abraham Gale.
Feb 19 A D 1786
 Elizabeth, daughter of Jonathan Sayre, born Octob 11 1785.
Feby 26
 Sarah daughter of Joshuah Davies, born Novr 14th 1785.
 Coe, son of Colvill Steward & Anna Brown, born June 17 1784.
Mar 5
 Anthony, son of John L. Moffat born —
Mar 20
 Mary, daughter of Isaac Carpenter, born July 4th 1782.
Apl 16
 Edward son of Edward McNeal, born Mar 5 1786.
May 14
 Samuel & Hannah son & daughter of Benjamin Carpenter born Apl 1, 1786.
 Phebe Maria, daughter of Joseph Denton & Hannah Yelverton his wife born
June 11
 *Samuel, son of Moses Philips & Sarah Wisner, his wife, born July 11th 1785.
June 18 1786
 *Baptized Joseph son of David Crawford born Mar 27 1786.

REGISTER OF BAPTISMS

Rhoda daughtr of Samuel Rackett born Augt 1785, of Blooming Grove.
June 25
Jonathan son of William Bodle.
Samuel son of Ichabod Lewis born May 3rd 1786.
*Daniel, son of Daniel Baily & Mary Tuthill his wife born Apl 7 1786.
July 16
Hannah daughtr of Coe Gale & Hannah Carpenter his wife born July 7 1786.
Augt 13
Rhebeeka daughter of Thomas Watkins & Lydia Ager, his wife.
Augt 20
Ezra Howell an adult.
Septr 15
Samuel McCormick son of Wm & Mary Shaw born
Mary daughter of Neal McLaughlin born July 27 -86.
Jesse Hall, son of Samuel & Mary Wickham born Feb 28 1786.
Septr 15 1786
Jenny, daughter of John McCarter, born Mar 12 1783.
Nancy born Jany 26 1785 daughter of John McCarter.
David born Octr 25 1782 born son of Ephraim Everett.
Freelove born June 30 1785, child of Ephriam Everett.
William born Feby 25 1772, son of Wm Stubs.
Samuel born Novr 27 1774.
Mary born Septr 25 1776.
David born Octr 22 1778.
Joseph born Novr 6, 1780.
Sarah born Septr 18 1782.
John born Augt 12 1784.
Elizabeth born June 16 1786, sons & daughters of ditt.
Octr 8
*Martin Luther, son of Elisha Reeve & Temperance, his wife, born 28th May 1785.
Novr 26
Anthony, son of Benjamin Jackson & Hannah Marvin, his wife, born Septr 19 1786.
Decmr 3
Daniel, son of James Keeler & Anna Fulton, his wife born 12 Octr 1786.
Abigail, daughter of Daniel Conkling.
Decemr. 24 AD 1786
Baptized Virgil son of Jonathan Swezy & Elizabeth Seward his wife, born 17 Septr 1786.
Jany 4 1787
Baptized Daniel Elsworth son of Benjamin Ludlum & Christian Bradner, his wife, born Novr 18 1786.
Jany 7
Liana, daughter of Eusebius Austin & Abigail Wood, his wife, born
Jany 14
Elizabeth, daughter of Allexander Cory & Martha Wells, his wife, Born Augt 27 1786.
Charles son of Charles Boreland born
Feb 4
Henry Laurens, son of Abiel Fry born July 5 1786.
Feb 11
Don Carlos, son of Archibald Hall & Polly Thomson his wife born Octr 19 1786.

REGISTER OF BAPTISMS

Feb 18
Levene, daughter of Joshuah Davis, born Augt 24th 1786.
Apl 9
William son of David Galaspy & Abigail Maypes, his wife, born 14 Decmr. 1786.
Benjamin son of John Bell & Keziah Maypes his wife born Octr 17 1786.
Apl 22 1787
Bradock son of Eliud Tryon born
May 13
Hezekiah Denton, son of Richard Welling & Mary Denton his wife born
Augt 19
Abner son of   Hulse born Feby 27 1787.
Septr 2
Ichabod, son of Uriah Terry & Bethiah his wife, born Mar: 25 1783.
Joshuah, son of Ditt. Born Apl 10 1787.
Septr 16
George Owens an adult.
Abel son of George Owens.
Catherine daughter of Abel Gale born 9th Octr 1787.
Octr 14
Israel Wells, son of Israel Wells, born May 3 1787.
Isaac Denton, son of Saml. Denton Junr. Born Apl 26 1787.
Elizabeth daughter of Asa Steward born Septr 10 1787.
Octr 26
Benjamin son of Nathaniel Bailey & Margrett Wickham, his wife, born Apl 25th 1783.
Abigail daughter of ditt. born Augt 1784.
Nathan son of ditt born Septr 10 1780.
Novr 8 1787
Baptized Abraham son of Allexander Bodle, born Apl. 1787.
Mary daughter of Samuel Boyd, born May 7th 1787.
Jany 6 1788
Mary daughter of Stephen Smith born Novr 11, 1787.
Jany 27
Abraham son of Edward McNeal born Novr 6 1787.
Feby 3
Baptized David son Frederick Saybott & Abigail Reeve, his wife, born Octr 30th 1787.
Keturah daughter of ditt born Septr 6 1787.
Joseph son of   Watkins born
Feby 8
Baptized Samuel son of Charles Tucker born
Julianah daughter of Charles Tucker born
Feby 10
Daniel son of Colvill Stewart born Novr 10 1786.
Feby 23
John Little son of John Little Moffat & Mary Yelverton his wife born Feby 12 1788.
Feby 24 1788
Dolly born Octr 19 1786 daughtr of Jesse Gale.
John Marvin born June 11 1787.
Abigail born Apl 29 1787 daughtr of Andrew Christie & Mary McWhorter his wife.
May 26
David son of Josiah Vail born Augt 30th 1787.

Israel Wickham son of Nathaniel Baily & Margarett Wickham his wife born Feby 11 1788.
June 8
Elizabeth, daughtr of Coll Moses Philips & Sarah Wisner his wife, Born 25 Octr 1787.
June 22
Mary Elmer the wife of Doctr. William Elmer.
John, son of John Smith, born Feby 26 1788 &
Robert son of ditt born the same day.
July 13
Anna daughtr of Samuel Moffatt born Novr 11th 1787.
Solomon son of Danniel Conkling born
July 20
*Abigail Anna, daughter of David Arnold, born Apl 12 1788.
Augt 31
Charles son of Wm Bodle.
Septr 28 1788
Baptized Hanibal Mason, son of Rueben Hopkins born Augt 8th 1788.
Octr 5
James Thomson son of Archibal Hall & Polly his wife born June 29 1788.
Octr 19
Israel, son of William Stubs, born May 28, 1788.
Novr 22
John, son of John Budd & Mary his wife born May 5 1788.
January 4th A Dom. 1789
Baptized Maria daugtr of Benjn Jackson & Hannah Marvin his wife, born Septr 20 1788.
Jany 11
*Hariet, daughter of Ichabod Lewis, born July 27 1788.
Jany 16
*Ebenezr son of John Keeler & Elizabeth Smith his wife born Novr 16 1788.
Isabel, †son of Wm. Wilson & Nancy McCurdy Born Septr 23 1784.
Daniel Butterfield son of Ebenezr Keeler & Nancy McNeal Born Octr 12 1777.
Ralph son of ditt born Aug 20 1785.
Allexander son of John McCarter born Feby 15 1787.
Jany 18
Jacob Aldrich son of Eluid Tryon born Octr 3 1788.
Jany 23
Elizabeth daughter of Samuel Wickham born Augt 28 1788.
*Elizabeth daughter of James Keeler & Ann Fulton his wife born Septr 28 1788.
*Henry Wisner, son of Joshuah Brown, Junr. & Tempe Wisner his wife born Apl 28 1788.
John Calvin son of Elisha Reeve & Temperance Reeve, his wife born Octr 1 1788.
Jany 23 1789, Baptized
Anna daughtr of Isaac Witters, born July 6 1788.
Allexandr born July 7 1788 son of John Bell & Keziah Maypes his wife.
Feby 8
Oliver born Decemr 8th 1788 son of Daniel Bayley & Mary Tuthill his wife.
Anna born Septr 27 1788 daughtr of Samuel Dunning & Catharine Price his wife.
Feby 22
Alfred born Septr 6 1788 son of Abiel Fray & Abigail his wife.

†(So in original).

REGISTER OF BAPTISMS

Mar 20
William son of William Wickham & Phebe Rose his wife.
George Clark son of ditt.
Joseph born Apl 24 1787 son of Joseph Conkling & Mary Pain, his wife.
Jonathan born Decemr. 2nd 1788 son of Jonathan Horton.
Jonathan Horton, son of William Jackson & Abigail his wife.
Apl 28
Gilbert born Decemr 1 1788, son of Andrew Cristie.
Millicent daughter of Benjamin Halsey & Millicent Forguson born Feby 1 1789.
May 31 1789
Baptized John, son of John Ludlum born
Juliana, an adult daughtr of Gilbert Vail & wife of Conkling Smith.
June 21
Mary daughtr of Frederick Seybolt, born Decemr 31st 1788.
July 5
John, son of Richard Welling & Mary Denton his wife.
July 19
James Goldsmith born Octr 31st 1789 son of Ezra Horton & Hannah Gardiner his wife.
July 26
*Joseph Wood born   son of Eusibius Austin & Abigail Wood his wife.
George Brown born Apl 5 1789 son of George Owen & Effy Brown his wife.
Augt 9
Columbus born June 28 1789 son of Nathaniel Bayley & Margarett Wickham his wife.
Augt 16
Laverna, daughter of Jonathan Bayley, born May 24-89.
Augt 23
Fanny born Decemr 28 1788 daughtr of Colvill Stewart & Joanna Brown his wife.
John Lee born June 20th 1789 son of Jesse Gale & Lueretia Lee his wife.
Augt 30 1789
Baptized Samuel White born   son of William Brown.
Septr 20
Margarett born June 15 1786, daughtr of William Graham.
Sarah born March 25, 1788, daughtr of ditt.
Septr 30
James born Apl 15 1789 son of John McCarter.
Mary born May 29 1789 daughtr of William Shaw.
Octr 27
*Christian born Apl 6 1787 daughtr of Thomas Gale.
Clarissa born May 7th 1788 daughter of Thomas Gale.
Novr 1
Nelle born Novr 23 1788 daughtr of Neal McGloughlen & Patience Boreland his wife.
Platt born   , son of Benjamin Coddington.
Jany 31
Harry son of Joseph Denton & Hannah Yelverton his wife born
John son of Anthony Carpenter & Mary Moffatt born
Collvil Bradner born Octr 28 1789 son of Benjn Ludlum & Christian Bradner.
Jany 31 1790
Baptized Thomas born June 14 1789 son of Jonathan Swezy & Elizabeth Seward his wife.
May 30
*Jonathan born Feby 27 1790 son of Stephen Smith.

Edward born Feby 6 1790 son of Edward McNeal.
June 6
Juliana born Mar 22 1790 daughter of Daniel Conkling.
Elizabeth born Jany 24 1786 daughter of Stephen Smith (son of Caleb).
Abigail born Augt 4th 1788 daughter of ditt.
June 12
Edward born Apl 7 1790 son John Suffern & Mary Myers his wife.
June 18
Daniel born Octr 31 1789 son of David Crawford.
June 20
David Clark born Feby 6 1790 son of Enos Case & Anna Clark his wife.
Thomas Watkins born Apl 1790.
Henry born   son of Henry Tucker & Rebeckah Gale, his wife.
Margarett born Decemr 11 1789 daughter of Asa Steward.
Septr 3 1790, Baptized
Andrew, son of Preserved Couley, born Jany 18 1781.
Preserved born Jany 12 1783 son of ditt.
Hannah, daughter of ditt. born Augt 31, 1785.
Anna born Augt 4 1788 daughter of ditt.
Novr 28
Baptized Elizabeth Gale wife of Coe Gale.
Thomas Waters & Benjamin Carpenter born Augt 3 1790 twin sons of Coe Gale & Elizabeth Waters, his wife.
Decmr 19
Mary Born Octr 25 1790 daughter of Edward McHenry & Sarah Stott his wife.
Decemr 26
Abigail born Octobr 28 1790 daughtr of Abiel Fry &
Jany 16 1791
Sarah born Octr 15th 1790 daughter of David Case.
Jany 21
*Sarah born   daughter of Ezekiel Roe.
*Elienor born   , daughtr of Ditt.
Samuel born   son of ditt.
Benjamin Budd born   son of ditt.
Catharine born   daughter of John Ludlum.
Jany 23 1791
Baptized Martha born Augt 13 1790 daughter of Ichabod Lewis.
Peter Mills born Feby 12 1790 son of Able G Smith & Mary Smith his wife.
Jany 28
Keziah born July 5th 1789 daughtr of John McDowell.
Feby 4
Mary born   daughtr of Charles Tucker.
Benjamin born   son of Cadmiel More.
Abigail born   Daughtr of ditt.
Kitsey born Jany 11 1787 daughtr of Joshuah Reeves.
Feby 20
Sally born   daughter of Joseph Hulse & Margrett Williams his wife.
Fanny born   daughtr of ditt.
Dille born   daughtr of ditt.
Apl 10
Hannah & Fanny, twin daughters of Benjamin Jackson born Decemr 17th, 1790.
Apl 15
John son of Charles Boreland born
Elizabeth born daughter of William Miller & Hannah Van Curah his wife.

Margaret born   daughter of ditt.
May 8th A D 1791
Baptized Rebeckah born Feby 24th 1791 daughter of James Horton.
June 5
Samuel born Novr 16 1785 son of William Wells.
Keziah born June 6 1788 daughter of ditt.
William born May 18 1790, son of ditt.
June 12
Barkus, born Feby 8 1791, son of Nathaniel Baily & Margrett Wickham his wife.
June 18
Mahetable born Apl 11 1791 daughter of Stephen Smith.
July 2
*Anna born June 24 1786 daughter of David Hawkins.
Sarah born Septr 24 1788 daughter of ditt.
Hilah born Jany 22 1791 daughtr of ditt.
July 10
Fanny born   daughter of William Bodle.
*Thomas Sanderfelt born   son of Eliud Tryon.
July 24
Alfred, born May 24 1791, son of William Stringham & Sarah Carpenter, his wife.
Augt 21
Colvill born May 27 1791 son of Colvill Steward & Joanna Brown his wife.
Octr 16 A D 1791
Baptized Benjamin Wells born Apl 25th 1791 son of Zacheus Case.
Novr 13
Coe born March 27 1791 son of Asa Smith.
Novr 18
Samuel born, June 4 1790 son of Josiah Vail.
*Effe born June 21 1789 daughter of John McLaughlin.
John born July 8 1791 son of Neal McLaughlin.
Decemr 25
Mary born   daughter of Thomas Monell & Elizabeth Hubard his wife.
Feby 12
Elizabeth born   daughtr of   Currin & Mehetabel Currin his wife.
John   born   son of ditt.
Moses born   son of ditt.
Feby 26
Tabitha daughtr of Charles Boreland born
Mar 2
Richard Wright & Henry Twin sons of Josiah Pierson born
Mar 6
Fanny born May 20th 1789 daughter of Joseph Conkling.
Hannah   born July 3 1791 daughtr of ditt.
Joseph born   son of Jesse Carpenter.
Clarissa born   daughtr of ditt.
Jesse born   son of ditt.
Hannah born   daughtr of ditt.
Goshen, Apl 15 1792
Baptized Nathaniel Roe son of Saml. Denton, Junr.
Apl 29
*Aaron son of Eusebius Austin.
Sylvester son of Daniel Conkling.

REGISTER OF BAPTISMS

May 13
  Sarah born   daughter of William Miller & Hannah Van Curah his wife.
  Margarett born Jany 30 1792, daughter of Daniel Baily & Mary Tuthill his wife.
May 27
  Andrew born Apl 1791 son of Saml. Dunning.
June 10
  Effe born   daughter of William Brown.
June 15
  William born May   1791 son of John McCarter.
June 24
  William Scot born   son of James W. Wilkins & Hannah Townsend his wife.
  Samuel born   son of ditt.
July 1
  John Seward born Apl 27 1792 son of Jonathan Swezy & Elizabeth Seward his wife.
  Delinda born March 25 1792 daughter of Reuben Hopkins & Hannah Elliott his wife.
July 29
  Abner born   son of Eneas Case & Ann Clark his wife.
Augt 26 1792
  John Baptized son of   Bell born May 23 1792.
  George Frederick son of   Saybolt, born
Septr 22
  Elizabeth born   daughtr of Henry Wells.
  Hannah born May 5 1792 daughtr of Andrew Jones.
Septr 29
  Stephen born   son of Stephen Smith.
Octr 7
  John born July 4th 1792, son of Benjamin Ludlum & Christian Bradner, his wife.
  Thomas Wickham born May 16th 1790, son of Benjamin Bradner & Mary Wickham, wife.
  Colvill born Decmr 23 1791, son of ditt.
  Isaac born Apl 17 1792 son of John Bradner.
Decemr 16
  Benjan. Conkling was born Augt 19th 1792 son of Stephen Smith, 3rd.
Apl 7 1793
  Benjamin born Decemr. 18 1791 son of Moses Hawkins & Catherine Harlow his wife.
Apl 14
  John born Feby 24 1793 son of John White & Effy Brown his wife.
Apl 21
  Joseph Wickham born Feby 7 1793, son of Nathaniel Tuthill Junr. & Martha Wickham, his wife.
Apl 28 1793 Baptized
  Jacob, son of Edward McNeal, born Jany 20th 1793.
May 5
  Elizabeth Conkling an adult.
May 19
  *Juliana born Septr 9 1792 daughtr of John Budd.
June 9
  David born March 11 1793, son of David Case.

REGISTER OF BAPTISMS

June 16
Dolly born Jany 27 1793 daughter of Colvill Steward & Joanny Brown, his wife.
June 30
*Thomas, born Novm 5 1792 son of Ichabod Lewis.
July 2
Gabriel born   son of William Cranse.
*Temperance born   daughter of William Cranse.
July 21
*Mary Scoit an adult.
Novr 9
Daniel born July 1 1782, son of Albert Foster.
*Abigail born August 5 1787 daughtr of Albert Foster.
George Corwin an adult.
Apl 3 1794
Abigaiil wife of Silas Peirson.
Matthew son of ditt.
Abigail daughtr of ditt.
Mary daughtr of ditt.
Silas son of Ditt.
May 4
Gabriel son of Gabriel Wisner & Elizabeth Waters, his wife, formerly
William son of Benjamin Bradner.
Hezekiah Denton son of Jacob Mills.
June 1st 1794
Baptized Henry born son of William Millar & Hannah Van Curah, his wife.
May 15
Mary born daughtr of Daniel Conkling.
May 21
Mary born   daughtr of James Carpenter & Mary Wells his wife.
Fanny born   daughtr of ditt   &
James born   son of ditt.
John Smith, Junr an adult.
Benjn Field born Oct 6 1793 son of Amos Mills & Mary Mills his wife.
May 22
Terry Owen, an adult.
*Ebenezer born   son of Jeremiah Jessup & Hannah Gale his wife.
May 29
Phebe born   daughtr of Enos & Ann Case.
July 5
Mary daughtr of Uriah Terry.
July 13
Susannah born   daughter of Adam Milspaugh & Jane his wife.
Juliet born Apl 13 1794 daughter of Eusebius Austin & Abigail Wood his wife.
Feby 14 1794
*Baptized Chauncy born June 14 1783 son of John Jackson & Phebe Everett his wife.
Augt 10
Jesse born   son of William Bodle.
Nov 16 1794
Lewis Dubois born Sept 15 1794 son of Asa Steward.
Feby 15 1795
Abner born Novr 27 1794 son of Saml. Dunning.
Mar 1
*Helen born Oct 17 1794 daughter of John McCarter.

REGISTER OF BAPTISMS

May 31
Abigail born Septr 29 1794 daughter of James Mitchell & Catharine Mac-Nicoll his wife.
June 7
Else & *Sarah twin daughters of Thomas Watkins & Lydia Eager his wife the children were born
June 7
Lucia a negro woman wife of John Bilson.
June 14
Nancy born March 1 1795 daughtr of Collvil Steward & Joanna Brown his wife.
June 21
Samuel born March 4th 1795 son of John White & Effy Brown, his wife.
July 19
Elizabeth wife of Uriah Terry.
Theophilus Howell born June 8 1783 son of Howell Peirson & Elizabeth More his wife.
Julia born Mar:30th 1785 daughtr of Uriah Terry & Elizabeth More his wife.
Abigail born July 28 1787.
Elizabeth born Jany 30 1790.
Hiram born May 5 1794 children of ditto.
Augt 23—A D 1795
Baptized Hannah born July 20 1795 daughtr of John Budd.
Elizabeth born July 27 1795 daughtr of Silas Peirson.
Sept 20
Nehemiah son of Stephen Smith born Nov 6 1794.
Mary born Jany 29 1794 daughtr of Moses Hawkins & Phebe Harlow his wife.
Maria born May 20 1795 daughtr of David Case.
John Herod born June 28 1795 son of Nathaniel Tuthill Junr. & Martha Wickham his wife.
Oct 4
Hiram born July 20th 1795 son of Danl. Conkling.
Oct 10
Bettridge born Augt 21 1795, Adam Milspaugh & Jane White his wife.
Oct 11
James born   son of Wm Bodle.
Nov 1
Susannah born June 24 1795 daughtr of Asa Smith & Sarah Carpenter his wife.
Nov 20
Mary born Augt 30 1794 daught of Jonathan Swezy & Elizabeth Seward, his wife.
January 31th 1796
Baptized Nathaniel born Nov 20th 1795 son of Daniel Baily.
Feb 7 1796
Scynthia born May 23 1779 daughter of John Carpenter & Abigail More his wife.
John Coe born May 4 1781 son of Ditt.
Benjamin born Apl 4 1783 son of do.
Abigail born Augt 9 1787 daughtr of do.
Mary born July 28 1789 daughtr of do.
Temperance born June 25 1791 daughter of do.
Isaac born Sept 18 1793, son of do.
Susannah born July 6 1795 daughtr of do.
Benjn. born Nov 4 1794 son of Benjn. Carpenter & Eunice Steward his wife.

Mar 13
 Samuel Denton born Jany 9 1796 son of   Mills.
May 20
 Lydia Eager born May 18 1796 daughter of Thomas Watkins & Lydia Eager his wife.
May 25
 Stephen born Augt 12 1787 son of Ananias Volantine.
 Mary born Sept 12 1789 daughtr of ditt.
 Keziah born Nov 3 1794 daughter of ditt.
June 26 1796
 Hannah born   daughter of Uriah Terry & Elizabeth More his wife.
 Hyram born Oct 30th 1795 son of William Millar & Hannah Van Curah his wife.
Augt 28
 George born Sept 16 1793 son of Anthony Carpenter.
 Temperance born June 7 1796 daughtr of Elisha Reeve & Temperance Reeve his wife.
Oct 8
 Baptized three for Luther Steward viz: Catharine born Apl 7 1783—Jesse Carpenter born Oct 7 1786 & Suzanna born Decemr 30 1788.
Oct 19
 Asa born Augt 7 1796 son Thomas Caldwell & Elizabeth Steward his wife.
Decem 4
 James Butler born Augt 30 1796 son of Stephen Smith.
Jany 29 1797
 Frances born daughter of Benjamin Bradner.
Feby 12
 William Wickham born   son of Jacob Mills.
 Sarah born   daughter of Stephen Smith.
Jany 1st 1797
 *John Gale born   son of Jeremiah Jessup.
May 7
 William Edward born June 15th 1796 son of Daniel Thorne & Mary Jones his wife.
June 3 1797
 Phebe Harlow an adult.
 Charles born son of John Jarvis a negro.
June 11
 Sally Ann born   daughter of James W. Wilkins & Hannah Townsend his wife.
 *Eliza Maria born   daughtr of ditt.
June 18
 Moses born June 9th 1796 son of Jonathan Dunning.
June 25
 Theresa born Sept 30th 1796 daughter of Joshuah Davies.
July 2
 Gilbert Bradner born   son of Benjamin Gale.
July 9
 Ira born   son of Moses Hawkins.
July 23
 Amzi born Mar: 14th 1797 son of John Harlow & Sarah Webb his wife.
Augt 20
 Sally born   daughter of Daniel Conkling & Suzannah his wife, 26th July 1797.

REGISTER OF BAPTISMS

Ann Mariah aged 11 months & 3 weeks daughter of John Smith & Nancy Elmer his wife.
Augt 31 1797
Baptized Mary born   daughter of Able Gale.
Sept 17
Nathan born   son of Silas Peirson.
Octr 1
Mary born   daughter of Ezehiel Roe & Mary his wife.
John Bradwick born   son of ditt.
Abigail Amitta born   daughtr of ditt.
Nov 19
Stephen Harlow born Nov 21th 1772.
Sarah born Jany 27th 1795 daughter of Stephen Harlow.
Decem 3
Olive Belknap born Oct 12 1797 daughter of David Case.
Jany 14 1798
Elioner born June 17th 1797 daughtr of Daniel Comfort & Phebe Fulton his wife.
June 10
Sarah daughter of the widdow of Samuel Smith, Junr.
Tempe daughter of Mrs. Monnel wife of Wm Monnel.
June 17
Jannet born Decembr 12 1797 daughter of John White & Effy Brown his wife.
July 1
Ira born Augt 18th 1797 son of Asa Smith.
John born   son of John Jarvis a negro.
July 8 1798
Absalom born Feby 3 1798 son of Jonathan Dunning.
    New Church in the Wallkill
Martha born Mar: 10 1798 daughtr of   Thomson.
    New church in Wallkill
July 22
Mary born Decemb 28th 1797 daughtr of Josiah Vail.
Septr 30
Adelina born   daughtr of Uriah Terry & Elizabeth More his wife.
Octr 13
Mary born Mar 31st 1798 daughtr of   Milspaugh.
Tamer a negro woman.
Octr 14
Benjamin born Feby 7 1796 son of Benjamin Carpenter.
Ferdinand born Septr 10 1798 son of Danniel Bayley.
Novr 11
Jane Graham born Augt 27th 1798 daughter of Stephen Smith.
Mar 3 1799
Maria, born Septr 10 1798, daughter of James Brown & Elizabeth Dunning, his wife.
Mar 15
Nathan born   son of Ezekl. Roe.
June 15
Mary daughter of Phineas Case & Deziah Tusteen, his wife.
Abigail duaghtr of ditt.
Sally ditt &
Usher Hampton son of ditt.
Kitty Deziah ditt.

REGISTER OF BAPTISMS

Hellen ditt.
Eliza ditt.
William son of Jeremiah Jessup.
July 28
Stephen born June 16 1799, son of Stephen Smith.
Augt 11
Oliver Edward born—son of Thomas Caldwell & Elizabeth Steward his wife.
Septr 1
Sarah Ann born March 30 1798 daughtr of Daniel Thorn & Mary Johns his wife.
William Holland born Septr 27 1798 son of David Reeve Arnell.
    Thus far examined & approved
       By order of the Presby.
          John Joline, Moderator.
Octr 5 1799
Baptized Benjamin Gale born 6th Septr 1794.
Sarah Gale born 29th May 1796 &
Anna Maria born 20th Apl 1798.
Children of David Mandeville Westcott & Keziah Gale, his wife.
Octr 6
William Rockwell an adult.
         Fishkill
Apl 15 1800
Theodore born Augt 20th 1799 son of Abraham Van Wyck & Susannah Haight his wife.
         Fishkill
Sally, William & Theodore born   , children of Theodore Van Wyck & Sally Young his wife.
June 15
Daniel Stodard born Octr 29 1799 son of Daniel Conkling.
July 20
Roger Townsend born   1800 son of James W. Wilkins & Hannah Townsend his wife.
Augt 21
Fanny born Novr 16 1799 daughter of Asa Smith.
John Elmer born Novr 27 1799 son of John Smith.
Septr 7
Elizabeth Wells & Robert McKune born July 7 1800 daughter & son of David Case.
Septr 14 1800
Baptized—born July 20 1800 son of John Budd.
Gilbert Hawkins born July 4 1800 son of Moses Hawkins & Phebe Harlow his wife.
Octr 4
Jane Born Apl 27 1800 daughter of David M. Westcott & Keziah Gale his wife.
Octr 5
Clarissa born   daughtr of John Jarvis a negro.
Richard Jones Born Feb 3 1800 son of Daniel Thorn & Mary Jones his wife.
Jany 25 1801
John Hull Born   son of Jacob Munson & Esther his wife.
Feby 6
Prissila Born Octr 3d 1800 Daughtr of Stephen Smith & Margaret Butler his wife.
May 3
Horrace Born   son of Benjn. Bradner.

REGISTER OF BAPTISMS

June 21
  Catharine Daughter of Allexander Cory.
  Benjamin his son
  Azubah
  Hannah & Maria his daughters

July 12
  Jane Born Jany 11 1801 Daughter of David Crawford, Junr. & Sarah Fitt his wife.

Octr 13 1801
  Malinda Born   daughter of   & Frances Monnel.

Octr 25
  Baptized Tempe Ann Born Augt 10th 1801 Daughtr of Joshuah Brown.

Novr 1
  Sally Born   Daughtr of Samuel Tucker.
  Charles Phillips born   son of   do.
  Lot Hawkins Born   son of do.

Decemr 6
  John Weathrow Born Apl 22 1800 Son of James Brown.

Decemr 18
  Andrew McDowell Born Marh 3 1801 Son of Richard Jackson & Mary Jackson, his wife.

Feby 7 1802
  Gabriel Born June 29 1801 Son of Gilbert Roberts & Elizabeth Shaw his wife.

May 22
  Sarah Born Mar: 17 1802 Daughtr of Asa Smith & Sarah Carpenter his wife.

June 26
  Juliann Born   Daughter of Jeremiah Jessup.
  Gabriel Smith Born   Son of Daniel Corwin.

July 4
  James Newton Born   Son of Thomas Caldwell & Elizabeth Steward his wife.

Septr 18
  Frances Matilda Born Septr 1 1802 Daughtr of James W. Wilkin & Hannah Townsend his wife.

Septr 26
  *Elizabeth Born May 27 1802 Daughter of David M. Westcott & Keziah Gale his wife.

Octr 24 1802
  Baptized Catharine Born Feby 17 1802 Daughter of James Brown.

Octr 30
  Susannah Born March 18 1796 Daughter of Benjamin Carpenter & Eunice Steward his wife.

Feby 16 1803
  Abigail Mary Born   Daughter of John Gale, Junr. & Frances Dunning his wife.
  Fanny Born   Daughtr of Do.

Apl 23
  Nancy Born Octr 12th 1802 Daughter of David Crawford Junr.

May 22
  Jonathan & Eliza Born Augt 23 1802 Son & Daughter of Stephen Smith & Margrett Butler his wife.

May 29
  William Born   Son of Eusebius Austin & Abigail Wood his wife.

REGISTER OF BAPTISMS

June 25
Emile Born Decemr 12 1802 Daughter of Stephen Jackson & Abigail Denton his wife.

June 26
Maria Born   Daughtr of Benjamin Bradner.
Aaron Born   son of John Jarvis a negro.

July 3
Joseph Reeves Born May 24 1803 Son of Stephen Smith.

Augt 3 1803
Baptized James Born Septr 25 1800 Son of Jesse Shepard & Ann Kinner his wife.
Harriett Born 4th Feby 1803 Daughtr of Do.

Augt 14
Sarah Ann Born Feby 15 1800 Daughtr of Thomas Carmer & Mary Gale his wife.
Hester OutWater Born Septr 7 1801 Daughtr of Do.

Octr 8
Thomas Edwin Born Jany 6 1803 Son of Hannah Arnold.
Robert Thomson Born Jany 7 1803 Son of Richard Jackson.

June 24
Charlotte Born   Daughtr of David M. Westcott & Keziah Gale his wife.
James Allexander Born   Son of James W. Wilkin & Hannah Townsend his wife.

Augt 24
Mary Ann Born June 8th 1804, Daughter of William Strain & Maria Strain alias Bell his wife.

Octr 6
Harriett, Born July 31 1804 Daughter of Stephen Smith & Margrett Butler his wife.

Octr 28 1804
Oliver Born   Son of John Budd & Mary Hawkins his wife.

Novr 25
*Daniel Strong Born May 1st 1804 Son of Joshua Brown &
          The Revd. Nathan Ker who baptized the persons mentioned in the preceding pages died in Dec. 1804 and the Revd. Isaac Lewis was installed in January 1806 who baptized the following mentioned Persons.—

April 4 1806
Mary Ann, daughter of Wid. Mary Eldred.

April 10
John Augustus, son of Stephen Smith & Sarah his wife, born May 3rd 1806.

Octr 4
*Henry, born July 20 1806 & *Ency born Feby 22, 1806, children of David M. Westcott & Keziah his wife.

Jany 5
Charlotte, Maria, Fanny, Jane & Lewis, children of Wid. Martha Dunning.
Mary, John, Joseph Harrison, Hiram, Nathan & Harriett children of Wid. Martha Coleman.

Jany 18
Margarett, Nathaniel, Anne, Elizabeth & Christian, children of Nathaniel Conkling Jnr. & Margaret his wife.

March 6
Hannah, born July 10 1797, Phebe, born Oct 10 1799, Elizabeth, born June 25 1802 & Sarah, born Decr 29 1804, daughters of Annanias Valentine & Elizabeth his wife.

REGISTER OF BAPTISMS

May 23
Phebe Maria, Aaron Jefferson, Elizabeth Carr & Letty McCord, children of Aaron & Mary Hetfield.
Jane, daughter of John & Julia Gale.

May 24
Sarah Mosier, wife of Jared Mosier.

May 31
Harriett Mead, daughter of Seth L & Sarah Poppino.

Octr 10
Samuel & Juliann, children of Samuel & Phebe Harlow.

Octr 18
Jacob, son of Thomas & Mary Casmer.

Novr 15 1807
Charity, Walter Brewster, Stephen Howell, Benjamin, Thomas, Hezekiah Howell, Jane Porter, Egbert, Eliza Margaret & James children of Benjamin Strong Esq & Susannah, his wife.

Jany 10 1808
Eliza Sophia, daughter of Revd. Isaac & Katharine Lewis.

July 10
Catharine, daughter of David M & Kezia Westcott.

Jany 1 1809
James Morrison, born Sept 25 1808, son of David R. & Mary M. Arnell.

May 6
William, son of John & Julia Gale.
Mariah, daughter of John & Dorcas Jarvis.

May 7
Phebe, wife of James Egbert.

July 2
William Augustus, son of Benjamin & Susannah Strong.

Augt 20
Sarah, Esther & Phebe, daughters of Mrs. Tibbits, White Lake.

Septr 30
Mary, Jane & Matilda, daughters of Wid. Mary Brown.

Oct 1
Mary Caroline, daughter of Joshua & Hannah Brown.

Oct 6
Selah, Hudson, Melinda, Eliza & Joshua, children of Joshua & Deborah Goldsmith.
John & Stephen, sons of Widow Mary Brown.
Cornelia, daughter of Aaron & Mary Hetfield.

Dec 27
Hilah Ann, Lewis, Dorothy, John Milton & Emeline, children of John Steward Ridgebury.

June 9 1810
David Mandeville, born March 14 1810, son of David M. & Kezia Westcott.

June 10
Samuel Vail, Hannah Vail, his wife & Michael Carpenter, Adults.

June 29
James, Julia, John Dunning, Jacob Arnout, William, Horace & Hannah, children of Samuel & Hannah Vail.
Eleanor, Sarah & Nehemiah, children of Wid. Dolly Carpenter.

Aug. 26
Isaac, born July 1, 1810, son of Revd. Isaac Lewis & Catharine, his wife.

Sept 2
Lewis Baldwin, born July 9 1810, son of Dr. David R. & Mary M. Arnell.

REGISTER OF BAPTISMS

Sept 20
Townsend, son of James W. & Hannah Wilkin.
Oct 14
Margaret Dolsen, wife of Fredk. Dolsen.
Decr 14
Mary, born March 19 1807, Eusebius Austin, born Oct 17 1808 & Elizabeth born April 1 1810, children of James & Elsa Gale.
Decr 21
Loisa Bodle & Allexander Bodle, Grandchildren of William & Sarah Bodle, whom they have adopted into their own family.
March 8 1811
Flemmon, child of Annanias & Elizabeth Valentine.
March 24
Isaac Lewis, son of James & Abigail Clason
April 27
, child of John & Julia Gale.
Sally—daughter of Samuel & Phebe Harlow.
Juliette—daughter of John & Dorcas Jarvis.
August 25
Susannah Frances, born April 29 1811, daughter of Benjamin & Susannah Strong.
August 31
William Bodle, son of Nathaniel & Mary Tuthill.
Novr 10 1811
John Sayre, son of John Crane & Abigail, his wife.
May 10 1812
John Bradner, born Octr. 11, 1811, son of James & Elsa Gale.
July 5
Mary, born June 21, 1793, John, born April 19 1799, Rachel, born Feby 19 1801, Eliza Ann born April 3 1808 & Juliet born April 30 1810, children of James & Phebe Egbert.
Mary, born Septr 11, 1806, daughter of Wid. Elizabeth Jackson.
Nathan, born May 17 1812, son of David M. & Kezia Westcott.
Septr 18
Simmony, Lewis & Isaac, children of Isaac & Tamar Hallock, Baptized by the Revd. Mr. King.
Novr 14
Hannah Newman an adult baptized by the Revd. Mr. Grier.
William, born Dec 14 1811, son of Annanias and Elizabeth Valentine, By the Revd. Mr. Grier.
Feby 8 1813
Jane, born Aug 5, 1812, daughter of Dr. David R. and Mary M. Arnell By the Revd Mr. King.
Total 116
Mr. Lewis

The Revd. Isaac Lewis was dismissed from his pastoral Relation to the Congregation in Goshen on the 12th July 1812 and the Revd. Ezra Fisk became its pastor in August 15 1813, who baptized the folowing persons.

Aug 22 1813
Henry Pribble, son of James & Abigail Clason.
Oct 9
Sarah wife of Samuel Butler.

1814 Feby 10
*Joseph, born Nov 13, 1813 & Abigail Juliana, children of Benjamin & Susanna Strong.
May 7
Benjamin, born Sept 11, 1813, son of James & Elsa Gale.
Phebe Elizabeth, born July 22 1813, daughter of Samuel & Phebe Harlow.
May 8
Julia—wife of Henry W. Denton adult.
Sally, wid. of Dan Hathway.
Solomon Carpenter.
Phebe Carpenter.
*Elizabeth—wife of Paul Masters.
*Elizabeth—wife of Jesse Smith.
Eleanor, daughter of Abrm. Vail.
Sally—Thomas & Rhoda James.
June 5
Jane, born Jany 29 1804, Henry, born Aug 25 1805, Robert Lawson, born Aug 9 1806 & Sarah, born Aug 8 1810, children of Wid. Sally Hathaway.
June 12
Jacob Conkling, William & Mary Ludlum, children of Daniel & Hannah Tooker.
*Emeline & Dolly Juliett, born April 21 1810, daughters of Solomon & Phebe Carpenter.
Frances Loisa, born April 13 1809, Asa Dunning born Jany 24 1811 & James Gale, born April 10 1813, children of James & Charlotte Wood.
Alanson, Eliza, William & Anna Fisk, children of Samuel & Mary Clason.
June 26
*Mary, Sarah & Nathaniel Johnson, children of William Kelsey dec'd. & Hannah, his wife.
*Thomas Borland, born Aug 6 1808, son of Andrew Noble & Eleanor his wife.
John Amron, Julia Ann & Sarah Elizabeth, children of Samuel & Sarah Butler.
Aug 5
Dolly, Jesse, Horace, Hiram & Bradner, children of Jesse & Elizabeth Smith.
Elizabeth Bull, born Sept 14 1813, adopted and grandchild of Jesse & Abigail Smith.
Aug 6
Jane, born June 29 1813, daughter of Isaac & Tamar Hallock.
Aug 7
Christiana wife of Thomas Hawkins.
Mary daughter of Joseph Brown.
Aug 25
John, Silas, Moses & Sarah, children of Paul & Elizabeth Masters.
Sept 16
*Elisha, child of Joshua & Deborah Goldsmith.
Albert Foster, born Aug 18 1812 & Christiana, born Aug.   children of John A. & Abigail Smith.
Novr 5
Benjamin Harlow, Debby Ann, Joseph, Phebe Jane, Cornelia, Emeline, Mary, Abel Birdsey & Margaret children of Abel B & Hannah Watkins.
Novr 6
Samuel Clason—An Adult.
*Sally—wife of Gabriel Smith.
Fanny—Wife of David Webb.
John Ainsly Smith.

*Mary—Servant of Thomas Waters.
Dinah wife of George Hubbard.
Novr 10
　Aaron Austin, born Aug 28 1810, Ellen, Henry Wisner & Frederick, born Oct 21 1812, children of Theophilus & Liava Dolsen.
　Emeline, Elizabeth & Theophilus, children of Frederick & Margaret Dolsen.
Jany 30 1815
　Juda, Jane, Charlotte & Harriett, children of Mary Servt. of Thos. Waters.
Feby 23
　Harriett, Milton, Emeline, Eliza Jane, Oscar & Hannah, children of Gabriel & Sally Smith.
March 4
　Mary Reeves, born Feby 14 1814, daughter of David R and Mary M. Arnell.
April 13
　William Augustus, born Sept. 24 1814, son of David M & Kezia Westcott.
May 7
　Joshua Goldsmith—　　Adults.
　William Noble.
　Charles Smith.
　Mary—Wife of William Edsall.
　Dolly—Wife of Timothy Wood.
　Mary—Wife of Gilbert Hawkins.
　Lois—Wife of Nehemiah Denton.
　John Jay Thompson.
　Mary—wife of Luther Harris.
June 11
　*Samuel Oakley, Frances Emily, Mary Allison, Isaac Lewis, Sarah Tusten, Juliet, born Aug 7 1810 & David Arnell, born Decr 19 1812, children of Joseph Wood Jr. Abigail his wife.
　Matilda, Richard Lewis, William Carpenter, born Apr1 27 1810 & Sarah Carpenter, children of Timothy & Dolly Wood.
July 16 1815
　Oscar, Alfred & Mary Jane, children of Luther & Mary Harris.
July 23
　Charles, son of Wid. Amy Morgan.
Aug. 5
　Andrew Jackson, son of John & Julia Gale.
Aug 6
　Martha—Wife of John Dunning.
　Mary Brewster & Anna Fisk, Adults.
Octr 15
　Emily, Samuel Ball, Electa Caroline and Jane, children of Josiah & Sarah Kitchell.
Nov 5
　Mary Elizabeth, daughter of James & Abigail Clason.
Nov 9
　Amanda, Emeline and William Henry, children of William & Elizabeth Howe.
　Jane—Servant of Elder Bailey.
　Scotta and Maria, Jane's Children.
Nov 10
　William S., Enos Stoddert, Sally Loisa & George Schuyler, children of Joshua & Nancy Conkling.
Nov 12
　Julia—Wife of Peter Gale.
　Rebecka Brown—Adult.

REGISTER OF BAPTISMS

John L'Hommidieu
Dolly—Wife of John L'Hommidieu.
Joshua Smith
Hester Smith.
Sarah Denton.
William McKoy.
Abigail, Wife of William McKoy.
Sally Maria Smith.
Hannah Jane Hawkins.
Elizabeth Maria Hawkins.
James Wolfe Dekay, Junr.
Elizabeth Smith.
Hilah Holley.
Nov 12 1815   Adults
Sally Maria Brewster.
Olivia Brewster.
Fanny Owens.
Ebenezer Bowers.
Mary Dunning.
Elizabeth Moore.
*Julianna Sawyer.
Nancy Horton.
Christian Vail.
Thomas White Gilbert.
Catharine Wife of John T. Wood.
Jeptha Marsh.
Mary Harrison.
Aden Gibbs—an Indian.
*Letitia Hill, free woman of colour.
Casar, Servt. of Dr. G. N. Phillips.
Rachel, Servt. of Stephen Smith.
Phana, Servt. of Dr. G. N. Phillips.
Katy, Servt. of Moses Phillips, Junr.
Jany 10 1816   Children
Littleton, Charles, Mary & Lewis, Phana's Children.
Jany 31
*Sally Butler, daughter of Andrew & Eleanor Noble.
Feby 9
Harrison Gale, child of William & Clarissa Otis.
Feby 14
Julia, Lucien, Jenette, De Nolkert, Orsamor & Everard Waldorf, children of Frederick & Eliz. Horton.
March 17
Hannah Maria, daughter of Wm. & Fanny Stephens.
March 20
Gabriel Tooker & Fanny, children of Peter & Julia Gale.
March 22 1816
Daniel & Eliza Baldwin.
Caroline, born June 15 1809, Martha & Thomas, children of William & Fanny Stephens.
Hannah, William & Mary, children of William & Mary Edsall.
March 27
Ira, William & Elizabeth, children of Widow Mary Smith.
May 11
Mary Moore, daughter of James & Charlotte Wood.

May 12   Adults
William Arnout.
Hannah Oakley.
James Sawyer.
Mary Gale.
Hilah Gale.
Susan Smith wife of Coe Smith.
Jeremiah Terbele.
Eunice Corey
George Evertson Arnout.
Sarah Taylor.
Deborah Smith—Wife of S. G. Smith.
Phebe Dunning.
John Gregg.
Maria Corey.
Israel Hendershot
Calvin Gardner Sawyer.
Nero Hunting &
Mary Hunting his wife.
Ralph, Servt of Dr. Phillips.
York, Servt. of Thos. Booth.
Betsey, Servt. of Willm. Stephens.
Jeffrey, Servt. of Moses Phillips, Junr.
June 16
Edward Ogden, child of Timothy B & Maria Crowell.
James Bradner, born Decr 29 1810, Elizabeth Conkling & Susan Conkling. children of John Gregg & Margaret, his wife.
July 1 1816   Children
Dolly ann—daughter of John A & Abigail Smith.
July 21
William—son of Gilbert & Mary Crawford.
July 30
Moses, Elizabeth, Benjamin Franklin, Harriett & Robert Wood, children of Benjamin & Hannah Sawyer.
Joshua—Servt. of Benj. Sawyer.
Susan Howell, Joseph Allison, Alanson, Richard Holly, James & Mary, children of William & Abigail McKoy.
Aug 10
Sarah, daughter of Josiah & Sally Kitchell.
Maria, daughter of Isaac & Tamar Hallock.
Adults
Mehitable, wife of Benjn. Conkling.
Isaac Bowers.
Mary Ann Phillips.
Richard Smith Denton.
Hannah Vail.
Elkanah Mills.
Hannah Moore.
Corelia Denton.
Susan—Wife of Charles Howell.
Juda Servt. of Jno. Steward Esq.,
Juda Servt. of William Phillips.
Jane Van Horan—free woman.
Prime Wisner—free woman.
Aug 26   Children

REGISTER OF BAPTISMS

Daniel Sullivan, George Alvin, Maria, Harriett, Caroline, Lucy Ann & Hester, children of Daniel & Mary Sloan.

Septr 10 1816   Children
Gilbert, Dolly, Sally Ann, William Edward, Michael Carpenter, Mary Ann, Nehemiah, Solomon & Ezra Fisk children of Nehemiah Denton dec'd & Lois his widow.

Novr 10   Adults
Lydia—Wife of Rainsford A. Ferris.
Phebe Loisa Corwin.
Henry Smith Youngs.
Deborah—Wife of Nathaniel Conkling.
George Whitman.
Margaret—Wife of Jacob Decker.
Mary Harris & Maria Smith Free women of color.

Jany 30 1817   Children
Dolly Maria—born Septr 4 1816, daughter of James & Elsa Gale.

Feby 13
Edward, Lewis Norton, Hiram, Gabriel, Emeline, Moses Hallet, George Wells & William Lawrence, Children of George & Mary Phillips.
John & James, Servt. of George Phillips.

Feby 27
Hannah—daughter of Abel B & Hannah Watkins.

March 13
William Arnell, son of Charles & Susan Howell.

March 14
Anthony, Charlotte, Jane, Abigail Austin, Elsa Tustin, Catherine & John, Children of John T & Catherine Wood.

April 13 1817   Children
Prudence Emily, child of Rainsford Ferris & Lydia his wife.

April 25
William Brown, Child of William Otis & Clarissa his wife.

May 3
George, child of James Classon & Abigail his wife.

May 4   Adults
Elizabeth Hudson wife of Eleazer Hudson.
Richard Smith.
Jesse Marvin.
John Halsey free man of color.
Silvia Halsey wife of John Halsey.

July 22   Children
*Betsey child of Phineas Rumsey & Margaret his wife.

July 27
James Gale, child of Wm. Goldsmith & Hila his wife.

Augt 2
Ann Maria, Phebe Adeline & William Lanson, Children of Colvin Corey & Sarah his wife.
Julia Child of John Gale & Julia his wife.
William Fisk Child of Thomas W. Bradner & Susan his wife.
Abram Clark Child of Thos. James & Rhoda his wife.
Mary Child of Richard S Denton &   , his wife.

Augt 3   Adults
Maria Goble wife of Thomas W. Goble.
Almira Van Duzer wife of Benjamin Van Duzer.
Dolly Maria—wife of Gilbert B. Gale.
Rufus Horton.

REGISTER OF BAPTISMS

Elizabeth, wife of Rufus Horton.
Morris Green Servt. of Joseph Wood, Junr.
*Rachel Bago, free woman of color.
*Lois Gardner, do.
Melinda, Servt of Gilbert B. Gale.
Jane Servt of James W Wilkin.

Sept 7   Children
Frances Almira Child of Jesse Marvin & Oliva his wife.

Nov 8
Sarah Schultz—daughter of Benjamin Strong & Susanna his wife.

Nov 9   Adults
Joseph Tolman.
Benjamin Van Duzer.
Mary Howell Wid. Philetus Howell.
Peter, Servt. of John Steward.

Nov 21   Children
Peggy, Thomas, Susan, Jane Ann & William Henry, Children of John J. Decker & Peggy his wife.

March 24 1818   Children
Thomas Jefferson, Maria Reid, Mehitable & George, children of George Whitman & Bethia his wife.

March 27
David, Horace, Sarah Elizabeth & John, children of Rufus Horton & Elizabeth, his wife.
Ann Maria, Child of James Wood & Charlotte his wife.

May 2
Harriet—daughter of Gilbert B Gale & Maria his wife.
John Wallace—son of T. B. Crowell & Maria his wife.
John Augustus—son of John Gregg & Margaret his wife.

July 11
John Barber, Adopted child of John Barber, Esq.
Temperance & Mary Jane, children of Samuel Horton & Sarah, his wife.
   The last three belong to Good Will Congregation.

Augt 1
Eliza Ann, George A, Charles B & Abigail Jane, Children of Daniel Foster & Sally his wife.
Walter Halsey, Frances Emily & Isaac, Children of Benj. Van Duzer & Almira, his wife.
Sarah Elizabeth, Anthony Denton, Nathaniel Crane & John, Children of Amzi L Ball & Jane his wife.
Charlotte Wood—Child of Calvin & Sarah Corey.
*Juliana Denton—child of Wm & Mehitable Noble.

Augt 2   Adults
*Elizabeth wife of Charles Bradner.

Augt 16   Children
George Gaulte—son of Joseph & Ann Tolman.

Augt 23
Dewitt Mortimer—son of Thomas & Elizabeth Ostrander.

Sept 6
Silvia, child of Francis & Phana Berbe, Servts. of Dr Phillips.

Sept 15
*David Reeves child of David R Arnell & Mary his wife.

Sept 27
Samuel Strong—son of Abel B & Hannah Watkins.

REGISTER OF BAPTISMS

Oct 31
Eliza Anderson—daughter of Thos W Bradner & wife.
Michael Boomhour—son of James Clason & wife.
Arminda, Mary Gale & Braddock, children of John L'Hommidieu & Dolly his wife.
Mary—daughter of Colvin & Sarah Bradner.
October 31 1818
Clarissa, Morris Green, Daniel Whitman, *Thomas Wisner & Mary Maria, children of Thomas W. & Maria Goble.
Nov 1
Mary Carpenter (adult)
Nov 13
Elizabeth, Hetty Kelsey & Thomas Lewis, children of Thomas & Deborah Mills.
Decr 4
Hilah Ann, Virgil & Sally, Children of John Conner & Elizabeth, his wife.
1819
William son of Eleazer & Elizabeth Hudson.
6
Elsa Jane, daughter of Wid. Jane Turner.
May 8
Benjamin son of Josiah Kitchel & Sally his wife.
Asa, Emily, Hannah & Theophilus Howell, Children of Coe & Susan Smith.
Cecilia—Child of Sally Hathaway.
Catherine—daughter of Nehemiah & Elizabeth Smith.
June 7
William Kelsey—son of Asa & Mary Dunning.
May 9   Adults
Daniel Whitman
*Hannah Whitman wife of Daniel Whitman.
Benjamin Ayers.
John C Green.
June 11 Children
Henry Jessup, Nathan C & Charles Heard, son of Abel Smith, Dec & Charity his widow.
Augt 31 1819
Hannah, Daniel, Harriett, Sarah June & Morris Green, Children of Benjamin & Mehitabel Conkling.
Sally Jane & Elizabeth, daughters of Harry & Abigail Smith.
Gabriel son of Timothy & Dolly Wood.
Frances, child of Thos. & Rhoda James.
DeWitt Clinton, son of Charles & Susan Howell.
Benjamin Bradner—son of Walter B & Fanny Strong
Nathan Stark—(Adult)
Pamelia Curtice do.
Children
Thomas Houston—son of John B Booth & wife.
July 31 1820
George Wilson—son of Abel B & Hannah Watkins.
Augt 5
Sarah Elizabeth, Phebe Ann & William Posten, children of Joshua Smith & Sarah his wife.
Ira Smith—son of Thomas W & Susan Bradner.
James—son of Gilbert B & Maria Gale.
Robert—son of Timothy B & Maria Crowell.

REGISTER OF BAPTISMS

Augt 5   Adults
Sevia Gibson.
Sylvester M Gregg.
James Wood—2nd.
James Foster.
Adeline Wells.
Elizabeth Jane Gardner.
George Milton Newman.
Isaac Mapes.
Emeline Tusten.
Julia Rumsey.
Miriam Smith—wife of Grant Smith.
James—son of Jacob & Hila Ann Vail.
Susan Maria—daughter of Samuel & Mercy Williams.
Elizabeth Moon.
Fanny—wife of Jno. Budd, Jun.
Hilinda Hawkins.
Maria Luckey.
Hannah Servt. of Joshua Goldsmith.
Augt 6 1820
Hennrietta—wife of Wm. Goldsmith.
Phillip Thomas, colored man.
Augt 19   Children
John son of Calvin G Sawyer.
Hannah Sawyer
Oct 27
*Gabriel son of John Steward Junr. & Martha, his wife, Deceased.
Nov 4
William Nitchie, son of Wm. & Sarah Phillips.
Walter, son of Benjm & Mehitable Conkling.
Martha Caroline, daughter of James & Charlotte Wood.
Mary, daughter of Amzi L & Jane Ball.
Ellen, daughter of John B & Harriet Booth.
Nov 5   Adults
Jesse Rhodes &
Maria Rhodes his wife.
Sarah Luckey
Sarah Jane Hall.
Ruth Smith.
Henry Conkling.
Laura Youngs.
Calvin Corey.
Harriet Barker.
Catherine Barker.
George W. Howell.
Carpenter Coleman.
Katy—Servt of Andrew Wilson.
Feb 20 1821   Children
Gabriel, Henry Denton, Oliver, Walter Halsey, Morgan, Charles & James, Children of James Lewis & Jane his wife.
May 6
Frances Satterly   adult.
June 10
Joshua, son of Wm. Goldsmith & Hilah his wife.

Augt 4
Mary Elizabeth, daughter of Charles & Susan Hawkins.
Augt 5
Sarah — Howell Adult.
Augt 13
*Mary Ann Child of Joseph & Ann Tolman.
Sep 16
David Reeves—Child of David Reeves & Mary M. Arnell.
Oct 27
Edwin—Child of John B & Harriet Booth.
Nov 3 1821   Children
Thomas, son of John Gale & Julia his wife.
Mary, John Milton & Betsey Ann, Children of Widow Frances Satterley.
Francis Evalina, Jane Dunning & Jeromus, Children of George W. Howell & Francis, his wife.
Mary Elizabeth, daughter of Calvin G. & Hannah Sawyer.
Nov 4
Betty wife of Peter Gale.
Jan 9 1822
Alfred, Mary Jane, Jerome, Frances, Julia Ford & Elizabeth Eunice, Children of Joshua Wells, the first four by a former wife & the last two by Catherine his present wife.
Jan 17
Emeline & Mehitable, Children of Orange Green & Mary his wife.
Jan 30
Mary Child of James & Jane Lewis.
Feb 7
Sarah Seely & Robert Seely, Children of William & Abigail McKoy.
May 4
Lois, Daughter of Colvin & Sarah Bradner.
May 5
Eliza, wife of Henry Waters.
Sarah Gale.
Eliza Hawkins.
Augt 3
Elsa Emily child of James Gale & wife.
Charles Norton, son of Theophilus & Mary A. Arnout.
Sept 21
Alexander, *Adeline, Eliza, Eunice, Mary, Anthony Drake & James Nelson, Children of John Halsey & Silvia his wife.
Nov 2
Thomas Scott, son of Thomas W & Susan Bradner.
Henry, Child of Harry & Abigail Smith.
Nov 3
Lydia Horton—wife of Squire Horton.
Nov 18
*Eleazer child of John Gale & Julia his wife.
Dec 23
Oliver Porter—Child of Nathan Stark.
Feb 5 1823
*George Whitfield Case adopted child & grandchild of James W & Hannah Wilkin.
May 3
Mary Ann, daughter of Timothy B. Crowell & Maria his wife.
Sarah, daughter of William Bradner & Frances E his wife.

REGISTER OF BAPTISMS

May 18
Mary Elizabeth, daughter of John & Julia Boak.
May 4
Nancy—wife of Daniel Reeve.
July 6 1823
Daniel Stephen & Charles Thompson, Children of Wid. Deborah Seward.
Augt 2
Robert—Child of James & Charlotte Wood.
Ogden—Child of Charles & Susan Howell.
Henry Denton, son of William & Mehitable Noble.
Sarah Jane, daughter of John B & Harriet Booth.
Mary, Alexander & Charles, Children of Samuel Jones Wilkin & Sarah his wife.
William Henry, son of Joseph & Ann Talman.
Sep 20
James & John, Children of John L'Hommidieu & Dolly his wife.
Maria L'Hommidieu, daughter of Thomas & Eliza Ostrander.
Sep 28
Daniel, son of Gilbert B & Dolly M Gale.
Margaret Emily, daughter of William & Rebecca Arnout.
Feb 8 1824
Samuel son of Calvin G & Hannah Sawyer.
March 3
Andrew Jackson, Sarah Elizabeth & Jesse Smith, Children of Anthony D Jones & Dolly his wife.
Nov 2 1823
Clarissa˜ Clark & Mary Burns, Adults.
May 1
Samuel Seward, Child of Thomas W & Maria Goble.
John Denton, son of Colvin & Sarah Bradner.
James Philitus, Sarah & Thomas Wells, Children of Coe Smith & Susan his wife.
Westcott—Child of Samuel J & Sarah Wilkin.
July 31
Thomas Scott, son of Wm & Sally Phillips.
Sarah, daughter of George W & Frances Howell.
Frances Emily, daughter of Wm & Mehitable Noble.
Mary Elizabeth, daughter of Horace T & Hannah Ball.
Charity, Child of Daniel & Sally Foster.
James Dolson, son of Wm Vail & wife.
Calvin Gardner, son of Moses & Elizabeth Sawyer.
Oct 15
Mary Ann, Harriet, John Nelson, Fanny Jane & Jonathan Horton, Children of John Budd & Fanny his wife.
Jonathan, Margaret & Martha, Children of Abram Vail & Harriet his wife.
Nov 6
Mary, daughter of Morris & Mary Taylor.
Frances, child of Timothy B & Maria Crowell.
Mary, daughter of Nathan & Mary Stark.
April 30 1825
Frances Adelia—Child of John & Margaret Gregg.
Mary & Jane, Children of Joshua Smith & Sarah his wife.
Mary Ann, daughter of John B & Harriet Booth.
Augt 6
Carolina, child of Charles & Susan Howell.

REGISTER OF BAPTISMS

Harriet Newell, daughter of Thomas W & Susan Bradner.
Reuben Mulford & Lorenzo, Children of Harris Rowley & Sarah his wife.

Augt 7
Florence Milton Crane—Adult.

Nov 5
Harriet, daughter of Harry & Abigail Smith.
William Wells, son of Horace & Hannah Ball.

Nov 8
Hector & Mary, Children of Widow Elizabeth Hudson.

May 6 1826
Elizabeth, daughter of Thomas W & Maria Goble.
Wm. Ira, son of Coe & Susan Smith.
Frances & Susan Emily, children of Aaron & Sally Van Duzer.

May 11
Sarah, Joseph, Lewis Oakley & Mary, Children of John T & Catherine Wood.

Augt 5
John Morrisson—Child of Morrison Taylor & Mary his wife.
Egbert Jansen, child of Anthony D Jones & Dolly his wife.
William, son of Saml. J Wilkin & Sarah his wife.
Clarissa Dolsen, child of Wm Arnout & Rebeckah, his wife.
Edward Ely—child of Noah Carpenter &   wife.
Harriet Emily, child of Thomas Mills & Deborah his wife.
Eliza Brown, child of Horace Denton & Adelaide his wife.

Nov 4
Joseph Emmons & Hannah Emily, Twins, Children of Amzi L & Jane Ball.
Harriet—Child of Abraham & Harriet Vail.
Oliver—Child of John & Fanny Budd.

Dec 13
Nicholas Evertson—Child of Wm & Sally Phillips.

Feb 3 1827
Marcellus Van Gieson—Child of James A & Jane Wilkin.

May 5
William Smith, child of Henry C Water & Eliza his wife.
Elizabeth, child of Moses Sawyer & Elizabeth his wife.

July 21
Mary Ethelinda child of Zecheriah N Hoffman & Elizabeth his wife.

Augt 4
Ann Maria—Child of George W Howell & Frances his wife.
Harriet—child of John B. Booth & Harriet his wife.
Alexander Corey—child of John Moore & Maria Corey.

Nov 3
Frances Maria—Child of Thomas W & Susan Bradner.

March 19 1828
Robert Simpson & Fanny, Children of Charles McCorn & Margaret his wife.

June 2
Hannah & Harriet, Children of Calvin G Sawyer & Hannah his wife.

July 21
Samuel Jones—Child of Samuel J Wilkin & Sarah his wife.

Augt 2
James Wilson—Child of Morrison Taylor & Mary his wife.
Samuel Denton—Child of Anthony D Jones & Dolly his wife.
Hannah—Child of Aaron Van Duzer & Sally his wife.
Edgar—child of Wm. Phillips & Sally his wife.
Phebe, Mary Mills & David, Children of Mary Hawkins, widow of Silas Hawkins.

REGISTER OF BAPTISMS

Nov 1
William Belknap—child of Noah Carpenter &
Fannelia—Child of Horace Ball & Hannah his wife.
Nov 2   Adults
Naomiette Moore
Mary Dodge.
Armanda Darby.
Dec 5
Bridget, Child of Henry C Waters & Eliza his wife.
Dec 18
Delia, Child of James Gale & Elsa his wife.
Feb 1 1829
Sarah Thompson wife of John J Thompson.
March 12
Mulliner Bull, James Bull & Gabriel, Children of John A. Smith & Jane his wife deceased.
Gideon Pelton child of J A. Smith & Mary his wife.
Charlotte & Hannah, Children of Joshua Smith & Sarah his wife.
May 2
William—Child of John Budd & Fanny his wife.
Susan & Frances, Children of Coe Smith & Susan his wife.
Susan Agnes, Child of John B Booth & Harriet his wife.
May 3   Adult
Frances Gifford Denton.
Augt 1
James Augustus, son of Thomas W. & Maria Goble.
George, son of George W & Frances Howell.
Mary, daughter of William & Frances E. Bradner.
Augt 2   Adult
Jane Wells.
Nov 7
Edward Ely Child of Theophilus Arnout & Mary Ann his wife.
Nov 8   Adults
Ila Watkins wife of James Watkins.
Mary Caroline Watkins.
Dec 15
Charles Carter—child of James H Gunug & Maria his wife.
Feby 7 1830   Adults
Deborah Goldsmith.
Melinda Owen.
Increase Stoddart Goldsmith.
May 1   Children
Horace Howard—child of Thomas W Bradner & Susan his wife.
Mary, Howard & Sarah, Children of John J Thompson & Sarah his wife.
May 2   Adult
Elsa Ann—wife of Nathaniel N Terrey.
July 31
James Edgar—Child of Charles & Jane Monell.
Robert—child of Moses & Elizabeth Sawyer.
Martha—child of Aaron & Sarah Van Duzer.
Phebe Ann—child of Chauncy & Rachel Smith.
John Denton—child of Henry C & Elizabeth Waters.
Nov 6
Juliet—child of John Budd & Fanny his wife.

REGISTER OF BAPTISMS

Frances Harriet, child of W. Arnout & Rebecca his wife.
Hannah Gale—child of Samuel J Wilkin & Sarah his wife.
Feb 6 1831
Beulah Ann wife of Henry Seward.
Julia Ann Seward—   Adults.
April 24
William Jackson—child of Nathaniel N Terry & Elsa Ann his wife.
April 30
Sarah Dorcas—child of Daniel Foster &   his wife.
John—child of Coe Smith & Susan his wife.
James Sidney & Thomas Thorne, Children of Thomas G. Evans, deceased
    & Mary Evans, his widow.
Grace—child of John I Thompson & Sarah his wife.
May 1   Adults
Abraham Purdy
Maria Cheeve wife of Jas. A Cheeve.
Hannah Waters Jones.
Mary Jones.
Sarah Elizabeth Jones.
Melinda Jackson.
Julia Ann Jackson.
Hiram Halstead.
John Howell.
Sally Jackson.
Nanny Maria Lusk.
Christiana Denton.
James Horton.
Mary Young wife of Calvin Young.
Abba Tupper.
June 13
Amira Corey.
Augt 6   Children
Mary Jane, Charlotte, William Henry & Harriet Louisa, Children of James
    A. Cheeve & Maria his wife.
Mary Ellen—child of Ebenezer & Maria Seely.
Bridget Wickham—child of Hezekiah G Cox, deceased & Catherine Cox,
    his widow.
James Howell & Nathan Coleman, Children of Abraham Vail & Harriet
    Vail his wife.
Melinda Ann, Child of John Moore & Maria his wife.
Emily & John Edward, Children of John Howell & Rebecca Ann his wife.
Lydia Hunt, Alvan, Susan Strong, Benjamin Strong, Hezekiah Howell, Samuel
    Jones, Jane Augusta, Francis Eliza & Julia Ann, Children of Abraham
    Purdy & Charity Purdy, his wife.
Augt 7 1831
Almira Vail.
Silas Rose.
Jane Vail Clark.
Sarah Jane Savage.
Clarissa Wilkin wife of Jas. D Wilkin.
Julia Ann Seward wife of Doct. Daniel Seward.
Eunice Mapes.
Ellen Mapes.
Mary Elizabeth Owen.
Mary Ann Moffatt.

Horace Elmer Dunning.
George Davis Dunning.
Sarah Bowers widow of Isaac Bowers.
Virgil Swezy Seward.
Oct. 27
James Mortimer, Daniel Thorne, Mary Thorne, Andrew McDowell, Edward Thorne, Harriet Thorne & Lewis Denton, Children of Andrew M. Jackson, deceased & Sarah Ann his widow.
Oct 29
Mary, Jane & Agnes, Children of John Wilson & Ann Susan his wife.
Frances Almira, Ira Smith & Albert Galatin, Children of Doct. John S. Crane & Sarah his wife.
Catharine Amanda—Child of Roswell Lewis deceased & Ellen his widow—adopted by Mrs. L—— Dolson.
Mary Ann—Child of Anthony D Jones & Dolly his wife.
Caroline—child of Calvin G. Sawyer & Hannah his wife.
Feb 2 1832
Elizabeth Rumsey—Adult.
Feb 11
Jane—child of John A & Mary Smith.
Oct 30 1831   Adults
Esther Vail.
Mary Vail.
William Poppino.
Jane Myers.
Abigail Payne.
Adeline Augusta Swezy.
Harriet Elizabeth Sweezy.
Susanna Mapes.
Abraham Smith
Samuel Rumsey.
Feb 12 1832   Adults
Robert Emmett Potter.
Milicent Strong Jackson.
Ency Adams wife of London Adams.
Julia Case wife of Daniel Case.
Horace Ball.
Mary Elizabeth Case   Sarah Helms wife of Reuben Helms.
Almira Helms.
Nancy Johnson wife of John H. Johnson.
Eliza Bodle.
Ira Coleman.
Emily Coleman wife of Ira Coleman.
Kezia Wood who was received in August having discovered that she had not been baptized.
May 5   Children
Caroline & James, Children of John & Ann Susan Wilson.
James All Saints—child of James A & Maria Cheeve.
Joanna—child of Gabriel & Sarah Owen.
Theodore Jason, Ann Eliza & Mary Caroline, Children of James D Wilkin deceased & Clarissa his widow.
May 6   Adults
Mary Corey wife of Lemuel Corey.
Sally Jane McCarter.

REGISTER OF BAPTISMS 141

Augt 4
George Hamilton & Caroline, Children of Andrew M. Jackson deceased & Sarah Ann his wid.
Susan, child of Charles Howell deceased & Susan his widow.
James, Mary Vail, Phebe, Ira & Moses, Children of Ira Hawkins & Hannah his wife.
Henry Melanclton, child of Thomas W. Bradner & Susan his wife.
William Arnell, Samuel & Andrew Jackson, Children of William McKoy & Abigail, his wife.
Mary Jane & Cornelia, children of Wm. Smiley & Christiana, his wife.
Joshua Reeve, child of Joshua Smith & Sarah his wife.

Augt 5 Adults
Elizabeth Ann Lusk.
George Washington Connor.
Jane Taylor—Colored.

Sept 13
Catherine Townsend & Daniel Hull, Children of Daniel H Tuthill deceased & Caroline his widow, adopted by J. W. Wilkin.

Oct 12 1832
John Carpenter—Child of Wm. Noble & Mehitable his wife.

Oct 20
Stephen, child of Henry Smith & Abigail his wife.
Mary Louisa, child of Moses Sawyer & Elizabeth his wife.
Mary Ellen & James, Children of John M. Gillespie & Harriet his wife.

Oct. 23
Elizabeth, Mary & James Smith, Children of Ichabod S. Oakley deceased & Ann his widow.

Rev. Dr. Fisk spent of Winter of '32, '33 at the South for the benefit of his health. During his absence Rev. John N. Lewis supplied his pulpit, & administered the ordinance of Baptism; as follows.—

Feby 3rd 1833
Charlotte, wife of Wm. J. Norris.

May 4th
Fanny Elizabeth, child of John Budd & Fanny his wife.

May 5th
Louisa, wife of Joseph Sayre.

June 19
Emily, Ann Eliza, Christiana, Joseph Warren, James & Julia, Children of Henry Scofield & Julia his wife.

June 23
Rebecca Jane child of John H & Nancy Johnson.

Augt 10
Caroline & Edward Wisner—children of Horace Denton & Adelaide his wife.
John Henry—child of John Wilson & Ann Susan his wife.
Gabriel Sayre—child of Gabriel Owen & Sarah his wife.
Nathan Cooper, Henry & Anna Elizabeth, Children of Henry Seward & Beulah Ann his wife.
Mary Elizabeth—child of Horace Crane & Nancy Maria his wife.
Virgil Case—child of Noah Carpenter &   his wife.

Augt 11 Adults
Anna Wood wife of Lewis Wood.
Phineas Rumsey.

Oct 15
Gabriel—child of Calvin G Sawyer & Hannah his wife.

REGISTER OF BAPTISMS

Oct 26
William Egbert, child of Wm Arnout & Rebecca his wife.
Almeda & Mary Jane, Children of Samuel Owen & Elizabeth his wife.
Daniel Wells, child of Virgil S Seward & Sarah his wife.
Sarah Elizabeth & Stephen Augustus, Children of Stephen Smith & Matilda his wife.
Oct 27
William Robinson, adult.
May 3 1834
Frances Emily, daught of Wm Bradner & Em'y his wife.
Jonathan & Henry Williams, Children of Jonathan Fisk & Susana his wife.
Augt 1st   By Revd. Furman—Baptised
Dolly Ann, Daughter of Wm B Smiley & Christian his wife.
Clarissa Wilkin, daughter of Anthony D Jones & Dolly his wife.
Jany 31 1835   By Revd. James R. Johnston—Baptised—
Theodore Augustus son of Hiram Phillips & Mary his wife.
Mary Elizabeth, daughter of —
May 2nd
Catherine Booth daughter of John B. Booth & wife.
Julia Rumsey daughter of Phinias Rumsey & wife
Margaret Carpenter daughter of Noah Carpenter & wife.
Augt 1st
Daniel Wells, son Moses Sawyer.
Frances—daughter of H Scofield.
John Jr. & Ann Duryea, children of Jas. G Thompson.
Daniel Denton—Elizabeth Horton & Andrew Jackson—children of John J Lusk & Letitia his wife.
Elizabeth Valentine—wife of Stephen Valentine.
Rachel Connelly wife of Constant Connelly,—adults.
Augt 9th
Child of Mrs Crane wife of Oliver Crane.
Oct 31
Emely Smith & Theodore—Children of Mrs Reeve.
Mary Elizabeth—child of Nehemiah Carpenter & wife.
Nov 1st
Abigail Denton—adult.
May 1st 1836
Scudder Newman & Ila his wife—adults.
Nov 5 & 6
Henry Duryea—Child of Virgil Seward.
Mrs. Mary Giles—adult.
Feby 4th 1837
Jas. Johnston—child of Joshua Smith.
John Smith child of William R. Smiley.
May 6th
Catherine Jane, child of Lotitia Lusk, wife of Jefferson Lusk.
Augst 5
Caroline, John & James Children of Widdow Gibs.
George Huston, child of James G. Thompson.
Sarah, child of Gabriel Owen.
Hannah, child of Phineas Rumsey.
James Wilkin—child of Anthony Jones.
Mary Eliza Black child of Anthony Wood.
Nov 4th
Juliette, child of George & Ann Halstead.

REGISTER OF BAPTISMS

May 11th 1838
Sarah Steward, child of George & Sally Newton.
Augst 5
Hannah, child of Hiram Phillips.
Jas. Johnston child of Wm. Wood.
1839   February 1st, Baptised
Elizabeth Denton wife of Theodore Denton & Horace E. Denton, adults.
May 4th
Elizabeth wife of John Wallace
   & Corlinda Molrience Newman—Adults.
Augt 3d
Sarah Ann Phillips—adult—Helen Child of Virgil Seward, Ezra Fisk child of Oliver Tuthill—Mary Ann Case, Joanna, Sarah, Nancy & Daniel children of Jas. C. Reeve.
Also May 4 & 5
Elizabeth & John Wallace children of John & Elizabeth Wallace—& Mary Elizabeth—child of Noah Carpenter & Richard Goldsmith & Margaret Ann children of Samuel Owen.
Nov 2d 1839
Antoinette Barker—adult.
Belinda Gale—adult.
Nancy Romain—adult.
Charles Bodle—child of R. E. Potter.
Sarah Elizabeth—child of P. Rumsey.
Jas & Elizabeth Strong—children of Mrs. Watkins.
Virgil—child of Jas. G. Thompson.
    The following Persons were baptised by the Revd. Dr. McCarter.
Jany 25th 1840
Solomon T Smith   adult.
Augt 1st
Harriot Elizabeth Phillips do.
Wm Henry child of Wm R Smiley.
Susan Emily   do   T. W. Bradner.
May 2nd
Mary Caroline do   do
Ann Eliza Wilson   do of John J. Lusk.
Oct 31st
Sarah & Benjm Strong do of Widow Colvill Bradner.
Rech'd Denton child of Anthony Jones.
Elizabeth Wells   do   of Horace Ball.
Thomas Spencer   do   " Sylvanus Schofield.
Feby 6 1841
Harriot Kitchel wife of Saml. B Kitchel.
Charlotte Wells widow of Dr. Wells.
Miriam Smith—adult.
May 2nd 1841
Sarah Carpenter wife of Danl. Carpenter.
Nov 1st
Wm Jansen & Mary Elizabeth, children of Danl. Gale & wife.
Sarah Frances child of Robt. E Potter & Mary his wife.
Jany 23 1842
Sarah Westcott & Horace William children of Horace W. Elliott & Charlotte his wife.
May 1st
Samuel Beyea &

REGISTER OF BAPTISMS

Sarah his wife &
Phebe Beyea.
John Little.
Eliza Vail &
Sally Ann Vail.

May 1843
Benjm. Franklin, Philander, Anna Louisa & Isaac B. M., children of Isaac Banker.

Augt 2nd 1845
Sarah Elizabeth, child of W. H. Ellott.
Jesse Augustus child of Jesse A. Case & wife.
Chas. Henry, child of Robt. E Potter & wife.
Martha Elizabeth, child of O. B. Tuthill.

Augt 2d 1845
Georgianna child of W Ackerman.
Joseph Farnum, child of R. L. Wood.
Alexander Langley, child of H Phillips.

Augt 1st 1846
Stephen H. Strong "adult".
Jane Elizabeth, child of D. A. Wood.

May 1st 1847
Chas. Franklin child of H. C Newman.

July 31st 1847
Helen, Henry Gunsey, Charles Edward & Frank Augustus, Children of Henry Merriam & wife.
Helen L. child of Mrs. Sarah Talmage.

Augt 3d 1842
Esther Hulse   Adult.
Louisa Webb   do.
Jas. J Reeve   do.
Jas. S Tuthill.
William A. Smith   do.

Augt 6th
Julia Schofield   do.
Barnard M Clark   do.
Alphus Gellet   do   "Col".
Clarrissa Smith   do.

Nov 8
Abigail Terry   do.
Wilmot C Terry   do.
Mary Howell   do.

May 3d 1843
Frances Jane Tuthill   do.
Oliver B. Tuthill   do.
Ann Romeyn   do.

Augt 5
Jas M. Steart   "col"   do.

Augt 3d 1844
Mary Stewart   "col"   do.

Feby 1st 1845
Termperance W. Owen   do.
John Jordon   do.

Feby 2nd
Ann Eliza Merriam   do.
Geo. P. Mapes   do.

Aug 3d 1846
Stephen Howell Strong   do.
May 1st 1847
Mary P Goldsmith   do.
Martha Maria Tuthill   do.
Aug 1st
Harriet E Goldsmith   do.
Nov 7th
Harriot E Carpenter   do.
Adeline Goldsmith   do.
Julia Ann Goldsmith   do.
Elizabeth Goldsmith   Adult.
Jas. Henry Child of
Eugene Franklin   do   of Alfred Wells.
Chas. Nelson   do   of Sylvestus Jervis.
Feby 5th 1848
Coe Howell, John Henry, Ida Jane, Ann Eliza & Jesse Case, Children of Bernard M. Clark and Abigail his wife.
May 6th
Juliett Wood, child of David A Wood.
May 8
Sarah Francis Gillispie, child of widow Harriot Gillspie Born 21st June 1838.
May 5th 1849
Mary Louisa Vanriper, adult.
Augt 6
Baptised by Dr. Cummins, child of Afred & Jerusha Harris.
Lewis Arnell, child of Alfred Wells & wife, baptized by Dr. Cummins.
Augt 16th
John Wilson—child of David Redfield, Baptized by Dr. McCartee at the House of John Wilson's.
       & wife
    Child of Alfred Harris & wife.
May 6th
Lewis Arnell, child of Alfred Wells & wife Baptized by Dr. Willm D. Snodgrass.
Nov 3
Mary Helen, child of John B Ackerman.
Mary Elizabeth child of Mary & Chas. Banks, people of color.
Nov 4th
Caroline Augustus Case, Audult.
Feby 2d 1850
Hiram, child of Hiram C. Newman.
Feby 3
Ann Eliza Crans, wife of Geo. H Crans, adult.
Mary Jane Gregory   do.
Margaret Lander   do.
Hector S Moore   do.
Goverin M Smith   do.
John Fitzgerald   do.
Hezekiah C Newman   do.
James T Reeve   do.
May 5th
Sarah Elizabeth Everett   do.
Sarah Mariah Denton   do.
May 5th 1850   Adults.

Frances Emily Conkling.
Harriot Ann Conkling.
Joseph Brewster.
Lewis Poppino.
Albert Foster Gardner.
Charles Wisner Poppino.
William Jackson Gardner.
Almeda Jones, widow of Andrew Jones.
Julia Webb, wife of Andrew Webb.
Clarrissa Jackson wife of H J Jackson.
Frances Eliza Moore, wife of John E. Moore.
Josephus Terbell.
Emily Poppino.
Elizabeth Belknap.
Ann Ferrand, widow of D R Ferrand.
Frances Jane Strong wife B. B. Strong.
Emily Smith, wife of Stephen Smith.
Mary Frances Swezy.
Elizabeth Thayre Denton.
Mary Thompson Strong.
Juliann Poppino.
Julia Ann Gardner.
Adeline Gardner, wife of Jas. Gardner.
Elizabeth Owen, wife of S. P. Owen.
William Poppino.
William Lewis Allison.
David Everett Gordon.
William Young Tuthill.
Charles Bodle Tuthill.
James Board Heard.
James Rockwell Vail.
Frances Elizabeth Greer, wife of G M Greer.
Phebe Ann Edsall, wife of Thos. Edsall.
Wickham Corwin Moffatt.
Elizabeth Lynch.
Emily Charlotte Ostrom, wife of J. W. Ostrom.
William Clark Foster.
Mary Tuthill, wife of Wm B. Tuthill.
Mary Beyea.
Levi Lewis Lockwood.
Augt 1st
Archibald Brown Bodle.
Mary Ann Bennett, wife of Gabriel Bennett.
Susan Elizabeth Young.
Sarah Frances Carpenter.
Mary Elizabeth Sinsebaugh, wife of A. H. Sinsebaugh.
William Corwin, Child of Wickham C Moffatt.
Sarah Elizabeth, Child of Sylvester J Jervis colored folks.
Augt 3rd 1850
Sarah Vanduzer, child of Aaron Vanduzer.
Joshua Smith   ditto of Gabriel Wood.
Frances Walker Lee, ditto of Newton F & Cornelia Lee.
Agnes & Sarah, Children of Asa & Sarah Dunning.
Jane & Julia Ludlum, ditto of John E & Frances Moore.
Benton, child of Ira & Jane Howell.

REGISTER OF BAPTISMS

Mary Elizabeth & George, Children of Geo. M. & Frances Grier.
Frances Tuthill & Thomas Evans, Children of Geo. M & Frances Grier.
Alexander Jackson Child of Jas. & Adeline Gardner.
Mary Jane   do   do   do   do.
Albert Smith Ferran, child of
Thomas Strong, child of Benjm. B & Francis J Strong.
Harvey Newton   child of Stephen Smith & Emily.
Sophia   do   do   do   do.
John Seely, Thomas Edsall & Edwin Sears, Children of Widow Almeda Jones.
Catharine, George Washington & Henry, Children of Adam H & Mary Elizabeth Sinsebaugh.
Sarah Smith, Frances Loiza & Jane Wells, Children of Benjamin Strong & Frances his wife.
Eliza Ward &   Children of Joshua W Ostrom and Emily Charlotte his wife.
George Howell, child of Hamilton J. Jackson & wife.

Feby 1st 1851
Geo. Howell, child of Hamilton J. Jackson.
Eliza Ann, Mary Jane, Emily, Julia Wheeler & Katharine, Children of John James Heard & wife.

May 2nd
Cornelia Smith child of Wm Smith & wife.
Henry G. McConnell child of Alfred Wells.
John Owen, Mary Elizabeth, Margaret Jane & William Nelson, Children of Nelson Owen.
Charles Webb,—child of Jane Goudy.

Index

ALLISON
  Henry 9
  Richard 9, 104, 108
  Mary 11, 12, 18, 79, 104
  Stephen 16
  William 17, 78, 109, 146
  Eliza 23
  John 48, 101, 109
  Martha 50
  Elizabeth 101, 108
  Margaret 102
  Sarah 103, 106

AGUR, AUGUR, AGER
  Jane 11
  Ebenezer 23
  Lydia 111

ALDRICH
  Bethiah 11, 106

ADAMS
  Eleanor 24
  Richard 29
  Matthew 52
  Emy 67
  Ency 140
  Loudon 67
  London 140

ALLEN
  Lemuel 12

ARMSTRONG
  Janat 12
  Martha 13
  Eunice 14
  Mary 15
  William 17
  Julia 24, 26
  Daniel G. 35
  Ella J. 46
  Archibald 50

ARNOLD
  William 15

  David 50, 101, 104, 105, 108, 110, 113
  Mary 50, 108, 110
  Hannah 101 124
  Elisha 104
  Elizabeth 105
  Abigail 113
  Jesse 110
  Thomas E. 124

AYRES, AYERS
  David 21, 37
  Randolph 38
  Julia E. 44
  Frank B. 47
  Benjamin 61, 76, 133
  Christian 61, 76
  Lucy 62, 75
  Hannah 62

AVERY
  Mary 16, 17

ACKERMAN
  John 71, 145
  Eliza G. 71
  Georgianna 144
  Mary Helen 145
  W. 144

ARCHER
  Joseph 16

AMES
  Elisha 17

ANDERSON
  Rhodana 19
  Walter 38
  Frances J. 42

ALBERTSON
  Hannah 21
  Clement 106

ABSLEY
  Jane 23

AMORY
  John 38
ASHMAN
  Jewet M. 46
ANDRUSS
  Robert H. 47
  Charles 47
  Kate H. 47
ASPELL
  Joseph 91
ANTILL
  John 81
ACKERLY
  Nathaniel 44
ACKLEY
  Hiram 28
  Minnie A. 47
  John T. 47
  Sarah J. 47
ANDREWS
  Joseph 27, 41
  Capt. J. 38
  Mary G. 72
  Isaac 72
  J. C. 41
AUSTIN
  Eusebius 26, 53, 78, 111, 114, 116, 118, 123
  Abigail 81
  Sarah 87
  Liana 111
  Joseph W. 114
  Aaron 116
  Juliet 118
  William 123
ARNELL, ARNILL
  Sophionia 34, 58, 76
  William 34, 59, 76, 122
  Charles 34
  David 54, 85, 90, 122, 125, 125, 126, 128, 132
  Hannah 54, 78
  Mary 55, 89, 125, 125, 126, 128, 132, 135
  James M. 62, 75, 125
  Puah 79
  Jesse 82
  Lewis B. 125
  Jane 126

ARNOUT, ARNOTT, ARNOT, ARNONT
  Peter 9, 50
  Jacob 10, 105
  Mary 13, 59, 135, 138
  Rebeckah 14, 136, 137, 139, 142
  Nathan 14
  Selah 19
  Abigail 19
  George 20, 53, 130
  James S. 23
  Julia 28
  Thophilus 28, 135, 138
  William 29, 58, 130, 136, 137, 142
  Margaret 92, 136
  Sarah 102
  Milliscent 105
  Charles N. 135
  Clarrissa D. 137
  Edward E. 138
  Frances H. 139
BURNS
  Francis 9
  Margarett 19
  William 20
  Mary 63, 136
BABCOCK
  James 9
  George 91
BALLARD
  John A. 41
BEEKMAN
  John 9
  Christian 16
  Ellsworth 79
BISHOP
  Gussie M. 46
  Jennie H. 47
BUTTERFIELD
  Jane 49
BURR
  Cloe 9
  Marcus, Rev. 44
BROCKWAY
  Cloe 9
BEETMAN
  Elizabeth 9

BARTLET
   Mary 10
   Hanes 19

BOYLE
   Elizabeth 10
   Edward 85

BRINSON
   Phebe 10
   Juda 90

BRIGS, BRIGGS
   Joel 12
   Jerome 41
   Lena R. 47

BRAND
   William 12

BRUNNING
   Margarett 12

BYARD
   Elizabeth 12

BARTON
   Stephen 13

BUCKBEE
   Russel 13
   Samuel 24

BINGHAM
   Phebe 14
   Hannah 105
   Hezekieh 105, 108
   Fanny 105
   Salmon 108

BIELLS
   Sybill 14

BRUYN
   Cornelius 15

BUSH
   Henry 15
   Juliann 63, 75

BELL
   John 15, 41, 112, 113, 117
   Robert 19
   Benjamin 112
   Alexander 113
   Maria 124

BOIALS
   George 15

BLANCHARD
   Ephriam 15

BRUNSON
   Suzanah 16
   Samuel 18

BLACKMAN
   Ichabod 16

BOWHANON, BOHANEN
   James 16
   Arabella 17

BUCHANAN, BUCANNAN
   James 18
   George 21

BARNEA
   Thomas 16

BIGGER
   Ann 17

BARTOLF, BERTHOLF
   Gilliam 18
   J. H. 43
   F. H. 47

BEMER
   Lydia 18

BELKNAP
   Samuel 18
   Joseph 20
   Jesse 22
   Elizabeth 146

BERKLEY
   Mary 19

BARKLEY
   George 20

BRAN
   John 19

BOUGHTON, BOUTON
   Samuel 19, 51

BURTIS
   John Gilbert 19

BLOSDOLL
   William 20

BURRELL, BURRILL
   Jonathan 20
   Charles 96

BEATEY
  Joseph 20
BERGER
  Francis 20
BAIRD
  William 21
BLOOM
  Peter 21
BARCLAY
  Samuel 21
BACHE
  William 21
BRUNDAGE
  Elizabeth 22
BENJAMIN
  Huldah 23
  Emeline 32
BUCKLE
  William 23
BEACH
  Esther 23
BOARD
  Nancy 24
  Ann 83
BIRDSLEY
  John W. 24
  Lina 24
  Mary 63
  Zina 63
BEARDSLEY
  Zebina 88
  John 90
  Mary 93
BURDSIEL
  Hiram 31
BEDFORD
  Susan 25
  ——— 32
  Sally Jane 35
  Huldah 67
  Benjn. 67
  Mrs. 97
BALDWIN
  Frances 25
  Elizabeth 60, 76

  Daniel 61, 75, 129
  Zechariah 79
  Eliza 129
BLAKELY
  Robert 25, 86
BURNHAM
  Joshua 26
BOAK
  Robert 26, 54
  John 28, 61, 76, 91, 136
  Thomas 29, 62, 75
  Mary 54, 91, 136
  Letitia 56, 76
  Jean 63, 75
  Sheba 80
  Julia 136
BARNUM
  David 27, 33, 84
  Lockwood 30
BANKER
  Isaac 28, 144
  James 32, 94
  Philander 34, 41, 70, 144
  Abraham 34
  Derick B. 34
  Angeline 41
  Daniel 41, 42, 46
  Hannah 41, 82
  Thaddeus 42
  Harriot 70
  Phebe 87
  John 87
  Benjm. F. 144
  Anna L. 144
  Mrs. 36, 96
BARBER
  Margaret 28
  John 132
BUGSBY
  Henry 29
BRAUSTEAD
  Juliet 29
BENEDICT
  Eli Starr 29
  Anna 84
  Smith 84
BARNES
  John 30

BOARDMAN
  Elijah 31
BRUSH
  Daniel 31
BROOKS
  Joseph 31
  Margaret 35, 36
  Hannah 101
BAYARD
  George 32
BLAIN
  Catherine 35
BLOCK
  Mary 35
BUGY
  Joseph 36
BARNETT
  Sarah 103
BATEMAN
  Theophilus 103
  John 103
BIRNEY
  Joseph 103
  William 103
  Abigail 103
BOSTWICK, BORTHICK, BATHRICK
  Samuel 36, 57, 77
BOWERS
  Isaac 59, 67, 90, 90, 93, 130, 140
  Sarah 67, 140
  Ebenezer 129
BURNETT, BURNET
  Daniel 54
  Rebeckah 102, 104, 107
BARKMAN
  Charles E. 47
BABCOOK
  Carrie 46
BEEBE
  Robert 39
BABBITT
  Charles C. 44
BEYEA
  Samuel 40, 70, 78, 143

  Archibald 42
  Mary 66, 146
  Sarah 70, 144
  Phebe 70, 78, 144
BARRETT
  Caroline 42
BLACK
  James T. 37
  Mary 63, 142
BARR
  John I. 41
BRIEN
  William 42
BALCOM
  Charles E. 43
BRINK
  Mrs. A. H. 47
  A. J. 47
BOWENS
  Ebenezer 57
BALE
  Jane 59
  Amzi L. 59
BOGUE
  Archibald 60, 88
BASURE
  Archd. 76
BADGER
  Jane 63
BIGARD
  Maxwell 69
  Rebecca 69
BOGART
  Jane 75
BROSS
  S. D. 72
BRANNON
  Charles 79
BEEKWITH
  Isaac J. 80
BRASTED
  James 82
BAGO
  Rachel 84

BOUNTY
   Dinah 87
BENTON
   Albert 29, 89
BRENTNEL
   John 95
BOND
   Jane An 95
BARRANS, BARRAN
   Mary 101
   Thomas 101, 102, 104
   Jane 101
   Jean 102
   John 104
   Agnes 102
BOYD
   Samuel 15, 110, 112
   Nathaniel 20
   John 24
   Mehitable 50
   Joshua 110
   Mary 112
BODEL, BODLE, BOODLE
   Alexander 9, 108, 112, 126
   Samuel 9, 106
   Snzannah 22, 100
   John 22, 107
   William 22, 53, 53, 72, 72, 78, 100, 103, 107, 109, 111, 113, 116, 118, 119, 126
   Mary 25
   Phebe 26, 53, 103
   Jonathan 27, 88, 111
   Adeline 30
   Archibald 30, 38, 146
   Sarah 53, 87, 100, 109, 126
   Fanny 57, 90, 116
   Eliza 67, 140
   Ann C. 72
   Betsey 81
   Nancy 87
   Daniel 106
   Amy 108
   Abraham 112
   Charles 113
   Jesse 118
   James 119
   Loisa 126
BOURLEN
   Tabitha 9, 103
   Patience 102

BOARLAND, BORLAND, BORELAND' BOORLAND
   Charles 11, 50, 109, 111, 115, 116
   Phebe 15
   John 18, 34, 88, 115
   Margaret 23, 109
   Dolly 23
   Rebecka 50, 94
   Elizabeth 53
   Thomas 53, 53, 96
   Abigail 56, 78
   Sophonia 58, 76
   Tabitha 83, 108, 116
   Patience 114
BENNET, BENNETT
   Abraham 15
   Mary 20, 146
   Jonathan 20
   William 20, 41, 42, 47, 85
   Maria 28
   Moses D. 28
   Gabriel 31, 39, 40, 96, 146
   Cornelia 32
   Eliza 38
   Abbe A. 43
   Sarah J. 44
   Schuyler 80
   Horace 89, 94
   Virgil 96
BROWN
   Joana 11, 114, 116, 119
   Elizabeth 13
   Nail 14
   Abigail 14
   Fanny 15
   Jane 16, 125
   Joshuah 16, 52, 113, 123, 124, 125
   Mary 18, 45, 52, 56, 81, 125, 125, 125, 127
   Effy 19 114, 117, 117, 119, 121
   James 21, 30, 71, 74, 121, 123, 123
   Alleexander 22
   Eleanor 24
   Joseph 24, 85, 127
   Ila 25
   Susan S. 33
   Amelia J. 35
   William 44, 88, 114, 117
   Frank M. 45
   Noah 46
   Hannah 52, 81, 125
   John 52, 123, 125
   Jo. 54
   Eunice 54

Rebecka 57, 100, 128
Matilda 58, 77, 125
Eliza 65, 74
Margaret 71, 74
Gilbert 79
Neal 83
Isaac 87, 87
Letitia 88
Ann 99
Moses 100
Archibald 100, 102
Thomas 102
Anna 110
Henry W. 113
Samuel W. 114
Joanny 118
Maria 121
Tempe 123
Catherine 123
Daniel S. 124
Stephen 125

BARKER
Sarah 13
Suzannah Milegan 19
John 23, 32, 76
Frances 26
Morris 27
Henry 30, 69, 94, 97
Jane 30
Catherine 30, 63, 75, 134
William 31, 67, 86, 94, 96
Jno. 61
Priscilla 61, 76
Harriet 63, 75, 134
Antionette 69, 143
Mary 92

BUDD, BUD, BUDDE
Mary 12, 82, 86, 110, 110, 113, 136
Juliana 21, 117
John 27, 27, 35, 38, 62, 82, 89, 90, 91, 97, 97, 110, 110, 113, 117, 119, 122, 124, 134, 136, 137, 138, 138, 141
Gilbert 29
Oliver 30, 124, 137
Harriett 36, 38, 136
William 41, 138
Fanny 41, 62, 134, 136, 137, 138, 138, 141
Julia 53, 83
Hannah 57, 119
Rebecca 89
Esther 105, 105

Jonathan H. 136
Juliet 138

BULL
Daniel 12
Charles 16
Thomas 16, 25
Samuel 16
Cadwallader 20
Anna 22
Richard 22
Sarah 25, 79
Hannah 25, 52, 82
Youngs 26
Peter M. 26
Jane 26, 28
Benjamin 27
Sally Jane 30
Lydia Ann 35
Hiram W. 45
John 52
Crisse 52, 70
Elizabeth 52, 80, 85, 127
Agnes 65
James 65, 82
Milicent 81
Dorothy 93
Experience 93

BREWSTER
James 17
Fanny 17
John 22, 52, 58, 84, 84
William 25
Olivia 27, 57 77, 129
David H. 33
Sally M. 56, 58, 76, 78, 129
Lottie 42
Joseph 73, 146
Elizabeth 39
Charlotte 73
Robert 84
Martha 88
Mary 52, 56, 77, 84, 128
Jno. 79

BAILY, BAILEY, BAYLEY, BAELY
Nathaniel 13, 22, 51, 53, 57, 64, 77, 102, 104, 112, 113, 114, 116, 119
Daniel 14, 53, 55, 58, 81, 97, 108, 111, 113, 117, 119, 121
Jonathan 14, 49, 110, 114
Temperance 20
James 21
Margaret 26, 117

John 27, 80, 108
Alexander H. 37
Bethiah 53
Ferdinand 61, 76, 121
Elias 100
Abigail 64, 90, 112
Mary 55, 86, 100, 102
Nathan 112
Samuel 100
Benjamin 112
Esther 104
Oliver 113
Isreal W. 113
Columbus 114
Barkus 116
Eliza 64
Laverna 114

BUTTLER, BUTLER, BUTLAR
Margaret 13, 108, 122, 123, 124
Mary 15
Marion—Miriam 17
Rachel 21
Elizabeth 22, 105
Sarah 30, 55, 78, 126, 127
William A. 38
Jane 48, 55, 87, 99
James 48, 55, 55, 90, 99, 101, 105
Samuel 55, 56, 78, 78, 101, 126, 127
Julia 63, 127
John 99, 127

BALL
Deborah 25
Sarah 26, 132
Frances 27
Milicent 30
Henry 42
John 132
Jane 76, 132, 134, 137
Amzi 76, 132, 134, 137
Hannah 136, 137, 137, 138
Horace 38, 41, 67, 91, 91, 95, 136, 137, 138, 140, 143
Anthony D. 132
Nathaniel C. 132
Joseph E. 137
Mary 134, 136
William W. 137
Elizabeth W. 143
Fannelia 138
H. 36

BOOTH
Jesse 17, 62, 75
Mary 18, 49, 73, 85, 136

Dorothy 20
Sally Maria 28
Alfred 37
John B. 37, 61, 62, 95, 133, 134, 135, 136, 136, 137, 138, 142
Sarah 37, 73, 78, 136
Matilda 43
Lois 48
Jane 56, 78
Harriet 62, 73, 134, 135, 136, 136, 137, 138
Thomas 56, 59, 78, 130, 133
Vincent 43
Ellen 73, 134
Hilah 62, 75
Charles W. 99
Lydia 99
William 99
Rhoda 98, 104
Edwin 135
Catherine 142
Susan A. 138

BRADNER
Mary 13, 38, 54, 72, 133, 138, 143
Christian 14, 74, 108, 111, 114, 117
John 14, 42, 54, 92, 117, 136
Margarett 17, 54
Benjamin 18, 54, 91, 117, 118, 120, 122, 124, 143
Abigail 19
Sarah 19, 42, 57, 133, 135, 135, 136, 143
Thomas 27, 33, 38, 58, 58, 71, 117, 131, 133, 133, 135, 137, 137, 138, 141, 143
Frances 28, 94, 120, 135, 137, 138, 142
Francis 59, 76
William 29, 60, 76, 118, 131, 135, 138, 142
Colvin 28, 133, 135, 136
Colvill 97, 117, 143
Maria 30, 63, 63, 75, 95, 124
Eliza 40, 71, 133
Emily 42
Anne 52
Suzannah 52
Susan 58, 131, 133, 135, 137, 137, 138, 141, 143
Charles 60, 132
Elizabeth 60, 85, 132
James 63, 88
Christianna 67
Harriot 71, 137

Ira 71, 133
Agness 72
Benoi 79
Horace 95, 122, 138
Isaac 117
Lois 135
Henry M. 141
Em'y 142
Mrs. T. J. 46
Jno. 52

CORTWRIGHT, COURTRIGHT,
CORTRIGHT (See Kortright)
  Susanna 9
  Ann 102

CLUFF
  Aulle 10

COOLY, COOLEY
  Unice 9
  Mary 9, 14
  William 10
  Sarah 11
  Anna 11
  Meriam 13
  David 13
  Abigail 14
  Danniel 14
  Esther 16
  Sybile 51
  Beriah 62
  Nathan 85
  Jesse 101
  James K. 103
  Isaac 99, 99, 101, 103

COULY, COULEY
  Mary 11, 17
  Experience 12
  Freegift 15
  Sybilla 19
  Hannah 19, 115
  Andrew 115
  Preserved 115
  Anna 115

COLEMAN
  Abigail 9, 103
  Johanah 10
  Micha 10
  Joseph 11, 98, 98, 124
  Phebe 12
  Sarah 13, 54
  Juliana 16
  Isaac 16
  Richard 20

John 25, 124
Phila 25
Julia 25
Christian 26
Fanny 27, 44
Joel 27
Harriet 28, 124
Ira 28, 68, 74, 140
Mary 43, 124
Alfred W. 46
Lewis E. 39
Roswell C. 42, 43
Anna A. 42
Annie 47
James C. 43, 44
Benjamin 48, 55, 95
Martha 48, 54, 78, 124
Nathan 54, 78, 124
Hannah 55
Eleanor 55
Carpenter 63, 75, 134
Emily 68, 140
Elmira 74
Maria 91
Gideon 81
Hiram 124

CRAWFORD
  Elizabeth 9, 14
  James 12, 102
  Mary 14, 19, 130
  Samuel 15
  Martha 19
  Jane 20, 51, 123
  David 51, 79, 99, 99, 102, 104, 108,
    110, 115, 123, 123
  Gilbert 58, 130
  John 108
  Joseph 110
  Daniel 115
  Nancy 123
  William 80, 104, 130
  Sarah 108
  Mr. 96

COLE
  Hittye 9

COCHRON
  Robert 10

CLEARWATER, CLARE WATER
  Charity 10
  Benjamin 20

CRONS
  Michael 10

CLARK, CLARKE
  Elias 9
  Elizabeth 9, 17
  George 16
  Vincent 17
  David 17
  Anna 18, 115, 117
  Annie 41, 145
  Richard 18
  Thomas 19, 83
  John 23, 37, 145
  Abigail 23, 145
  Julia 27
  Stephen 28
  Abner 28
  Hosea 35
  Harriet 39
  Sally Ann 39
  Sarah N. 41
  Clara W. 42
  Anson 42, 42
  J. Howard 43
  William 45, 82
  Clarissa 63, 136
  Jane 66, 139
  Bernard 71, 144, 145
  Coe 74, 145
  Dennis 82
  Rebecka 83
  Ida Jane 145
  Jesse C. 145
  Widow 80
  Miss. 82

COREY, CORY, CORRY
  Isaac 10
  Gabriel 12
  John 13
  Allexander 15, 54, 88, 111, 123
  Lueiana 16
  Mary 19, 24, 68, 140
  Juliana 22
  Hannah 29, 56, 123
  Fanny 30
  Maria 30, 57, 123, 130, 137
  Zube 34
  Oliver D. 37
  Patience 48
  Azuba 56, 123
  Catherine 56, 123
  Benjamin 56, 77, 123
  Eunice 58, 130
  Sarah 59, 71, 76, 78, 131, 132
  Amira 66, 94, 139
  Fanelia 67
  Lemuel 68, 140
  Charlotte 71, 132
  William 71, 77, 78, 131
  Abigail 77
  Thurston 93
  Martha 93
  Elizabeth 111
  Ann Maria 131
  Phebe A. 131
  Colvin 59, 131
  Calvin 62, 71, 75, 76, 132, 134

CHANDLER
  Hannah 10
  John 11, 100
  Samuel 12
  Charles 28
  Mary 100
  Sarah 100
  Lydia 102

CORNWALL
  Mary 10

CHAPMAN
  Syble 10
  Asa 13

COYKENDALL
  ———— 11

CULP
  Catherine 11

CARY
  Elizabeth 12
  Adam I, 70

CHRIST (See Crist)
  Catherine 12
  Martha 95
  P. 95

CRIST (See Christ)
  Philip 34, 35
  Mary 35
  Rufus 84

CONNEL, CONNELL
  Gabriel 12
  Jennie 46

CLINTOCK
  Mary 12

CAMPBEL, CAMPBELL, CAMBLE, CAMPBLE
  Edward 12, 93
  Mary 12, 20

James 19
Margarett 22
COX
  Reeves 12
  Catherine 12, 65, 139
  Bridget 45, 73, 139
  Hezekiah 65, 130

CODDINGTON, CODINGTON
  Joseph 13, 16
  Mary 20
  Benjamin 51, 144
  Platt 114

CRAIG
  Francis 15
  James J. 29

CRANE
  Stephen 13, 53, 78
  Willam 17, 91
  Sarah 18, 140
  Benjamin 19, 25, 67, 80, 86
  Affai 21
  Mary 21, 91, 141
  John 27, 29, 34, 38, 40, 55, 66, 89, 90, 94, 101, 126, 140
  Floyd 40, 41, 43, 44, 46
  Melissa 46, 74
  Abigail 55, 126
  Horace 64, 75, 141
  Eve 67
  Frances 71, 137, 140
  Philip 86
  Betsey 86
  Lydia 101
  Peggy 101
  Florence M. 137
  Ira S. 140
  Albert G. 140
  Nancy M. 141
  Oliver 142

CARMEN, CARMAN
  Elizabeth 14
  Thomas 79

CONNELLY, CONNELY, CONOLY
  Hugh 14
  Constantine 31, 94
  Constant 69, 96, 142
  Rachel 69, 96, 142

CARROWAY
  Suzanah 14

CORWIN, CORWINE
  Eli 14, 90
  Permela 17
  Nathan H. 28
  Samuel H. 34
  Jason 39, 42, 44, 47
  J. Wells 44
  Hannah 53, 85
  George 51, 118
  Mehitable 51
  Daniel 53, 54, 92, 123
  Adeline A. 67
  Sally 74
  Phebe 59, 77, 131
  Gabriel S. 123

COOPER
  Esther 15
  Christian Eliza 21
  Mary 21
  Jonah 30
  John 40, 42, 45
  Thomas 51
  Stephen 94

CUNNINGHAM
  Archibald 15
  Thomas 20
  Jane 23
  John 27
  Wid. Maria 29

CURTIS, CURTICE
  Thomas 16, 52
  Elizabeth 18
  Pamelia 61, 76, 133
  Charity 99
  Noah 99, 101
  Keziah 99
  Suzannah 101

COOKE, COOK
  William 16
  John 20
  Hannah 21
  Richard 45
  Abigail 64

COMSTOCK
  Ann 16
  Elisha 19
  Stephen 72, 74

CARMICHAL
  John 16

CRANCE, CRANSE
  Suzanah 17
  Elizabeth 17

Obediah 71
Gabriel 118
William 118, 118
Temperance 118

CONLY
Abby 17

CLEVELAND
Benjamin 18

CARR
Catherine 18
George 22, 81
William 26
Sarah 37
Robert 45

CARNAGEN
Margaret 18

CALDWELL
Thomas 18, 52, 120, 122, 123
Mary 21
Martha 21
William W. 29
Elizabeth 52
Margaret 52
James 52, 79, 123
Asa 120
Oliver E. 122

COPSE
Abigail 18

CUTTER
Ebenezer 18

CLANCY
Jane 73

COURTNEY
Francis 19

CLEMENT
Sarah 20

CONNER, CONNERS, CONNOR
Charles 20
William 22
Julia 28
Dolly 28
Elizabeth 27, 133
Jared 30
John 38, 82, 133
Sally 33, 66, 80, 133
Virgil 133
James 96

George W. 33, 68, 94, 141
Hilah Ann 133

CROCKER
Jesse 20

CARMER
Thomas 22, 54, 124
Mary 54
Sarah Ann 124
Hester O. 124

CLEARMAN
James 23

CONGER
David 23
Abigail 23

CROSBY
Joshua 24
Jacob 30
J. B. 46

CROWELL
Sarah 24
Timothy 56, 78, 82, 82, 130, 132, 133, 135, 136
Maria 56, 130, 132, 133, 135, 136
William 82
Samuel 87
Edward O. 130
John W. 132
Robert 133
Mary Ann 135
Frances 136

COWDREY
Col. John 25

CRABTREE
Margaret 27
Betsey 27
Harriet 31
Clarissa 32
Huldah 82
Sarah 93

CLASON, CLASSON
Mary 27, 55, 127, 128
James 55, 126, 126, 128, 131, 133
Abigail 55, 126, 126, 128, 131
Samuel 55, 56, 65, 127, 127
Isaac L. 126
Henry P. 126
Eliza 127
William 127
Alanson 127

Anna F. 127
Michael B. 133
George 131

COULTER
  Benjamin 31

CLEVES
  Julia 27
  Thomas 81

CLINTON
  Charles 32

CABREY
  Phebe Ann 34
  Jane 68
  John 68

CARP
  Samuel 34

COLWELL
  Mrs. Sally 35

CRANS
  George 35, 41, 41, 70, 70, 73, 145
  John S. 37
  Letitia 51
  Wilhelmus 51
  Synthia 70
  Moses B. 72
  Ann E. 73, 145

CASTLE
  George 36

CARTERS
  Mary 38

CASTERLING
  Mary 38

COURTIER
  Isabella 40
  David 40

CHEBEE
  Mr. and Mrs. 36

CHEEVE
  Maria 66, 139, 139, 140
  James 66, 90, 92, 139, 139, 140
  Mary J. 139
  Charlotte 139
  William H. 139
  Harriet L. 139

COLLEY
  Patty 83
  Nathan 87

COAN
  Michael 40

CRONK
  Ellen 40

CARSON
  Samuel 41
  Ann 41

CLISSOLD
  Edward 41

CONDIT
  Emeline 66

CROSS
  Adam G. 69

CLAWSON
  John 72
  Abigail 78
  Samuel 78, 78
  James 78
  Mary 78

CURREN, CURRIN
  David 98, 98
  Elizabeth 116
  Mehatable 116
  Moses 116
  John 116

CALKIN
  Abigail 98

COLT
  Hannah 98

CRISZER
  Mary 99

COE
  Moses 104
  Sarah 104
  Ann 104
  Benjamin 104

COMFORT
  Daniel 121
  Elioner 121

CASMER
  Jacob 125
  Thomas 125
  Mary 125

CRUTTENDON
  Maria 60

CONDON
   Harry J. E. 46

COYLE
   Libby 46

CARLING
   Alfred 44

CASSADY
   Marrietta 47

CHRISTMAN
   Uphila J. 44

CHEESEMAN
   Jane E. 43

CONNING
   George 44

CUDDEBACK
   Augusta T. 45

CORNING
   Sarah 56
   Wm. 56

CULLEN
   Joanna 44

CHRISTIE, CRISTIE
   Fannie 45
   Andrew 112, 114
   Abigail 112
   Gilbert 114

CHAMPION
   B. R. 46

CASE
   Amy 9, 49, 104
   Zacceus & Zacheus 11, 87, 106, 108, 110, 116
   David 11, 26, 53, 63, 65, 68, 85, 93, 106, 108, 110, 115, 115, 117, 119, 121, 122
   Elizabeth 13, 87, 96, 105, 122
   Danniel 13, 24, 38, 67, 85, 106, 140
   Jesse 13, 37, 144
   Joshuah 16, 83
   Hephzibal 17
   Enos 18, 21, 115, 118
   Eneas 117
   Joseph 20, 37, 105, 105, 108
   Helen 24, 122
   Julander 26
   Charlotte 26
   Delia 26
   William 26, 62, 75
   Wheeler 28, 93, 94
   Peggy 28
   Benjamin 26, 116
   Catherine 29, 72
   Usher 34, 64, 121
   Nathl. L. 37
   Keziah 28
   Olive 28, 121
   Maria 30, 119
   Phebe C. 38, 72, 118
   Mary 35, 53, 67, 91, 97, **106, 121,** 140
   Kitty 61, 76, 121
   Jane 62, 75
   Abigail 63, 121
   Eunice 63
   Deziah 54
   Julia 67, 68, 140
   Margaret E. 72
   Caroline 73, 145
   Birdsey 83, 88, 110
   Phinehas 82, 121
   Charles C. 82
   John 85, 104, 105, 108, 110
   Wilmot 88
   Hannah 88, 106, 108
   George 88, 135
   Patience 91
   Evelina 92
   Virgil R. 94
   Isaac 104
   Esther 105, 108
   Sarah 105, 115
   Julianah 108
   Gideon 110
   Abner 117
   Ann 118
   Sally 121
   Robert Mc. 122
   Eliza 122

CONKLING, CONKLIN, CONCKLIN
   Daniel 10, 31, 50, 110, 111, 113, 115, 116, 118, 119, 120, 122, 133
   Francess 12, 39, 146
   Nathaniel 17, 26, 38, 39, 44, 53, 53, 54, 59, 81, 83, 86, 95, 124, 131
   Mary 19, 58, 89, 99, 104, 118
   John 20, 99
   Joseph 20, 21, 31, 59, 84, 95, 99, 102, 104, 107, 110, 110, 114, 116
   Elizabeth 21, 23, 117, 124
   Helen 21, 90
   Bathia 22, 53, 87

Julia 25
Ruth 25
Margaret 25, 54, 86, 124
Nancy 29, 56, 128
Hannah 30, 79, 109, 116, 133
Martha 31, 53, 84, 85
William 32, 128
Enos 32, 88, 128
Henry 39, 62, 75, 134
Fanny 40, 116
Ely S. 44
Benjamin 51, 53, 59, 80, 109, 130, 133, 134
Harriet 34, 38, 133, 146
George 40, 128
James 46
Joshua 56, 63, 88, 97, 128
Eleanor 59
Mehitable 59, 93, 130, 133, 134
Sarah 63, 133
David 82, 83, 109
Lucretia 84, 107
Deborah 59, 131
Samuel 102
Julianah 110, 115
Abigail 111
Solomon 113
Sylvester 116
Hiram 119
Sally 120, 128
Suzannah 120
Anne 124
Christian 124
Morris G. 133
Walter 134

CARPENTER
James 9, 23, 54, 84, 97, 102, 118, 118
Moses 9, 99, 108
William 9, 105, 106, 108, 110, 138
Samuel 9, 49, 99, 100, 106, 109, 110, 110
Michael 9, 53, 55, 78, 125
John 10, 22, 56, 77, 94, 94, 99, 100, 102, 103, 114, 119, 119
Ruth 10, 11, 20, 103
Rhoda 11, 107
Carman 11
Mary 11, 23, 48, 54, 60, 87, 107, 107, 110, 118, 119, 133, 142, 143
Elinor 11, 53, 55, 92, 100, 103, 125
Keziah 12
Benjamin 12, 21, 50, 53, 55, 80, 92, 102, 105, 107, 108, 110, 119, 119, 121, 123

Elizabeth 13, 16, 17, 21, 52, 66, 99, 99, 99, 99, 100
Isaac 13, 110, 119
Nehemiah 13, 49, 56, 66, 125, 142
Suzannah 13, 50, 51, 103, 107, 119, 123
Jesse 13, 103, 116, 116
Martha 15
Waight 17
Priscilla 18, 49
Unice 18, 110
Eunice 55
Sarah 18, 36, 39, 50, 61, 70, 99, 99, 103, 108, 116, 119, 123, 125, 143, 146
Hannah 11, 19, 57, 77, 79, 103, 106, 108, 110, 111, 116
Rebekah 19
Louis 21
Dorothy 22
Amelia 24
Daniel 25, 39, 45, 70, 82, 88, 103, 103, 104, 107, 143
Nathaniel 25, 102, 107
Horace 27
Frances 27, 100
Noah 36, 54, 63, 78, 96, 102, 102, 104, 107, 110, 137, 138, 141, 142, 143
Abigail 49, 50, 100, 119
Gilbert 49, 107, 108, 110
Richard 49
Lydia 50, 81
Solomon 25, 51, 55, 70, 78, 93, 127, 127
Dolly 53, 85, 125, 127
Phebe 55, 78, 101, 127, 127
Emeline 62, 87, 127
Robert 70, 104
Susan 70, 80
Harriet 73, 145
Mercy 84
Jane 94
Catherine 94
Colvill 99, 99, 101, 103
Margaret 99, 109, 142
Joseph 102, 102, 103, 104, 105, 116
Jemy 105
Charity 107
Clarissa 116
Fanny 118
Temperance 119
Scynthia 119
Anthony 114, 120
George 120

Edward E. 137
Virgil C. 141

DAINS, DANES
  Abigail 9
  Mary 9
  Danniel 11
  John 13
  Martha 14
  David 15
  Elizabeth 23

DEANS, DEAN
  Tabitha 10
  Johannah 12
  David 86
  Hannah 86
  Amanda 93

DENN
  Daniel 12

DECKER
  Temperance 9
  Jemima 12
  Martin 16
  Mary 21
  Cornelius 21
  John 25, 77, 132
  Jonah 28
  Benjamin 30
  Isaac 38
  Sarah J. 46
  Margaret 59, 77, 131
  Lucas 67, 74
  Jane 92, 132
  Rebeckah 86
  Susan 86, 132
  Jacob 59, 131
  Peggy 132, 132
  Thomas 132
  William H. 132
  Jack 83

DE FREES
  James 9

DARBY
  Nancy 9
  Armanda 138

DUGLASS, DOUGLAS
  Wm. 11
  Adam 83

DUN, DUNN
  Hannah 11
  Sally 31

DOUGHERTY
  Rebeckah 11
  Ann 29, 60, 76
  John 86
  Quinton 87
  Daniel 93

DOUGHTY
  Lizzie B. 41
  Sarah A. 44

DOLSON, DOLSEN
  James 12
  Frederick 24, 55, 126, 128, 128
  Theophilus 35, 56, 78, 86, 128, 128
  Margaret 55, 126, 128
  Leana 56
  Lina 78
  Phebe 80
  Liava 128
  Aaron A. 128
  Ellen 128
  Henry W. 128
  Emeline 128
  Elizabeth 128
  Mrs. L. 140

DORSON
  Deborah 14

DENNY
  Phebe 15

DOBBINS
  Anthony 15, 24, 83, 85

DILL
  John 16

DODGE
  Mary 65, 138

DE CAMP
  Maria 67
  John 67

DOYLE
  James 16

DOLPH
  Robert 17

DEVOE
  Mary 17

DIER
  Susannah 18

DURLAND
  Rozanah 18
  Phebe A. 44

DOTY
   Samuel 19

DeKAY, DECAY
   Jacob 19
   Fanny 20
   Christian 21
   Hannah 22
   Margaret 23
   Horace S. 36
   James 57, 63, 77, 129
   Julia 63
   Jacobus 80
   Mary 101

DURYEA, DURYEE
   Hannah 21, 100, 101, 101
   Hilah 22
   Martha 23
   Henry 31, 36, 40, 71
   Eliza 31, 31
   Sarah 33
   Tillah 39
   Alpheus 40
   Cornelia 40
   Nancy 68, 74
   Garritt 88
   Yores 100
   George 100, 101

DAY
   Elizabeth 21

DICKY
   John 22

DAVY
   Jonathan 30

DUSENBURY, DUSENBERRY
   Samuel 30
   William 30, 33, 34
   Sarah 33
   Daniel 33
   Zeno 34
   Theodore 39

DOOLITTLE
   Charles 30
   Joseph 52
   Abigail 52

DOWNIE
   James 39

DELANCEY, DELANCY
   Bridget 40
   Mary 41

   James 42
   John 88

DOUGALL
   Susan M. 42

DALY, DALLEY
   Joseph H. 43
   Mary A. 43

DONNELLY
   Johanna 43

DUER
   John 25, 80, 84, 85
   Mrs. 43

DENNISTON
   George 46, 47

DYKEMAN, DIKEMAN
   Ed. 45
   Carrie M. 46

DUTCHER
   Arthur M. 45

DEWITT
   Mary E. 47

DUNDY
   Margaret 44

DALTON
   Katie 46

DE HART
   Sarah A. 45

DELAVAN
   Newton K. 45

DEMAREST
   James 47

DAVIDSON
   Maria 68

DUBOIS
   Hannah 81

DUNLAP
   Abraham 82

DILLEN, DILLON
   Sally 84
   David 92, 95
   Mary 95

DENER
   ——— 87

DUNING, DUNNING
  Deborah 9
  Isaac 10
  James 10, 54 54, 82, 97, 105
  Mary 12, 22, 54, 58, 61, 77, 85, 88, 106, 129, 133
  Phebe 13, 59, 76, 130
  Lois 13
  Elzabeth 13, 21, 21, 67, 121
  Ebenezer 14, 54
  Keturah 14
  Hannah 14
  Sarah 15, 23, 42, 54, 93, 146
  Eleoner 18
  Juliana 20
  Margaret 21, 86, 103
  Samuel 21, 85, 94, 100, 103, 106, 109, 113, 117, 118
  Abraham 21
  Fanny 22, 124
  Abijah 24
  David 25
  Festus 26
  Gabriel 28 57, 77
  Emily 28
  Charlotte 25, 124
  Maria 26, 124
  Asa 26, 27, 30, 97, 133, 146
  Jane 27, 124
  Sheba Ann 29
  Jonathan 30, 120, 121
  Lewis 31, 124
  Hamilton 32
  Charles T. 43
  Martha 54, 56, 91, 124, 128
  Jno. 56
  John 128
  Timothy 54, 89, 102, 105, 107
  Horace 67, 140
  George 67, 67, 74, 93, 140
  Nathaniel H. 95
  Betsey 100
  Phanah 102
  Oliver 107
  Catharine 109
  Anna 113
  Andrew 117
  Abner 117
  Moses 120
  Absalom 121
  Frances 123
  William K. 133
  Agnes 146

DRAKE
  Ruth 10, 106
  James 11
  Mary 11
  Hannah 14
  Elizabeth 15, 43
  Benjamin 15
  Samuel 18
  Curtice 18
  Jonathan 21
  Francis 22
  Eliza 26
  Clarissa 28
  Abigail 29, 48
  Antoniette 30
  Emily 30
  Wid. Ann 31
  John L. 44
  Sarah 60
  Jermiah 60, 95
  Lavinia E. 70
  Joseph 79
  Nathaniel J. 84
  Rufus 91

DENTON
  Martha 11
  James 12, 28, 92, 106
  Mary 14, 17, 22, 32, 58, 77, 105, 112, 114, 131
  John 14, 77, 80, 90, 102, 102, 105
  Joseph 14, 25, 26, 95, 108, 110, 114
  Samuel 15, 35, 105, 112, 116
  Hannah 16, 20, 96
  Jacob 18
  Sarah 19, 28, 28, 38, 46, 57, 102, 129, 145
  Henry 20, 34, 55, 80, 127
  Nehemiah 21, 33, 56, 82, 83, 128, 131
  Jane 23, 93
  Thomas 25, 91, 102, 109
  Catherine 28
  Elizabeth 28, 29, 57, 69, 102, 143, 146
  Theodorus 28, 69
  Hezekiah 30, 66, 93
  Michael 32, 34, 131
  William 34, 38, 96, 131
  Richard 35, 59, 84, 130, 131
  Julia 55, 89, 127
  Lois 56, 128, 131
  Cornelia 59, 76
  Corelia 130
  Dolly 62

Adelaide 64, 65, 137, 141
Frances 65, 138
Christian 66
Solomon 66, 131
Esther 67
Eliza 68, 137
Horace 69, 137, 141, 143
Abigail 69, 105, 123, 142
Christiana 74, 139
Adeline 75
Anthony 81, 108
Benj'm. 92
Lewis 93
Gabriel 106
Gilbert 109, 131
Phebe Maria 110
Isaac 112
Harry 114
Nathaniel R. 116
Sally Ann 131
Ezra F. 131
Edward W. 141
Caroline 141
Theodore 143
Mrs. 81
Jno. 58

DAVIES (See Davis)
   Elizabeth 10, 19, 107
   Richard 12
   Elsy 15
   Andrew 17
   Juliana 17
   Peter 17
   Christian 106
   Joshua 106, 110, 120
   Sarah 110
   Theresa 120

DAVIS (See Davies)
   Charity 29
   Jewett 40
   Hannah 48
   Joshua 52, 79, 103, 112
   Azubah 54, 103
   Ruth 87
   Levene 112

EVERETT
   James 9, 28, 53, 83, 86
   John 10, 17, 29
   Daniel 10, 48, 84
   Julianah 19, 53, 106
   Sarah 22, 87, 145
   Mary 23
   Benjamin 24, 106

William 28, 35, 37
Charles J. 42
Frank G. 46
Ephriam 48, 106, 106, 111, 111
Elizabeth 48, 85
Cornelia 87
Phebe 103, 118
Walter 106
Lydia 106
Hephzibah 106
Freelove 111
David 111

ENSIGHN, ENSIGN (See Insign)
   James 11, 99
   Osman 99
   Ruth 105

ELMER
   William 11, 52, 53, 84, 113
   Michael A. 23
   Horace 24
   Mary 53, 80, 87, 113
   Phillis 93
   Nancy 121

EVERSON
   Abigail 11

EVERTSON
   George 28

ELLIOTT, ELIOT, ELLIOT
   Mary 26
   Sarah 28, 59, 72, 77, 78, 143, 144
   Elizabeth 30, 60, 76
   Horace 32, 94, 143
   Frances M. 32
   Henry W. 37, 78
   Ethelinda 37, 60, 92
   Charles 39, 47
   William 60, 92
   Charlotte 60, 70, 73, 76, 143
   Benjamin 88
   Hannah 107, 117
   W. H. 70, 144
   H. W. 32, 72

EVANS
   Elizabeth 12
   Mary 65, 139
   Thomas 65, 92, 139
   John 102
   William 102
   Ann 102
   James S. 139

ELLISON
   Ann 48

ELLIS
   Deborah 12
   Lucy 13
   Sarah 66
   William 66
   Mary 71
   Joseph 71
   James 84, 84
   David H. 92

EAGER
   Lydia 13, 119, 120
   William 15, 16
   Martha 17, 18
   James 17
   Edward 19
   Ann 19
   Sarah 20, 37
   Jason 20
   Easter 21
   John 26
   Elsa 27
   Agnes 68
   Thomas 82

EATEN, EATON
   Allexander 13
   Eliza 39
   James M. 39

ERWINTON
   Suzannah 17

EGBERT
   John 29, 61, 75, 126
   Mary 29, 126
   Rachael 31, 61, 75, 126
   Juliet 32, 126
   Phebe 55, 125, 126
   James 55, 79, 125, 126
   Eliza Ann 126

EARLES, EARL
   Rachel 18
   John 42
   Isaac T. 46

ELDRED
   Sarah 21
   Sussanah 22
   Everet 22
   Mary 26, 124
   Mary Ann 28, 59, 76

EDMONSON
   David 21

ESTILL, ESTELL
   Jonathan 21
   Eliza 30

ELY
   Edward 25, 90

EDSALL
   Julia 29
   Hannah 29, 129
   Almeda 33
   Selah 33
   Seely 37
   J. Seely 43
   Mary 56, 67, 83, 96, 128, 129
   William 56, 96, 128, 129
   Thomas 83, 146
   James 94
   Phebe Ann 146

EGILES
   Mary 35

EDWARDS
   Ogden Jr. 38

ESCHELMAN
   James R. 46

ECKERT
   Addie L. 46

EGERTON
   ——— 88

ELEMS, ELMS
   Elizabeth 106, 108, 110

FINCH
   Solomon 9, 53
   Christian 10
   Rhoda 11
   Samuel 13, 107
   Mary 16
   Keziah 17, 20
   Allison 17
   James 19
   John 21, 48, 107
   Deborah 53, 85
   Ruth 99

FOSTER
   Albert 9, 53, 91, 103, 105, 118
   Mary 10
   James 11, 61, 96, 134

William 23, 36, 56, 85, 103, 146
Hannah 23, 105
Abigail 24, 105, 118, 132
Daniel 24, 57, 118, 118, 132, 136, 139
Annis 25
Caroline 31
Samuel 35
Abby Jane 35
Phebe 56
Sally 57, 78, 132, 136
Elizabeth 84
Eliza Ann 132
Charles B. 132
George A. 132
Charity 136
Sarah D. 139
——— 97

FORGUSON, FORGERSON, FURGURSON, FERGUSON
James 10
Millicent 17, 114
Richard G. 17
Allexander 18
Amelia A. 38
Stauts 60
Stewart 76
Robert 98
Nancy 98

FELLER
Tobias 10

FAULKENER
John 11
William 17
Letty 24
Charles W. 47

FARRIER
Esther 11

FULLER
Phebe 11
Jepthah 13
Jedediah 14

FRY, FRYE, FRAY
Abiel 15, 51, 79, 109, 111, 113, 115
Charles 109
Abigail 109, 113, 115
Henry L. 111
Alfred 113

FALLS, FALL
William 15

Betsey 83
Sarah 97

FORSYTHE
Anna 15

FAIRCHILD
Eleazar 16
Amy 52

FRANKLIN
Elizabeth 16

FORT
Hannah 16

FLEMING
George 17

FOULPROUCK
Chaunrod 17

FARNAM
Sarah 19

FREEMAN
Jonathan 20
Robert 37
Mrs. 51

FELTMAN
Jane 20

FRENCH
John 21

FERRIS, FARRIS
Diantha 21
Lydia 59, 76, 131, 131
Rainsford A. 59, 131, 131
Reynsford A. 76
Prudence E. 131

FREEDINBURGH
Hezekiah 21

FULLERTON
Daniel 22, 42
Angeline 42

FARRAND, FERRAND, FERRAN
David 27
Hiram 37, 39, 39
Ann 146
Albert S. 147
D. R. 146

FINN
Robert 29
Mary W. 32

FITZGERALD
   Sidney S. 30
   John 45, 73, 145
FIELDS
   Fanny 30
FISK
   Ezra 26, 27, 33, 56, 95
   Harriett 31, 62
   Esther 56, 67, 74
   Anna 56, 77, 128
   Susanna 59, 67, 128
   Jonathan 59, 67, 74, 77, 142
   Diannah 70
   Susan 77
   Simon 97
   Henry W. 142
FISHER
   Eve 35
FURMAN
   Mary Ann 38
FAUCON
   Maurice 39
FREELIGH
   Carrie A. 40
FALIN
   Julia 40
FORTNER
   Eunice 42
FORCHEE
   Rufus 45
FARRELL
   Maggie 46
FLETCHER
   Jennie E. 46
   Emma 46
FINK
   Mary 65
   Alexander H. 65
   Herman 89
FOX
   Huldah 81
FINDLEY
   James 87
FULTON
   Anna 111, 113
   Phebe 121
FITT
   Sarah 123

GREEN
   Elizabeth 9
   John 9, 61, 76, 133
   Isreal 13
   Joshua 23
   Maria 24
   Asaph L. 39
   George W. 44
   Deborah 53, 84
   James 53, 59, 76, 84
   Mary 57, 71, 77, 135
   Orange 57, 77, 135
   Emeline 135
   Mehitable 135
GOBLE
   Benjamin 9
   Thomas 24, 60, 76, 86, 131, 133, 136, 137, 138
   Selah S. 29
   Clarrisa 31, 31, 133
   Maria 60, 76, 131, 133, 136, 137, 138
   Dolly M. 76
   Morris G. 133
   Daniel W. 133
   Samuel S. 136
   Mary Maria 133
   Elizabeth 137
   James A. 138
   G. B. 76
GRIFFEN, GRIFFIN
   Ebenezer 12
   Mary 17
   Elizabeth 23
   Letitia 29
   Jane 43
   Emma C. 47
   Pierre 90
GILES, GILLIS, GILIS
   Charles 12
   Elizabeth 15
   Hannah 16
   Jennet 55
   Mary 69, 142
   John 69, 96
   Jane 95
GLASPAY, GALLISPAY, GALLASPY, GALLESPY, GALASPY, GILLISPIE, GELLISPY, GILLESPY
   David 12, 112
   Margarett 15
   Joseph 17

John 19, 25, 31, 141
Sarah 20, 145
Elizabeth 21
Harriet 62, 141, 145
Mary 73, 141
William 112
James 141

GOLDSMITH, GOOLDSMITH
  Elizabeth 11, 30, 62, 73, 75, 145
  Caleb 11, 16
  Mary 13, 18, 24, 35, 37, 73, 145
  Elisha 15, 80, 87, 127
  Benjamin 18
  Patience 21
  Stephen 22
  Thomas 25
  Gabriel 26, 35, 73
  Joshua 29, 55, 56, 62, 97, 125, 127, 128, 134, 134
  Francis 31
  Melinda 35, 62, 125
  Susan H. 37
  Keziah 37
  Harriet 38, 73, 145
  Louis 41
  Deborah 55, 65, 93, 95, 125, 127, 138
  Hudson 57, 77, 125
  Selah 57, 125
  William 62, 93, 131, 134, 134
  Henietta 62, 134
  Hilah 57, 77, 131, 134
  Prudence 62
  Increase 65, 138
  Adeline 73, 145
  Julia 73, 145
  Abigail 102
  Eliza 125
  James G. 131

GARRISSON
  Abigail 12

GERSHIMER
  George 13

GODFRY
  Mary 13

GREAG, GREGG
  Hugh 14, 60, 76
  John 25, 59, 94, 96, 130, 130, 132, 136
  Susan 38, 69, 130
  James 38, 39, 130
  Martha 59

Jane 60, 76
Silvester 61, 75, 134
Margaret 94, 96, 130, 132, 136
Elizabeth C. 130
Frances A. 136

GARNER
  Jesse 15

GARDNER, GARDINER
  Samuel 16
  Hannah 17, 28, 32, 114
  Mary 18, 24, 147
  James 29, 146, 147
  Phebe 29
  Frances A. 37
  Eliza J. 62
  Lois 86
  Dublin 94, 95
  Elizabeth J. 134
  Adeline 146, 147
  Albert F. 146
  William J. 146
  Julia Ann 146
  Alexander J. 147

GIDNEY
  William 15

GRAHAM, GRAHAN, GORHAM
  William 15, 84, 114
  Mary 17
  Richard 22, 51
  Jane 25
  Mehitable 27
  Christopher C. 33
  Phillip 45
  Ann 51
  Frances 74
  Sarah 114
  Margaret 114

GALAWAY, GALLOWAY
  Elizabeth 16
  Leah 19
  George 20

GOLD
  John 17

GARY, GAREY, GERREY, GARRY
  Anna 17
  Benjamin 20
  Elizabeth 20
  Stewart 21

GILCHRIST
  Agness 20

John 19, 25, 31, 141
Sarah 20, 145
Elizabeth 21
Harriet 62, 141, 145
Mary 73, 141
William 112
James 141

GOLDSMITH, GOOLDSMITH
Elizabeth 11, 30, 62, 73, 75, 145
Caleb 11, 16
Mary 13, 18, 24, 35, 37, 73, 145
Elisha 15, 80, 87, 127
Benjamin 18
Patience 21
Stephen 22
Thomas 25
Gabriel 26, 35, 73
Joshua 29, 55, 56, 62, 97, 125, 127, 128, 134, 134
Francis 31
Melinda 35, 62, 125
Susan H. 37
Keziah 37
Harriet 38, 73, 145
Louis 41
Deborah 55, 65, 93, 95, 125, 127, 138
Hudson 57, 77, 125
Selah 57, 125
William 62, 93, 131, 134, 134
Henietta 62, 134
Hilah 57, 77, 131, 134
Prudence 62
Increase 65, 138
Adeline 73, 145
Julia 73, 145
Abigail 102
Eliza 125
James G. 131

GARRISSON
Abigail 12

GERSHIMER
George 13

GODFRY
Mary 13

GREAG, GREGG
Hugh 14, 60, 76
John 25, 59, 94, 96, 130, 130, 132, 136
Susan 38, 69, 130
James 38, 39, 130
Martha 59

Jane 60, 76
Silvester 61, 75, 134
Margaret 94, 96, 130, 132, 136
Elizabeth C. 130
Frances A. 136

GARNER
Jesse 15

GARDNER, GARDINER
Samuel 16
Hannah 17, 28, 32, 114
Mary 18, 24, 147
James 29, 146, 147
Phebe 29
Frances A. 37
Eliza J. 62
Lois 86
Dublin 94, 95
Elizabeth J. 134
Adeline 146, 147
Albert F. 146
William J. 146
Julia Ann 146
Alexander J. 147

GIDNEY
William 15

GRAHAM, GRAHAN, GORHAM
William 15, 84, 114
Mary 17
Richard 22, 51
Jane 25
Mehitable 27
Christopher C. 33
Phillip 45
Ann 51
Frances 74
Sarah 114
Margaret 114

GALAWAY, GALLOWAY
Elizabeth 16
Leah 19
George 20

GOLD
John 17

GARY, GAREY, GERREY, GARRY
Anna 17
Benjamin 20
Elizabeth 20
Stewart 21

GILCHRIST
Agness 20

Rebeckah 18, 49, 81, 83, 99, 115
John 19, 22, 32, 51, 54, 55, 79, 79,
  80, 87, 88, 109, 114, 123, 125,
  125, 126, 126, 128, 131, 135,
  135
Hilah 20, 58, 130
Dorothy 21
Mary 21, 22, 27, 31, 51, 58, 77, 110,
  121, 124, 126, 130, 143
Peter 23, 50, 57, 77, 78, 99, 99, 102,
  106, 106, 128, 129, 135
James 24, 55, 57, 126, 126, 127,
  131, 133, 135, 138
Catherine 25, 112
Thomas 26, 49, 53, 54, 81, 86, 109,
  114, 114, 115, 131, 135
Clarissa 27, 55, 78, 114
Maria 27, 132, 133
Harry 27, 35, 83, 83
Gilbert 27, 57, 60, 77, 120, 131, 132,
  133, 136.
William 28, 58, 77, 94, 96, 125, 143
Colvin G. 35
Esther 53, 78, 99, 99, 102
Juliana 53, 91, 102
Elizabeth 54, 94, 107, 115, 126
Phebe 54, 107
Able, Abel, 54, 98, 98, 100, 102,
  105, 107, 112, 121
Julia 55, 57, 77, 125, 125, 126, 128,
  128, 129, 131, 135, 135
Elsa 55, 82, 126, 126, 127, 131,
  135, 138
Abigail 58, 96, 123
Dolly 60, 112, 131, 131, 136
Sally 63, 75
David 69
Belinda 69, 143
Eusibius 71, 126
Daniel 80, 99, 136, 143
Patty 83
Henry 85, 85, 96
Nathaniel 98
Jacob 99, 105
Hezekiah 100
Fordine E. 101
Jane 107, 125
Jesse 107, 108, 112, 114
Martha 108
Highly 109
Abraham 110, 110
Gabriel 110, 129
Keziah 122, 122, 123, 124
Fanny 123, 129
Andrew J. 128

Harriet 132
Betty 135
Eleazer 135
Delia 138
Mrs. 96
P. 53

HORN
  Danniel 9

HOLLY, HOLLEY
  Hannah 9
  Silas 10
  Hester 10
  Mary 11, 14, 15
  Martha 11
  William 11, 83
  Daniel 13
  Joseph 23
  Abigail 23
  Sally 24
  Richard 25, 83, 86
  Jesse 31
  Hilah 57, 77, 129
  Lewis H. 76

HILL
  Martha 9
  Peter 10
  Susanna 14
  Tilton 16
  Rebecca 29
  Adeline 30
  Henry 45
  Jane A. 45
  H. B. 47

HAFF, HUFF
  Abraham 10
  Mary 14
  Abigail 16

HIGGINS
  Catherine 10

HUBARD, HUBBARD
  Joshua 10
  George 90, 128
  Elizabeth 116
  Dinah 128

HUMPHRY
  Ann 10

HALLETT, HALLET
  Moses 11
  Nathan 14

HOHAMER
　Philips 11
HOMES
　Margret 12
HOLMES
　Samuel 23
HARDEN
　Mary 12
　Stephen 16
HARDING
　Avis 25
HENNISON
　Sarah 12
HIMSON
　Benjamin 13
HAWKS
　Ruth 13
HODGE
　William 13
HUNNELL
　Mary 14
HUNT
　Nathaniel 14
　Samuel 14
　Cornelia 43
　Joseph 92
HART
　Andrew 15
　Rachel 18
HOPPER
　Elizabeth 15
HULL
　Sarah 16
　Samuel 23, 85
　Adelaide 61
　Charles 95
HUFFMAN, HOFFMAN
　Henry 17
　Mary 22, 137
　Zechariah 30, 137
　Elizabeth 60, 137
HOERY
　John 17
HANDLEY
　Edward 18

HARRISON
　Nathaniel 18
　Mary 22, 58, 129
　Anna 64
　Wm. H. 64
HOSACK
　Simon 18, 19, 51
HORSE
　Christien 19
HARRINGTON
　James 19
　Harriot 70, 74
　Jubel 70
HAMMON
　David 19
　Peter 21
HAMMOND
　David 28, 66
　Catherine 36, 70
　Jane 37
　Emily 37, 66
　Sarah Ann 93
HANGAN
　Isaac 19
HENRY
　John 20
　Rachel 20
HIZAR
　Rebekah 20
HUSTEN
　James 21
HOUSTON
　Jane 26
　Anthony 33
　Henry 34
　John 38, 39
　Eliza 67
HAYS, HAYES
　William 21
　Richardson 29
HANYAN
　Elioner 21
HOSIER
　Margaret 22
HIGBY
　Elleoner 23
　Peter 27

HARTHEWAY, HATHAWAY, HATHWAY
  Dan 23, 55, 79, 81, 81, 127
  Jane 30, 127
  Cecelia 35, 133
  Robert 37, 127
  Sally 55, 127, 127, 133
  Henry 127
  Sarah 127

HELMS, HELM, HELIMS
  Temperance 23
  Mary E. 40
  Sarah 67, 140
  Reuben 67, 140
  Almira 140
  ——— 68

HOUSE
  Phebe 23
  Mary E. 41

HALL
  Lewis 24, 36
  Harriet 33
  Alvira 36
  Rosanna 36
  Martha 43
  Archibald 50, 111, 113
  Abigail 53
  Daniel 53
  Sarah 54, 62, 75, 103, 134
  Timothy 54
  Don Carlos 111
  Polly 113
  James T. 113
  Dr. J. 37

HINCHMAN
  William 24

HASLETT
  Elizabeth 25

HETFIELD, HATFIELD
  Betsey 25
  Phebe Maria 27, 125
  Letitia 30
  Cornelia 33, 125
  Thoms 41, 78
  Aaron 55, 83, 125, 125
  Mary 55, 96, 125, 125
  Jane 78
  Moses 81, 105
  Dick 82
  Adonijah 105
  Elizabeth C. 125
  Letty Mc. 125
  A. 25

HANFORD
  David 26

HUTCHINS, HUTCHINGS
  Sally 27
  Fanny Maria 39
  Harriet O. 41
  E. W. 39

HUDSON
  William 24, 133
  Eleazer 27, 88, 131, 133
  Jonathan 30
  Ebenezer 60
  Elizabeth 60, 131, 133, 137
  Amanda 64, 75
  Horace 83, 84
  Abigail 83
  Sarah 84
  Maria 86
  John 92
  Mary 97, 137
  Hector 137

HANEHETT
  Florinda 28

HAYNES
  John 28
  Peter 41
  Jacob 42, 43

HOBBY
  Lewis H. 30, 61
  Abigail 61, 88

HOYT
  Hezekiah 30
  David 31, 95
  Mrs. Jane 35
  Jesse O. 40
  H. V. D. 44
  Edward 95
  Widow 95

HARRIS
  Alfred 32, 34, 36, 37, 40, 61, 72, 128, 145, 145
  Luther 36, 56, 128, 128
  Oscar 41, 61, 128
  Mary 56, 66, 74, 77, 128, 128
  David 66
  Jerusha 72, 145

HENDRIE
   Robert C. S. 32, 71
   Mary C. 65, 71

HEARD
   Charles 33
   John 40, 45, 147
   Jennie V. D. 45
   James B. 146
   Eliza Ann 147
   Mary Jane 147
   Emily 147
   Julia W. 147
   Katherine 147

HALSTEED, HALSTED, HALSTEAD
   Lois 14
   Wilmott 19
   George 34, 142
   Hiram 66, 139
   Eliza A. 67
   Michael 104
   Esther 104
   Margarett 104
   Juliette 142
   Ann 142

HANIS
   Mary Jane 35

HALHEIDER
   Henry 36

HAIGHT
   D. H. 41
   Suzannah 122

HENDERSON
   William H. 41

HOOPER
   Nathan 36

HOSFORD
   Henry 42

HEPBURN
   Rev. S. C. 43

HILLMAN
   Nicholas 43

HUFFNAGLE
   Mrs. E. K. 44

HALLOCK
   Mary A. 44
   Dewitt C. 45
   Emma 47

   Isaac 54, 126, 127, 130
   Tamar 54, 126, 127, 130
   Simmony 126
   Lewis 126
   Jane 127
   Maria 130

HAGGERTY
   James M. 44

HAWLEY
   Mary A. 45

HEALY
   John J. 46
   Mrs. John J. 47

HOTALEN
   Malvin 46

HEMMAN
   Leman 46

HOWE, HOW
   William 56, 77, 128
   Elizabeth 56, 90, 128
   Amanda 128
   Emeline 128

HUGHES
   Molly 79

HERRICK
   Francis J. 46

HOMAN
   Susie A. 47

HENDRICKS
   Philip 46

HOLMAN
   George W. 47

HARDINE
   Alex J. 47

HENDERSHOT
   Israel 59, 130

HOUGHTON
   Theophilus L. 59
   S. L. 76

HUNTING
   Mary 58, 76, 130
   Nero 58, 130

HERTON
   Susannah 77

HURTIN
   Jno. G. 25
   Harriet 91
   Christian 93

HIGSON
   Mary 90

HULSE
   Joseph 9, 115
   Jacob 10, 106, 106
   Sarah 10, 37
   Ann 11, 44
   Benjamin 11, 14, 106
   James 15, 106
   Mehatable 15
   Mary 15, 19, 90
   Martha 17
   Charity 22
   Edward 23, 37, 90, 94
   Samuel 27, 85, 102
   Juliann 30, 104
   Andrew 36, 70, 94
   Lewis E. 36
   Hudson K. 42
   Chauncy S. 44
   Frances C. 44
   Oliver O. 46
   Elisha 48
   Elizabeth 48, 82
   John 50, 100, 102, 104, 107, 109
   Esther 70, 144
   Sylvester 100
   Abigail 100, 102, 104
   David 109
   Abner 112
   Sally 115
   Fanny 115
   Dille 115
   ——— 112

HULTSE (See Hulse)
   William 86

HOPKINS
   Elizabeth 10
   Adelaide 23
   Rebecka 24, 107
   Gilbert 26, 44, 45, 97
   Hannibal 29, 39, 55, 89, 113
   James 38, 41, 42, 44
   Alfred D. 42
   Henry D. 44
   Benjamin B. 51
   Reuben 53, 53, 78, 78, 107, 109, 113, 117
   Hannah 53, 78

   Mary 55, 73, 78
   Delinda 57, 77, 117
   Elliott 81, 82
   William H. 109
   H. M. 73
   Miss 97

HAWKINS
   David 12, 54, 90, 106, 110, 116, 137
   Oliver 20
   Anna 24, 116
   Sarah 27, 54, 116
   Silas 27, 61, 91, 137
   Benjamin 28, 117
   Ira 29, 67, 74, 120, 141
   Samuel 30, 34, 67
   William 30
   Elizabeth 30, 57, 77, 129
   Matilda 34
   Cornelia 36, 71
   John 40
   Floyd 47
   Kate 47
   Christiana 53, 127
   Mary 56, 61, 78, 78, 106, 110, 119, 124, 128, 135, 137, 141
   Hannah 57, 77, 129, 141
   Hilinda 62, 75, 134
   Eliza 63, 70, 135
   Moses 62, 117, 119, 120, 122, 141
   Phebe 62, 137, 141
   Gilbert 56, 78, 122, 128
   Mahala 79
   Thomas 82, 127
   Margarett 110
   Hilah 116
   Charles 135
   Susan 135
   James 141

HARLOW
   Mary 16, 22, 27
   Samuel 17, 54, 55, 125, 126, 127
   John 21, 120
   Hannah 22, 103
   Sarah 22, 121
   Sally 27, 126
   Elmore 35
   Phebe 54, 119, 120, 122, 125, 126, 127
   Corlinda M. 69
   Benjamin 81, 89, 101, 101, 103
   Catherine 117
   Amzi 120
   Stephen 121, 121
   Juliann 125

HALLSEY, HALSEY
  Benjamin 17, 114
  Adeline 88, 135
  James 89, 135
  Silvia 90, 135
  John 92, 135
  Millicent 114
  Alexander 135
  Eliza 135
  Mary 135
  Eunice 135
  Anthony D. 135

HORTON
  Silas 9, 36, 86
  Anna 9, 53, 107
  Ann 104
  Susannah 9, 56, 104
  Elihu 10
  Mary 11, 66, 69, 74, 86, 89, 106, 132
  Thomas 11
  Sarah 12, 74, 106, 110, 132, 132
  Ezra 17, 114
  Samuel 15, 132
  James 18, 27, 34, 50, 66, 68, 69, 74, 74, 81, 81, 87, 92, 114, 116, 139
  John B. 21, 25, 132
  Gilbert 24
  Frederick 21, 57, 91, 129
  Barna 24, 27, 53
  Jeremah 25
  Nancy 28, 58, 129
  Richard S. 27, 84
  Caroline 30
  Jenet 31
  Charlotte 34
  William 34, 35, 36, 95
  Margaret 36, 84, 85
  Jane 36
  Vashti W. 39
  Fannie E. 44
  Selah 59, 76
  Elizabeth 60, 67, 129, 132, 132
  Rufus 60, 131, 132, 132
  Clarissa 64, 75
  Lydia 63, 91, 135
  Fred 80
  Catherine 87
  Egbert 93
  Beyea 94
  Barnabas 102, 104, 107
  Justus 102
  Abigail 106
  Jonathan 106, 109, 114
  Juliana 109
  Rebeckah 116
  Lucien 129
  Jenette 129
  Horace 132
  David 132
  Temperance 132
  Julia 129
  De Nolkert 129
  Orsamor 129
  Everard W. 129
  J. S. 37
  O. 80

HOWELL
  Theophilus 13, 20, 93, 96
  Elizabeth 13
  Margaret 14
  Deborah 15
  Benjamin 15, 22, 52, 54
  Mary 16, 37, 60, 69, 71, 78, 132, 144
  Hannah 16, 71, 91
  Obediah 19
  Jane 19, 73, 135, 146
  Eunice 25
  James 25, 35, 50
  Susan 26, 45, 59, 130, 131, 133, 136, 136, 141
  Suzie R. 44
  Epinetus 27
  George 35, 62, 63, 134, 135, 136, 137, 138
  Sarah 39, 52, 98, 135, 136
  Dewitt 39, 43, 133
  John 40, 42, 43, 66, 66, 139, 139
  Carpenter 44, 45
  Daniel 45, 62, 75
  Ann 45, 73, 137
  Sylvanus J. 45
  Ezra 50, 111
  Miriam 54
  Philetus 60, 84, 132
  Rhoda 63, 75
  Frances 62, 135, 136, 137, 138
  Rebecca 66, 139
  Joshua 69
  Hester 86
  William 93, 106, 131
  Horatio 96
  Emily 97, 139
  Hezekiah 98
  Archibald T. 83
  Edw. 106
  Charles 59, 83, 94, 130, 131, 133, 136, 136, 141
  Jeromus 135
  Carolina 136

Ira 73, 146
Benton 146
Ogden 136
Widow 96
Mrs. S. 37

HULBERT, HOLBERT, HOLBART
Ephriam 17
Peter 18
Jesse 30
Jonas 36
Susan T. 41
Adrian 42, 44, 46, 69
James 69
Hannah 69
Mary 79
Jerusha 102, 102
Samuel 102, 104
Joshuah 104

IMBLER
Mary 15

IVERY
Christian 18

INGRAM, INGRAHAM
John 19
Maria 56

INSIGN (See Ensign)
Silas 27

INGERSOL
Parmelia 30

IRVING
Austin 34

IMPSON
Joseph 90

IRWIN
James 93

IRELAND
Jean 63

JESUP, JESSUP
Jeremiah 9, 51, 54, 83, 118, 120, 122, 123
Daniel 17, 41
Mehitable 27, 59
Andrew J. 43, 44
Seneca 43
John 53, 83, 120
Hannah 54, 87, 88

William 57, 77, 122
Juliann 57, 77, 123
Sally 58
Isaac 81
Peggy 91
Ebenezer 118
Mrs. 57

JONES (See Johns)
Nathan 12
Elizabeth 13
Hannah 15, 29, 36, 37, 49, 66, 101, 117, 139
Michael A. 23
James 23, 36, 142
Ambrose 24
Anthony 28, 136, 137, 137, 140, 142, 142, 143
Clarissa 28, 142
Mary Ann 31, 39, 66, 101, 120, 122, 139, 140
Samuel 32, 49, 101, 137
Andrew 32, 33, 42, 43, 117, 136, 146
Phebe Ann 36
Fannie 39
Denton 41
Horace 41
Gabriel B. 43, 44
Dolly 57, 136, 137, 137, 140, 142
Sally 60
Sarah 66, 136, 139
Jesse S. 136
Egbert J. 137
Rech'd D. 143
Almenda 146, 147
John S. 147
Edward S. 147
Thomas E. 147

JENINGS, JENNINGS, JENNING
Benjamin 15, 16
Mary 15, 73
Jesse 18
Asa 22, 24
Melissa 40, 74
Frances 71
Nathl. 71

JOHNSON
Abigail 11
Peter 15
Hannah 18
Catherine 19
Isaac 19
James 20, 41, 97
Ieronimus 23

Henry 24
John 27, 67, 87, 140, 141
Jane 29
Margaret 39
Frances C. 41
Caroline 41, 71
Asher 47
Jothan C. 47
Nancy 67, 140, 141
Delinda 77
Rebecca J. 141

JANSON, JANSEN
Cornelius 15
Egbert 27, 63, 96
Asa 40
Frances 63, 87, 95

JOHNSTON
John 17
O. M. 44
Wm. 57
Delinda 57

JOHNES, JOHNS (See Jones)
Andrew 19
Mary 21, 122
Saml. 104
Michael 104

JACK
Lydia 20

JOLINE
Revd. John 21, 22
Mary 25
Ellen 61, 76

JAYNE
Stephen 24
Charles N. 37
Dewitt C. 37
Emily 37

JUMP
Juliana 33

JAY
Nathaniel M. 43

JENKINS
Carrie 44

JUDSON
William 45
Bertha 45

JAMES
Rhoda 63, 75, 127, 131, 133
Thomas 63, 75, 89, 127, 131, 133
Sally 127
Frances 133
Abram C. 131

JORDEN, JORDON
John 72, 144

JACKSON
Hannah 9, 18, 66, 100, 104, 115
Hamilton 9, 34, 35, 97, 110, 147, 147
Daniel 10, 74, 140
Henry 11, 23, 50, 53
William 12, 30, 37, 38, 44, 45, 53, 62, 90, 94, 100, 114
John 12, 20, 26, 87, 100, 103, 118
James 14, 16, 35, 140
Enoch 15
Jane 17
Elizabeth 18, 20, 53, 97, 103, 126
Richard 20, 27, 54, 83, 97, 123, 124
Mary 20, 29, 46, 57, 63, 89, 123, 126, 140
Fanny 21, 64, 75, 115
Stephen 22, 64, 79, 102, 124
Abigail 22, 23, 53, 64, 84, 92, 104, 114
Samuel 23, 110
Sarah 23, 31, 66, 74, 140, 141
Jonathan 24, 114
Margaret 25
Michael 25, 54, 80, 88, 100
George 25, 141, 147, 147
Martha 26, 48
Epinetus H. 27
Gilbert B. 27
Gabriel 29, 103
Emily 29, 124
Charles T. 31
Josiah S. 33
Milicent 33, 67, 74, 140
Edward 34, 140
Thomas J. 36, 39, 41, 107
Allie M. 45
Dolly S. 47
Phebe 49, 100
Ann 54, 92
Olivia 61, 76
Eleanor 65, 75, 108
Sally 66, 139
Julia Ann 66, 139
Julia 110
Melinda 66, 139
Andrew 66, 93, 123, 140, 141
Joel C. 81, 82
Joseph 86
Robert 87, 124

Anthony 94, 111
Mehetable 97
Benjamin 100, 102, 104, 107, 108, 111, 113, 115
Maria 113
Chauncy 118
Lewis D. 140
Harriet T. 140
Caroline 141
Clarissa 146
H. J. 146
G. B. 61, 76
A. M. 74

KNAP, KNAPP
Jabez 9, 28
Mary 9
Mary Ann 35
Abigail 9, 12, 101
Sarah 12, 16, 101
John 12, 13, 16, 20, 42, 64, 80, 101
Nathaniel 13
William 14
Jonathan 14
Elizabeth 15, 25
Ruth 18
Azuba 19
Elijah 27
Melinda 28
Catherine 34
Dolly 35
Ranselaer 42
Millicent 50
Fanny 82
Polly 83
Julia 101
Joseph 101
Zubah 101
Stephen 104
James 104, 107
Milla 104, 110
Zephaniah 104, 104, 107, 110

KIMBEL, KIMBLE
Peter 9
Able 10
Azubah 14
Phebe 15
Jane 20

KNIGHT
Catherine 10
Rachel 10
Nicholas 13
Prudence 19
Julia 24

KEELER
Ezra 11
Daniel 31, 111, 113
James 50, 99, 111, 113
Elizabeth 99, 113
Ebenezer 99, 113, 113
Thomas 99
Jane 99
Nancy 99
Ralph 113
John 113

KOONZ
William A. 44

KELLUM
Moses 11
Elizabeth 13

KING
Mary 11
John 12
Clement 12
Andrew 14, 17, 21
Sarah 26
Gilbert 57, 77
Nancy 58
Jerusha 104

KINNER
Jeremiah 12
Keziah 18
Anna 53, 81, 99, 101, 103, 124
Rosanna 82

KINNEY
Isaac 12

KID
James 12

KEARNEY
Catherine 15

KETCHAM
Mary 17, 52
Joseph 41
Jemimah 98
Phillip 98
Allexander H. 104
——— 104

KER, KERR
Hannah 17, 98
Catherine 18, 98
Margaret 20, 51, 98
Elizabeth 21, 51, 99
James 94

Oliver L. 98
Nathan 98
Ann 98
Mary 99

KORTRIGHT (See Cortwright)
Lydia 25
Sarah C. 39

KELSEY
Hetty 26
Mary 27, 127
Thomas 27, 89, 89, 90
Sarah 30, 127
Jeremiah 30, 94
Hannah 55, 84, 127
Nathaniel 43, 47, 95, 127
Jane 72
William 80, 127
J. P. 72

KITCHELL, KITCHEL, KETCHELL
Nancy 27
Amelia 28
Jane 31, 128
Benjn 37, 133
Sarah 39, 128, 130
Sally 56, 130, 133
Josiah 56, 56, 90, 128, 130, 133
Harriet 70, 143
Samuel 70, 128, 143
Emily 128
Electa C. 128

KINSLEY
Hudson 32

KINSEY
Laura E. 45

KREBS
John M. 38

KITNER
Jane 39

KIPP
Richard A. 43, 43

KNIFFEN
Mary 44
S. Logan 44

KILLIS
Diana 63, 75

KIZER
Robert 89

LITTLE
James, 9, 49
Archibd. 9
Suzannah 13
William 13, 35, 35, 36, 37
Experience 15
Esther 15
Sarah 16, 65
Mary 16, 66, 74, 77
Sally 24
Orpha 27
S. Frances 35
Charles 35
John 35, 65, 69, 70, 144
Julia H. 37
Francis 64, 75
Adelaide 64
Adeline 75
Eliza 65, 74
J. 36

LYNCH
David 10
Stephen 21
Mrs. 82
Elizabeth 146

LOVE
Elizabeth 10

LAMOREAUX
John 11

L'HOMEDIEU, L'HOMEDEAU,
L'HEOMIDEAU
John 11, 25, 57, 77, 129, 133, 136
Juliana 23
Hudson 30
Eliza 57, 77
Cornelia 59, 76
Dolly 57, 129, 133, 136
Braddock 84, 133
Mary 22, 133
James 136
Arminda 133

LANE
Elizabeth 11
Samuel 26

LETTS
Abraham 12, 42

LYON
Martha 13
Mary 23

LATTY
    Moses 14
LEWIS
    Mary 12, 28, 73, 135
    Alletta 22
    James 23, 61, 62, 104, 134, 135
    Thomas 24, 118
    William 24, 90, 108
    Samuel 24, 81, 111
    Polly 27
    Martha 28, 85, 115
    Hannah E. 46
    Isaac 24, 26, 54, 125, 125
    Jane 61, 134, 135
    Catherine 29, 54, 58, 78, 125, 125, 140
    Parson 78
    Loisa C. 80
    Ichabod 79, 102, 104, 106, 108, 111, 113, 115, 118
    Oliver 102, 134
    Morris 106
    Hariet 113
    Eliza S. 125
    Gabriel 134
    Henry 134
    Walter H. 134
    Charles 134
    Morgan 134
    Ellen 140
    Roswell 91, 140

LUDLUM
    Nathaniel 14
    Benjamin, 14, 108, 111, 114, 117
    Francess 16
    Isaac 24, 108
    John 26, 79, 99, 114, 115, 117
    Christiana 30
    Colvin 33, 83, 84, 90, 114
    Hezekiah 37, 44
    Jane M. 40
    Catherine 48, 115
    Daniel 79, 111
    Elsa 81
    Anna 84
    George 99
    Christian 89
    Mary 99, 105
    Sarah 105

LATHROP, LATHROOP
    Benjamin 14
    James M. 45
    Mattie A. 45

LANDON
    Laban 15
LUDLOW
    Peter R. 16
LACKEY
    Isabel 15
LUCKEY, LUCKY
    George 27
    Charles C. 47
    Maria 62, 134
    Sarah 62, 75, 134
LARDON
    Benjamin 17
LIBOLT
    Mary 17
LYBY
    Agnis 18
LINDERMAN
    John 19
LINDSEY
    Hugh 20
LEE
    Miriam 21
    Lueretia 107, 114
    Newton F. 146
    Cornelia 146
    Frances W. 146
LISH
    Peter 23
LAROE
    Rebeckah 26
    Crynus 32
LAUGHLIN
    Martha 28
LUSK
    Margaret 25
    Anna 25
    Ann Eliza 143
    Sally 25
    Benjamin 28
    John 30, 68, 96, 142, 143
    Elizabeth 64, 68, 75, 141, 142
    Francis 64, 83
    Frances 75
    Nancy M. 66
    Nanny M. 139

Latitia 68, 142, 142
Hannah 84
James 90
Jane 91
William 93
Daniel D. 142
Andrew J. 142
Jefferson 142
Catherine J. 142

LOCKYER, LOCKYEAR
Thania 30
Morris 59
Grace A. 87

LORD
George W. 35

LEDDEL
Samuel W. 36
Henrietta M. 36

LAWRENCE
James 38
William A. 41
John 41
Kattie 45

LOCKWOOD
Levi 39, 42, 45, 146
Fannie E. 42

LOOCKEE
Cornelius H. 40

LAMALINE
Franklin 41

LAMB
John C. 43

LA FORGE
Emma 44

LATEER
Jennie 45

LYAN
A. H. 46

LOMMIS, LOOMIS
Juliann 63, 75

LICKNER
Margaret S. 72

LANDER
Margaret 73, 145

McBRIDE
Mary 9
John 9
Janett 11
James 20
Patrick 24
William 27, 89
Wellington 45, 46
Belle 46
Widow 89

McCAMBLY, McCAMLY
John 9, 10
Sarah 14

McCONNELY
Duncan 10, 105
William 105

McCURDY
Lydia 10
Archibald 17
John 18
Agnes 101
Nancy 113

McVAUGH
Alexander 11, 104
Eilinor 11, 104

McCOUN
Elizabeth 10

McNISH
Clark 10, 107
Ruth 49, 98
Margaret 50
Joshua 92, 107
Mary 108

McVEAGH, McVAEGH
Benjn. 10
Elizabeth 14

McDUGALL, MacDEUGAL
Ellinor 11
Hannah 13

McCUNE
Phebe 13

MacNEAL, McNEAL
Rebeckah 11
John 12, 21, 98, 101, 102
Abigail 21, 100
Martha 22, 105
Isaac 22, 103
Hannah 23

Edward 98, 100, 103, 105, 107, 109,
 110, 112, 115, 117
William A. 101
Thomas 101, 107
Joseph 102
Margaret 102
Abraham 112
Nancy 113
Jacob 117
James 109

McCORY
 Allexander 14

McGOWEN
 Lydia 14
 Jane 100
 John 100
 James 100
 Mary 100

McCLINTOCK
 Mary 14
 George 20

McHENRY
 Thomas 15
 Edward 18, 51, 115
 Benjamin 106
 Daniel 106, 106, 108
 Jane 106
 Mary 115

McWILLIAMS, McWILLIAM
 Elizabeth 16
 Agness 17
 Isabel 19

McKINSTRY
 John 16

McCOBB
 Mary 17

McGLOUGHLIN, McGLOUGHLEN,
 McGLOUCHLIN, McGLAUGHLIN
 John 17
 Catherine 18
 Mary Ann 41
 Jennie 45
 Tabitha 100
 Patience 100
 Neal 100, 104, 109, 114
 Thomas 104
 Isabella 109
 Nelle 114

MacCLURE
 William 19

McCLEAR
 Sarah 23

McCLARE
 Mary 24

McDANIEL
 Roger 19

McINNES, McINNIS
 Peter 19
 Orphia 30

McCORMICK
 Sarah 19
 Jane 20
 Elizabeth 20

McMUN
 Elijah 19

McHUGH
 Martha 20

McCAIN, McCANE
 Abigail 20, 51
 Amelia 43
 Sarah D. 43

McCORD, McCHORD
 Elizabeth 20
 Jackson 23
 Caroline 30
 Sarah 32
 Letty 37
 Andrew L. 37

McCARTY
 Elioner 21
 Sarah Ann 71

McCARTHY
 John 21
 Mrs. 51

McCOY, McKOY
 William 23, 57, 129, 130, 135, 141
 Phebe 27
 Susan 29, 130
 Abigail 57, 129, 130, 135, 141
 Alanson 130
 Richard H. 130
 James 130
 Mary 130
 Joseph A. 130
 Sarah S. 135

Robert S. 135
Samuel 141
Andrew J. 141

McHANNEY
  Margaret 21

McCORKEY
  Mary 24

McLAUGHLIN, McLAUGHLEN
  Eleanor 24
  Rachael 31
  Mary 31, 36, 63, 111
  Alexander T. 39
  Nancy 87
  Daniel 86
  James 91
  Widow 91
  Frances 96
  Neal 102, 106, 111, 116
  Charles 106
  Peter 102
  John 116, 116
  Effe 116

McPHERSON
  William 24

McGEE
  James 25

McCOLLUM
  Joseph 25

McELROY
  Samuel 26
  Ann Maria 36

McDONALD
  John 27
  Bridget 80
  Abigail 83

McVEY
  Adin 28
  Sarah 29
  John 29
  Milton 30
  Alexander 90

McCARTER
  Harriett 32
  Sally Jane 68, 140
  Allin 99
  John 99, 100, 100, 102, 105, 106, 111, 111, 113, 114, 117, 118
  Annanias 102

Mary 105
Margarett 106
Jenny 111
Nancy 111
Allexander 113
James 114
William 117
Helen 118

McGONAGEL
  Thomas 33

McCARTEE
  J. G. 36
  Mrs. 36
  P. M. 36
  Margaret B. 70
  Isabella G. 71
  Davis B. 71
  Mary M. 71

McBRYSON
  P. 37

McNAUGHTON
  Mary 40

McNALLY
  Mary Ada 42

McMINN
  Lizzie 43

McEWEN
  George 45

McMULLEN
  William 49

McCORN
  Charles 64, 75, 137
  Margaret 64, 137
  Robert S. 137
  Fanny 137

McCREA
  Elizabeth 65

McCATER
  Jesse B. 72

McCOLLOUGH
  Joseph W. 81

McKINNEY
  Matthew 85

McGREGOR
  Alexander 88

McDOWELL
  Abigail 100
  John 100, 103, 104, 106, 115
  Elizabeth 100, 104
  Martha 103
  George 106
  Keziah 115

McCRADDE
  Jane 104

McWHORTER
  Mary 112

MacNICOLL
  Catherine 119

MARVIN
  Elihu 9
  Abigail 22
  Stephen 23
  Sally 24
  Sarah F. 40
  Jesse 27, 60, 76, 131, 132
  Floyd 40
  Olivia 57, 132
  Jane P. 60
  Frances A. 132
  John F. 71, 112
  Amelia 71
  Hannah 102, 108, 111, 113

MORE, MOORE
  James 10, 95
  Saml. 10
  Abigail 10, 16, 49, 115, 119
  Hannah 11, 32, 59, 130
  Elizabeth 11, 24, 58, 119, 119, 120, 129
  Peter 12
  Usher H. 13
  Anna 13, 17
  Kadmiel 13
  Cadmiel 115
  William 13, 98
  David 13, 17, 20, 49, 98, 98, 100, 101, 106, 108
  Margaret 14, 24
  John 15, 30, 41, 41, 44, 103, 103, 137, 139, 146, 146
  Jon 31
  Wilmot 19
  Wilmut 98
  Lydia 20, 100
  Mary 20, 26, 31, 31, 98, 98, 100

  Benjamin 16, 115
  Reuben 22
  Sarah 23
  Juliana 26, 53
  George 26
  Melinda 27, 139
  Henry 31
  Josephine 43
  Andrew J. 45
  Julia 44, 146
  Elihu 32
  Cynithia 28
  Naomiette 65, 138
  Beulah 51, 106
  Charles C. 95
  Eunice 98
  Walter 101
  Daniel 103
  Dolly 103
  Thomas 108
  Hector 73, 145
  Maria 139
  Alexander C. 137
  Jesse 103
  Frances 146, 146
  Jane 146
  Phebe 106

MACE
  Gideon 10
  Leah 11

MOFFATT, MOFFITT, MOFFAT
  Samuel 10, 50, 53, 80, 105, 109, 113
  Mary 15, 67, 108, 109, 114, 139
  Elizabeth 22, 105
  Suzannah 23
  Ann 22, 26, 51, 113
  Wickam 40, 146, 146
  Sarah 53, 90
  John 108, 109, 110, 112
  Anthony 110
  William C. 146

MEGEE
  Sarah 10

MARSTON
  Ephriam 10
  Ruth 17

MANNY
  Anna 11
  John 29
  Lois 100
  James 100
  Sarah 100

MIERES
  Cornelius 11
MYERS
  David B. 45
  Jane 67, 140
  Mary 115
MAPES, MAYPES
  David 10
  Smith 10
  James 11
  Abigail 12, 112
  Hannah 11, 13, 19, 99, 104
  Isreal 13
  Jemimah 13
  Enos 14
  Melesent 14
  Stephen 14
  Samuel 16
  Erastus 17
  Phebe 19
  Rumsey 25
  William 26, 41
  Edward 31
  John 32, 41
  Thos. 39
  Isaac 62, 93, 134
  Eunice 66, 139
  Susanna 67, 140
  Ellen 66, 139
  George 72, 144
  Widow 90
  Henry 99
  Keziah 15, 99, 112, 113
  Mary 101
  Daniel 102, 102

MONNEL, MONNELL, MONELL, MUNNELL
  William 11, 121
  James 13, 32, 138
  Rebecca 28
  John 32, 37, 71, 93
  Charles 37, 65, 94, 138
  Francis E. 37
  Frances 52, 123
  Jane 65, 138
  Mary 101, 116
  Tempe 121
  Thomas 116
  Malinda 123

MILLER, MILLAR
  William 11, 14, 115, 117, 118, 120
  Catherine 12, 13
  Mary 13
  James 13
  David 19
  John 20, 31, 31, 34, 68
  Samuel 23
  Christian 24
  Thomas 26
  Walter T. 26
  Maria 28
  Sally 28
  Reuben 34, 35
  Eliza 36
  Sarah 46, 117
  Juliann 57
  Clarissa 68
  Phillip 82
  Margaret 82, 116
  Elizabeth 115
  Henry 118
  Hyram 120

MUSKINNOS
  Adam 11

MAN, MANN
  Levi 11
  Elias 46

MUNROE, MANROE
  Angus 12
  Esther 12

MURDOCK
  James 12

MANHCART
  John 13

MATHEWS, MATTHEWS, MATHES
  Elizabeth 14
  Triphenal 14
  Sally 26
  Samuel 30
  Rebecca 37
  Raymond 76
  Thomas 47

MOSIER
  John 12
  Jared 22, 55, 125
  Ida 23
  Ruth 50, 105
  Sarah 55, 125
  Jonathan 105
  James 105
  Abigail 105

MOSHER
  Daniel 17

MARTIN
  Esther 13
  Walter 16
  John S. 38
  Joseph 38, 54
  Margaret 54
  Cynthia 66
  Alexander 91

MORRIS
  Sarah 15
  Christian 15
  Robert 16
  William B. 32

MOTT
  Unis 16
  Samuel 19
  Sarah 19

MAINS
  Elizabeth 16

MEEKER
  Elizabeth 16
  Hannah 23

MONGER
  Abigail 16

MEDDAUGH, MEDAUGH
  Deborah 16
  Mary 21

MILLS
  Ebenezer 16
  Thomas 25, 60, 84, 133, 137
  Harriett 27, 137
  Deborah 60, 133, 137
  Alfred 63, 90
  Elkanah 97, 130
  Amos 118
  William 120
  Mary 118
  Benjamin F. 118
  Hezekiah D. 118
  Samuel D. 120
  Hetty K. 133
  Elizabeth 133
  Jacob 118, 120
  ——— 120

MULOCK
  William 17

MORRISON
  Hamilton 18, 28
  William 21
  Andrew 24
  John 58, 77

MORRISION
  Violet 32

MELLONY
  John 18

MILSPAUGH, MILLSPAUGH
  Peter 19, 22
  Mary 22, 121
  Stephen 29, 33
  William 33
  Virgil 37
  George 41
  Charles 42, 42, 44
  Sallie 45
  Adam 52, 118, 119
  Mowbray 60
  Mabey 76
  Rachel 81
  Suzannah 118
  Jane 118
  Bettridge 119
  Dr. 31

MOON
  Elizabeth 62, 134
  Silas 19

MANSOR
  Huldah 20

MURRAY
  Allexander 20
  Warren 40
  Henry S. 42
  Matthias K. 93

MANDEVILLE, MANDEVILL
  Anna 22
  Cornelia 85
  Henry 96

MERRILL
  Richard 23

MITCHELL
  Jabez 24
  James 51, 119
  Abigail 119

MERRIAM
  Henry 33, 42, 144
  Charles 41, 42, 42, 43, 44, 144
  Nancy 65, 74
  Samuel 65, 74, 92

Helen 144
Frank A. 144
Ann Eliza 144

MERRIMAN, MERIMAN
Ann Eliza 72
H. 72

MURTHA
Thomas 36

MAGINNESS
Margarett A. 37
Mrs. 37
Joseph 37

MULVEY
Ellen 41

MARSHALL
Mary R. 38

MARTINE
William H. 44

MEEHAM
Francis J. 46

MILBURN
Niall 46

MULLIGN
Elizabeth 38

MUTH
Charles 42

MORGAN
Annie T. 42
Milton 43
Elizabeth 43
Amy 56, 78, 128
Charles 128

MARCLAY
J. Iwing 44

MAURICE
John 45

MOEILD
Christopher P .37

MASTIN
Ephriam 49

MORSE
Chancey E. 47

MUNSON
Esther 52, 122

John H. 122
Jacob 122

MASTERS
Paul 55, 127, 127
Elizabeth 55, 85, 127, 127
John 127
Silas 127
Moses 127
Sarah 127

MARSH
Jeptha 58, 76, 129

MATHER
Raymond 60, 60
Sally 60, 76
Benj. 76

MOIR
John 60, 76, 76
Isabel 60, 76
Jennet B. 61, 86

MINTHORN
John 79
Nat C. 79

MICHENS
Thomas 81

MIDDLEBROOK
Abijah 85

METCALF
Susan 93

MILLARD
Hannah 103
Elisha 103
Anna 103

NEWKIRK
Charity 10
Mary 12
Rachel 15
Matthew 35

NEELY, NEALY
Isabella 10
Elenor 14
Jane 15, 29
Deborah 19
James 21
Mary 45
Thomas 49
Margaret 49

NOBLES, NOBEL, NOBLE
  Jabez 13, 80
  Sarah 22
  Andrew 24, 55, 81, 82, 93, 129
  William 27, 56, 96, 128, 132, 136, 136, 141
  Eleanor 55, 129
  Mehitable 59, 132, 136, 136, 141
  Lois 88
  Julia 88, 132
  Thomas B. 83
  Sally B. 129
  Henry D. 136
  Frances E. 136
  John C. 141

NIVER
  Hannah 19

NICKOLSON
  Mary 20

NICOLI
  John 21

NEWTON
  Sally 24, 66, 74, 143
  George 33, 143
  Sarah S. 143

NOLAN
  Lizzie 46

NORRIS
  James 29
  Ann 38
  William 63, 68, 75, 95, 141
  Charlotte 68, 95, 141

NORTHY
  John 39

NELSON
  Thomas 45

NANNY
  Harrison S. 46

NOSTRAN
  Abigail 102

NEWMAN
  George 31, 62, 74, 75, 85, 96, 134
  Melinda 35
  Wm. H. 38, 43
  Arthur 46
  Hannah 46, 55, 126
  Hezekiah 46, 73, 145
  Julia 62
  Mary 62, 84, 95
  Scudder 69, 84, 142
  Ila 69, 142
  Nelson 70
  May 70
  Corlinda M. 69, 143
  Hiram 46, 78, 144, 145
  Platt 84
  Sarah 96
  Charles F. 144

OWEN, OWENS
  Nathaniel 9, 49
  John 10, 24, 91, 147
  Margarett 11, 143, 147
  Jonathan 12, 19, 91
  Mary 11, 37, 67, 139, 142, 147
  Tabithy 13
  David 13
  Abigail 15, 109
  Hannah 16, 50
  Terry 16, 52, 118
  Sarah 17, 22, 41, 67, 140, 141, 142
  Juliana 23
  Daniel C. 30
  Samuel 30, 39, 72, 142, 143
  Maria 35
  Oscar 37
  Harriet E. 37
  Joanna 39, 91, 140
  Schuyler 39, 41, 42
  Maggie 42
  Annie E. 46
  William 46, 147
  Gersham 50
  George 51, 112, 112, 114
  Fanny 57, 129
  Elizabeth 62, 75, 142, 146
  Gabriel 63, 67, 74, 140, 141, 142
  Melinda 65, 138
  Temperance 72, 144
  Elsa 81
  Christian 89
  Richard 95, 143
  Eleazar 109
  Abel 112
  Almeda 142
  Nelson 147
  Mrs. 37
  S. R. 38

OLIVER
  Thos. 11
  David R. 18
  James 38

OLDFIELD
    Keziah 11, 49, 98, 98
    Patience 12
    William 16, 46
    Mary 49
    Joseph 98

OSBORN, OSBOURN, OZBOURN, OSBORUNE
    John 11
    Abraham 12
    Phinehas 18
    Dan'l 19
    Mary 19
    Phebe 21
    Robert 42
    Hilah 58

OAKLY, OAKLEY
    Jeremiah 12
    Margarett 14
    John 15
    Ann 34, 141
    Isaac R. 44
    Sarah E. 44
    Hannah 58, 130
    Eliza A. 67
    Ichabod 67, 94, 141
    Mary 95, 141
    James S. 141
    Elizabeth 141

OTIS
    William 27, 129, 131
    Clarissa 55, 78,129, 131
    Harrison 129

ODELL, ODLE
    Hannah 16
    Isaack P. 31
    Daniel 64, 75
    Jesse 88
    John 88
    Sophronia 91

OSTROM
    Dr. 37, 38, 39, 40
    G. W. 43
    Gunning B. 45
    Emily C. 146, 147
    J. W. 146
    Joshua W. 147
    Eliza W. 147

OGDEN
    Mary E. 45

O'NEILL, O'NEAL
    ——— 38
    Mrs. C. E. 46
    Deborah 59
    Daniel 72

OSTRANDER, OSTRAND
    Eliza 57, 77, 136
    Morris 64, 75
    Thomas 132, 136
    Elizabeth 132
    Dewitt M. 132
    Maria L. 136

PARSHILL, PARSHALL
    Samuel 10
    Keziah 14

PERSAL
    Caty 19

POWELL
    Elizabeth 10

PECK
    Mary 11, 99, 102
    John 99
    Thomas 99

POPHAM
    Francis 11

PARISH
    Mary 11
    Irene 12

PARSON, PARSONS
    Theophilus H. 11
    Lewis H. 33
    Frank O. 46
    Mr. 93

PRICE
    Elizabeth 13
    John 28
    Ann E. 40
    Catherine 41, 113

PENNY, PENNEY
    John 13
    James 19

PEARSON, PEIRSON, PIERSON
    Abigail 12, 118, 118
    James 13, 80, 93
    Elizabeth 15, 119
    Silas 16, 51, 85, 118, 118, 119, 121
    Anna 24, 80

Ila 26
Maria 27
Henry 31, 116
Sarah M. 42
Eliza 64
Josiah 116
Richard W. 116
Matthew 118
Mary 118
Howell 119
Theophilus H. 119
Nathan 121

PAIN, PAINE, PAYNE
   Esther 12
   Samuel 12
   Unis 17
   Prosper 18, 34
   Jemimah 18
   Phebe 23
   Daniel 26
   John 31, 33
   Alexander 38
   Cornelia W. 44
   Jonah K. 44
   Henry C. 46
   Julia 64
   Ann 66
   Rosswell 66, 92
   Abigail 67, 140
   Mrs. 79
   Widow 88
   Mary 114

POPYNO, POPINO, POPPINO
   Danniel 13
   Richard 18
   William 23, 60, 67, 140, 146
   Adeline 29
   Bradner 31
   Emily 39, 146
   Julia 23, 47
   Juliann 146
   Seth 54, 80, 125
   Sarah 54, 125
   Hannah 60
   Harriett M. 125
   Charles W. 146
   Lewis 146
   J. J. 92

PELLETT, PELLET
   Abigail 14
   Assenath 19
   Obediah 21

PETIT, PETITT
   John 39
   Hannah 49

PAULY
   Mary 14
   Moses 17

POLLEY
   Hugh 16
   Jane 16

PARK
   Amos 14

POFF
   Peter 15

PUFF
   Sunanah 17
   Elizabeth 19
   Margrett 19
   Henry 37

PLUMMON
   William 16

PORTER
   Erastus 16
   Esther 26

PATTEN
   David 20
   Elizabeth 24

POTTER
   James 20
   Robert 23, 35, 67, 87, 140, 143, 143, 144
   Jane H. 63
   Frances E. 64, 75
   John 92
   Charles 143, 144
   Sarah E. 143
   Mary 143

PRINDEL
   Elizabeth 21

PALMER
   Deziah 22
   Lemuel 35
   James 35

PLOUGHMAN, PLOWMAN
   Juliana 22
   Peter 25
   Phebe 26
   John 30

Mary 30
Tuthill 32

POOL
  Catherine 28

PERRY
  Abraham 32

POUND
  Thomas 34

POTTS
  Daniel 35

PERRIT
  Peletiah 38

POST
  Adeline L. 40
  Carrie D. 43
  Belle M. 45
  Annie J. 46

PHILCOX
  William 43

PLOUGHER
  Annie 43

PUFFER
  Marietta A. 45

PAUL
  William 48
  Charles 86

PEPPARD
  Jacob 59

PURDY
  Jane A. 39, 139
  Benj. 39, 139
  Susan 39, 139
  Abraham 66, 139, 139
  Charity 66, 139
  Alvan 139
  Samuel J. 139
  Frances E. 139
  Lydia H. 139
  Hezekiah H. 139
  Julia A. 139

PHILLIPES, PHILLIPS, PHILIPS
  George 19, 59, 109, 131
  Mary Ann 28, 59, 68, 91, 130, 131, 142
  Harriet 29, 68, 70, 74, 74, 143
  Sarah 51, 69, 100, 105, 134, 143
  Moses 51, 55, 58, 68, 74, 81, 85, 100 100, 103, 105, 109, 109, 110, 113, 129, 130, 131
  William 54, 55, 59, 78, 80, 80, 83, 103, 130, 131, 134, 136, 137, 137
  Eliza 55, 80
  Dr. 58, 85, 91
  Sally 55, 78, 136, 137, 137
  Hiram 63, 68, 131, 142, 143
  Caroline 65, 74
  Emeline 66, 131
  Maria 68, 74
  Julia 68, 74
  Elizabeth 68, 94, 113
  Margaret 69
  Adaline L. 70
  Charles 80
  Nelly 83
  Elsa 87
  Henry 91, 109
  Edward 97, 131
  Louis 109
  Gabriel 109, 131
  Samuel 110
  Thomas S. 136
  Lewis N. 131
  Nicholas E. 137
  Theodore A. 142
  Hannah 143
  Alexander L. 144
  Edgar 137
  N. 59
  H. 144

QUICK
  Matthias 11
  Jeminah 24
  Peter 24
  Cornelius 24

RACKET, RACKETT
  Samuel 9, 103, 107, 111
  Martha 103
  Rhoda 103, 111
  Hannah 107

ROADS, RHODES, RHOADES, RHOADS
  John 9
  Jesse 28, 62, 62, 75, 75, 134
  Suzannah 48
  Maria 62, 75, 134

RYAN
  Ruth 9
RISE
  Sevier 9

REED, REID
  John 9, 12
  James 11, 46
  Phebe 12
  Moses 15, 17
  Mary 15
  Azuba 19
  Asenath 19
  Rachel 21
  Elizabeth 21
  Margaret E. 42
  Sidney 46
  Polly 80

RODGERS, ROGERS
  Rebecah 9, 22
  Solomon 10
  Jonathan 10
  Samuel 11
  Moses 14
  Daniel G. 14
  Mary 15
  Robert 18
  Benjamin 19
  Margaret 23
  Nancy 24
  Elizabeth 25
  Jason W. 25
  John 27

RAND
  Abraham 11

RIDMAN
  Catherine 10

ROE
  Suzannah 10, 50
  Patience 12
  Ezekiel 12, 115, 121, 121
  Juliana 15
  Elizabeth 15
  William 18, 31
  Joshua 21, 81
  Sarah 22, 115
  John 24, 121
  Lewis 26
  Mary 43, 51, 121
  Nathl. 50
  Elienor 115
  Samuel 115

  Benjamin B. 115
  Abigail A. 121
  Nathan. 121

ROWLIN, RAWLINE, RAWLINS
  Margarett 13
  Jennie L. 47
  Emily S. 47

RANDALL, RANDEL, RANDLE, RANDOL
  Peter 14, 91
  Anna 17
  Margarett 17
  Abigail 79
  Mrs. 81

RICKEY
  Andrew 14
  Isreal 48
  Rebeckah 49

RAY
  Thomas 14
  Jane 16
  Edward H. 46
  William V. 46

RANER
  Samuel 15

REEVES, REEVE
  Nathan 9
  Bathia 11
  Elisha 13, 17, 53, 108, 109, 111, 113, 120
  Temperance 13, 108, 111, 113, 120
  Abigail 15, 109, 112
  Joshuah 16, 83, 115
  Hannah 16, 97
  Submit 18
  Isaac 24, 83, 85
  Enoch 25
  J. Cooper 28
  Thomas 32
  James 32, 36, 37, 61, 64, 70, 73, 78, 95, 97, 143, 144, 145
  Sarah 30, 37, 72, 74, 143
  Ann Eliza 33
  Chaplin S. 33
  Dolly 37
  Charles 40, 41
  Franklin 31, 31
  Nancy 41, 63, 136, 143
  Joanna 41, 92, 143
  Adeline 61
  Chapman S. 67

Daniel 63, 89, 136, 143
Elizabeth 67
Charlotte 71
Mary M. 71
Mary Ann C. 143
Gabriel P. 73
Cooper 97
Miss 97
Rebeckah 103
Martin L. 111
John C. 113
Kitsey 115
David 135
Emely 142
Theodore 142
Mrs. 142
T. T. 36, 37

RUMSEY
  Daniel 9
  Nathan 14
  James 14
  David 16
  Jemima 17
  Juliana 20
  Mary 25
  Emily 30
  Sarah 31, 143
  Obadiah 30
  Phineas 24, 31, 31, 32, 36, 55, 65, 68, 84, 94, 95, 95, 131, 141, 142, 142
  Samuel 33, 61, 67, 85, 85, 140
  William A. 46
  Margaret 55, 86, 131
  Elizabeth 61, 67, 88, 94, 140
  Julia 62, 134, 142
  Eliza 65
  Phebe 84
  Betsey 84, 131
  Hannah 142

ROBINSON
  Margarett 18
  James 25, 88
  William 30, 68, 95, 141
  Mrs. 36
  Martha 37
  George 37
  Benjamin 52, 55, 84
  Mary 48, 55, 95
  Catherine 63, 70, 75

RUSSEL
  Judah 18
  Sadie R. 47

ROCKWELL
  Esther 18
  William 122

RICE
  Anna 18

ROY, ROYS
  Nancy 19, 24
  Robert 30
  Edwin L. 43

REDNER
  Henry 19

RAPALYA
  Joshua 20

ROSE
  Joseph 21
  Jacob D. 22
  Hester 25
  Silas 66, 139
  Sarah 70
  Phebe 103, 114

RAYNEY
  William 21

ROW
  Nathaniel 22

REDDING
  Phinehas 22

REEDER
  William H. 26

REYNOLDS
  Samuel 28, 85, 86
  Mary 29
  Ida 47

ROSS
  John J. 29, 96
  M. P. 41
  Jeheil 52
  Calvin 52
  Joanna 52
  Deborah 55, 78
  Rhoda 63, 75
  Sarah 72, 74
  Charles 72, 74
  Anthony 91

REDFIELD
  David 32, 33, 39, 40, 40, 42, 46, 73, 73, 145

Edgar P. 46
Ann E. 73
John W. 145

RYSDEK
  Wm. 33
  Ella 46
  Garrett 96

RANDOLPH
  Newton 35, 96
  Hattie 41
  Mrs. 96
  ——— 94

ROMAINE, ROMAIN, ROMEYN,
  ROMEYNE, ROMINE
  ——— 37
  John 37, 70, 72
  Nancy, 69, 143
  Ann 72, 144
  Benjamin 97
  Miss 97

RANKLIN
  Sarah J. 37

RIKER
  James, Jr. 39

RINE
  Edward 40

ROYCE
  William B. 43

RYERSON
  Mary 45
  Annie 46

ROBERTS
  Gilbert 52, 123
  Elizabeth 52
  Gabriel 123

ROWLY, ROWLEY
  Sarah 61, 76, 137
  Haines 61
  Harris 76, 137
  William 105, 105
  Reuben M. 137
  Lorenzo 137

RIDER
  Sarah 104

SEEWRIGHT
  Elizabeth 9

SPRINGSTEEN
  Christopher 9

SIMONTON
  John 9
  Wm. 37

SHEPARD
  Mary 9
  Daniel 9
  Jesse 124
  James 124
  Harriett 124

SLOTT, SLOOT, SLOAT
  John 10, 106, 106
  Elizabeth 15
  James 35

SEALY, SEELY
  Thaddeus 10
  Joannah 10
  Samuel 10, 12, 24
  Millescent 12
  Bazaleel 12
  Elijah 13
  Sarah 13
  Israel 14
  Suzannah 21
  Catherine 22
  Mary 23, 139
  James 23
  Jonas 37
  Saly Ann 28
  Ebenezer 30, 139
  Hannah 87
  Maria 63, 75, 139
  Edmund 36, 38
  Robt. 89

STEPHENSON
  William 10

STEPHENS
  Jemimah 11
  William 25, 57, 59, 77, 77, 129, 129, 130
  Fanny 57, 129, 129
  Chiliam 59
  Hannah 83, 129
  Ebenezer 86
  Caroline 129
  Thomas 129
  Martha 129

STEVENS
  George 30

SPREAG
    Milly 10

SALMON, SOLMON, SOLOMON
    Mary 11, 24
    Hannah 11, 24
    Sarah 13
    Phineas 14, 87
    Stephen 18
    Katy 25
    Lois 28
    Polly 26
    Catherine 21, 105
    Gideon 82
    Joanna 59, 84
    Nathaniel 105

SWARTHOUT, SWORT-HOUT
    Moses 11
    Ralph 14
    Aaron 15

SHAPPE
    Ashkenar 11

SKINNER
    Daniel 12

SANDS
    Charity 12

SANS
    David 28

SAYBOLT, SAYBOTT, SEYBOLT, SAIBOLT
    Francess 12
    Frederick 15, 112, 114
    John 16, 99
    Phebe 17
    Rebeckah 17
    Catherine 19
    Katarena 99
    David 112
    Keturah 112
    Mary 114
    George 117

STEBBINS
    George 30

SHA, SHAW
    Marcum 12
    Mary 20, 88, 111, 114
    Dorinda 34
    John 38
    Edward P. 46
    Henry 86
    Charity 88
    Reuben 89
    Samuel 111
    William W. 89, 111, 114
    Elizabeth 123

SIMMERS
    Sarah 13

SUMMERS
    John 30

SPENCER
    Henry 14

SCOIT, SCOTT
    Abigail 14
    Mary 21, 51, 118
    Hattie S. 46

SHORT
    John 14

SIMSON
    Benjamin 14

STEEL
    William 14
    F. H. 47

SULLIVAN
    George 15
    Patrick 43

SYMONS, SIMONS, SIMMONS
    Agness 15
    Benjamin 19
    Charity 90

SHIPPY
    William 15

SHULTS
    Lydia 15

SAMSON
    Rachel 15

SOPER
    Anna 16

SCHENKLING
    Jeremiah 16

STOTT
    Martha 16
    Mary 17
    Sarah 18, 115

Judah 20
Anna 20

SWALES
   Naney 16

STRINGHAM
   Patience 17
   William 18, 18, 48, 99, 116
   Phebe 99
   Margarett 99
   Alfred 116

STAGG
   Peter 17
   Jemimah 20

STAGE
   Joseph D. 38, 42
   Hiram T. 42
   Mary J. 73

STORM, STORMS
   Hannah 19
   Jane H. 72
   Peter 72

SNYDER
   Daniel 20

SWEET
   Hannah 20
   Kittie 46

SMILEY, SMYLEY
   Mary 20, 47, 141
   William 30, 32, 65,, 141, 142, 142, 143
   ——— 39
   Eliza 65, 74
   Christiana 65, 141
   Cornelia 142
   Christian 142
   John S. 142
   Dolla Ann 39, 142, 142

SHONCH
   Mary 21

SOODEN, SODON
   Thomas 21, 85, 91
   Lydia 24
   Elizabeth 25
   Jane 27
   John 92

SAVAGE
   Jane 21
   Henry 21

John 22
Sarah 66, 139

SACKRIDER
   Daniel W. 21

STANBRAUGH
   Servia 22

SINCEBAUGH, SINSABAUGH
   Margaret 22
   William 38, 40
   Elizabeth B. 38
   A. H. 38, 39, 146
   Kate 40
   James B. 40
   Anna 42
   Henry 44, 147
   Nellie J. 47
   Mary E. 146, 147
   Adam H. 147
   George W. 147
   Catherine 147

SOUTHERLAND, SOUTHERLIN
   David 22
   Elizabeth 23
   Rachel D. 30

SMELLIGER
   Manuel 22
   Nancy 24
   Margaret 30

STRAIN
   Archibald 23
   William 124
   Mary Ann 124
   Maria 124

SIDWAY
   William 23, 84

SLOWWATER
   John 23

SPROUGHT
   Phebe 24
   Margaret 24

SPRINGER
   Phebe 24

SATTERLY, SATTERLEY, SATURLY
   Jonas 25, 101
   John 26, 135
   Betsey Ann 36, 70, 135
   Frances 63, 95, 134, 135

Elnathan 100
Samuel 100, 101
Sarah 100, 101, 101
Mary 135

SKELLINGER
Oliva 27

SAVENY
Mary 30

STURGE
Clarissa 31

SHERWOOD
Benjamin C. 33

SILSBY, SILSBEE
John 34
George 84
——— 79

STEPPENFIELD, STEPPERFIELD
John F. 35
Kezia 66

SCUDDER
Walter 35
Francis 64, 75

STACKHOUSE
——— 35

SANDFORD, SANFORD
Mary Ann 36, 45
Ezra 40
Emma E. 41
Capt. 41
N. C. 45

SERRELL
James E. 37
Mr. and Mrs. 37

SEARS
Capt. 37
Sarah 38
Richard 41, 41

SHAFER
William 37

SNODGRASS
James 37
Charlotte 38, 39, 40, 41, 43, 45
El. K. 38, 39, 40, 41
Alex. 38
George V. 39, 40, 42
Archibald 39
Saml. S. 39, 42, 43

Thomas 40, 41
R. D. 41
Robert D. 43, 44
Annie 43
Emma 45

SEARGEANT
William 39

SCOFIELD, SCHOFIELD
John 38
Frances 40, 142
Henry 63, 71, 141
Julia 39, 71, 141, 144
James 39, 141
Christianna 73, 141
Emily 95, 141
Ann E. 141
Joseph W. 141
Sylvanus 143
Thomas S. 143

SIP
Cornelius J. 39

SHELDON
Henry A. 40

SHINE
John 41

SLAUGHTER
Samuel 41, 44
Benjamin 58

SING
William 43

STEINER
John 43

SAMUEL
Charles H. 44

SEARLES
Sarah C. 45

STUART
Ellen 45

STANTON
Wm. H. 45

STAATS
Dubois 45

SLAWSON
John B. 46

SEASE
   David A. 47

STAFFORD
   M. B. 47
   Charlotte E. 73

SCHOONMAKER
   T. D. 47

STUBBS, STUBS
   William 48, 50, 110, 111, 111, 113
   Mary 50, 110, 111
   Samuel 111
   David 111
   Joseph 111
   John 111
   Sarah 111
   Elizabeth 111
   Israel 113

STARK
   Nathan 61, 63, 69, 75, 133, 135, 136
   Mary 63, 69, 75, 136
   Oliver P. 135

SLACK
   Nathan 76

SPRINGSTED, SPRINGSTEAD
   Sevia 80
   Aaron 86

SCANTLING
   John 91

SUTTON
   Daniel S. 93
   Widow 93

SAXTON
   Sarah 93

SHERMAN
   Margarett 102
   Henry 102

SUFFERN
   John 115
   Edward 115

STRONG
   Catherine 10
   Vincent 25
   Walter 28, 38, 125, 133
   Benjamin 26, 27, 29, 33, 34, 36, 38, 55, 55, 82, 82, 89, 90, 92, 93, 125, 125, 126, 127, 132, 133, 147, 147

Ellis 29
Abigail 33, 127
James 33, 40, 125
Hezekiah 33, 125
Mary 40, 146
Jane 40, 60, 125, 147
Sarah 41, 68, 132, 147
Jennie W. 43
Frances 47, 146, 147, 147
Susannah 55, 125, 125, 126, 127, 132
Eliza 68, 125
Maria L. 71
Stephen 72, 125, 144, 145
Amy 80
Joseph 82, 127 *
William 82, 125
Egbert 93, 125
Charity 125
Thomas 125, 147
Fanny 133

STEWARD (See Stewart)
   Colville 11, 110, 116, 118, 119
   Luther 12, 54, 78, 106, 120
   Eunice 12, 119, 123
   Elizabeth 18, 53, 68, 106, 107, 112, 120, 122, 123
   Susan 24
   Mary 29, 55, 86, 95, 107
   John 54, 55, 55, 86, 92, 95, 107, 125, 134
   Asa 53, 84, 112, 115
   Kezia 54
   Edward 66, 74
   Maria 68
   Sarah 68
   Martha 86, 134
   James 95
   William 106
   Silas 106
   Coe 110
   Margarett 115
   Dolly 118
   Nancy 119
   Suzanna 120
   Lewis D. 125
   Catherine 120
   Jesse C. 120
   Dorthy 125
   Hilah Ann 125
   Emeline 125
   Gabriel 134

STEWART (See Steward)
   Silas 11, 102, 104

Mary 11, 99
Margarett 14, 36, 68
Cornelia 36
James 37
Eliza J. 37
John 39, 99, 104
William 93
Gabriel 99
Nathaniel 102
May 104
Sarah 104
Elinir 108
Daniel 112
Colvill 112, 114
Fanny 114

SEWARD
  John 15, 53, 60, 87
  Daniel 20, 25, 90, 136, 139, 142
  Hector 30, 89
  Elizabeth 31, 109, 109, 111, 114, 117, 119
  Henry 31, 33, 65, 74, 139, 141, 142
  Virgil 31, 33, 36, 38, 40, 67, 68, 140, 142, 142, 143
  Fredk. W. 47
  Mary 53
  Deborah 62, 88, 136
  Jno. 62
  Beulah Ann 65, 74, 139, 141
  Julia Ann 65, 66, 139, 139
  David 66
  Sarah 68, 142
  William 89
  Charles 89, 136
  Nathan C. 141
  Anna E. 141
  Helen 143

SAWER, SAWYER
  Temperance 12
  Sarah 16, 107
  Benjamin 18, 33, 58, 96, 107, 130
  Elizabeth 25, 30, 49, 64, 130, 136, 137, 138, 141
  Calvin 28, 59, 77, 130, 134, 135, 136, 136, 137, 140, 141
  Moses 29, 33, 62, 64, 75, 89, 92, 107, 130, 136, 137, 138, 141, 142
  Franklin 32
  Robert 33, 36, 64, 65, 75, 130, 138
  William 40
  James 49, 58, 77, 107, 130
  Hannah 57, 58, 93, 96, 130, 134, 135, 136, 137, 140, 141
  Catherine 58, 77

Juliann 58, 87, 129
Eleanor 92
Mary 107, 135, 141
Matthew 107
John 134
Samuel 136
Harriet 130, 137
Caroline 140
Gabriel 141
Daniel W. 142

SAYRE, SAYRES, SAYER
  Mary 13, 52, 99, 99, 102
  Hannah 21, 101
  Jemima 22
  Archibald 23
  Martha 23, 42, 106
  Elizabeth 23, 110
  Abigail 24
  William 26, 38, 40, 41
  Joseph 34, 68, 95, 97, 98, 101, 101, 141
  Jonathan 52, 98, 99, 104, 106, 108, 110
  George M. 42
  Roswell M. 43
  Margarett E. 37
  Louisa 68, 97, 141
  Frances A. 95
  Thomas 98
  Stephen 98, 101, 102, 109
  Jermimah 104
  Else 108
  Ann 109

SWEZY, SWEEZY
  Elizabeth 22, 50, 109, 109
  Jonathan 23, 50, 81, 109, 109, 111, 114, 117, 119
  Dolly 26, 100
  Adaline 34, 67, 140
  Moses 35, 38, 39
  Harriet 38, 67, 140
  Horace 42, 69, 109
  David 54, 86, 96, 100, 107
  Abigail 54, 86, 100, 107
  Morris 82
  John 107, 117
  Virgil 111
  Thomas 114
  Mary 119, 146

SLOAN
  Mary 56, 77, 131
  Daniel 56, 77, 131
  George A. 131

Maria 131
Harriett 131
Caroline 131
Lucy Ann 131
Hester 131

SMITH
Hannah 9, 13, 22, 25, 36, 48, 52, 59, 61, 84, 105, 128, 133, 138
Sarah 9, 9, 16, 22, 26, 29, 36, 40, 41, 47, 50, 51, 53, 57, 66, 69, 71, 74, 85, 87, 103, 105, 120, 121, 123, 124, 133, 136, 136, 138, 141, 142
Israel 9, 103, 103
Samuel 9, 36, 96, 101, 121
Dolle, Dolly 9, 28, 57, 128, 130
Hester 10, 27, 57, 77, 129
Martha 10, 98
Meriam 11
Miriam 26, 62, 133, 143
David 11
Mary 12, 18, 21, 25, 26, 26, 27, 48, 56, 58, 64, 65, 66, 70, 72, 74, 77, 78, 98, 99, 104, 108, 112, 115, 129, 136, 138, 140
James 11, 18, 81, 98, 108, 120, 136, 138, 142
Enos 12, 23
George 13, 26, 32, 56, 78, 83, 98
Joseph 13, 16, 82, 88, 92, 124
Solomon 13, 38, 38, 39, 41, 45, 50, 51, 70, 143
Allexander 13, 98
Tabitha 13, 61
Stephen 13, 28, 29, 33, 41, 41, 53, 56, 57, 58, 58, 61, 82, 83, 89, 100, 102, 102, 105, 105, 108, 112, 114, 115, 116, 117, 117, 119, 120, 120, 121, 122, 122, 123, 124, 124, 124, 129, 141, 142, 146, 147
Amy 14
Henry 14, 22, 30, 30, 34, 36, 51, 68, 88, 94, 96, 97, 101, 105, 109, 133, 135, 141
Caleb 14, 18, 34, 104, 115
Rachel 14, 61, 75, 99, 138
Elizabeth 14, 23, 27, 35, 49, 56, 57, 58, 85, 96, 109, 113, 115, 127, 127, 129, 129, 133, 133
William 15, 24, 38, 41, 71, 74, 82, 108, 129, 133, 137, 144, 147
Benjamin 15, 18, 25, 27, 41, 45, 56, 66, 78, 104, 106, 117
John 15 20, 20, 24, 28, 29, 32, 33, 35, 43, 49, 52, 53, 56, 61, 65, 74, 78, 84, 103, 103, 106, 108, 110, 113, 118, 121, 122, 124, 127, 127, 130, 138, 139, 140
Lenah 16
Sibyl 16
Juliana 16, 51
Abigail 17, 20, 23, 53, 54, 56, 56, 57, 84, 91, 95, 100, 115, 127, 127, 130, 133, 135, 137, 141
Joel 18
Abel 18, 29, 61, 85, 98, 115, 133
Margarett 18, 53, 105
Esther 18, 36
Frederick 19
Isaac 19, 21, 49, 49, 80
Suzanah 20, 23, 119
Unice 20
Charley 20, 21, 56, 128, 133
Ellioner 20, 53
Ezra 21
Wate 21
Wait 108
Catherine 21, 50, 100, 108, 133
Fanny 22, 103, 122
Elisha 23
Prissylla 23, 28, 105, 122
Robert 23, 37, 113
Archibald 24
Harriet 26, 36, 36, 83, 124, 128, 137
Grant 26, 62, 92, 134
Coe 26, 58, 116, 130, 133, 136, 137, 138, 139
Joshua 26, 35, 57, 71, 84, 97, 104, 129, 133, 136, 138, 141, 142
Susan 27, 58, 130, 133, 136, 137, 138, 139
Hila Ann 28
Ruth 29, 62, 134
Frances 29, 138
Phebe 30, 51, 84, 103, 133, 138
Eliza 30, 123, 128
Sally Maria 30, 57, 129
Sally Jane 34, 133
Sally Ann 34
Sally 53, 127, 128
Jonathan 30, 50, 56, 81, 82, 114, 123
Christiana 30, 127
Hector 31, 97
Chauncey 31, 34, 138
Hiram 30, 94, 127
Jesse 32, 40, 56, 92, 127, 127, 127
Thomas 32, 36, 40, 136
Abraham 33, 67, 95, 99, 140
Gabriel 36, 41, 53, 88, 97, 127, 128, 138

Emily 37, 94, 133, 146, 147
Emiline 37, 62, 128
Horace 37, 61, 64, 90, 127
Jane 38, 61, 89, 121, 136, 138, 140
H. Elizabeth 40
Mrs. W. C. 40
Lydia Ann 41
J. Augusta 41
Cornelia 42, 147
Theodore 42, 46
Wickham 46
Horton 47
Matthew 49, 108, 109
Deborah 51, 58, 81, 130
Asa 51, 116, 118, 119, 121, 122, 123, 133
Harry 57, 83, 133, 135, 137
Patience 57, 77, 100
Joanna 57, 77, 102
Richard 60, 131
Daniel 61, 81, 91, 98, 100
Charity 61, 133
Matilda 62, 142
Abba 66
Lemuel 66
Clarrissa 71, 144
Caroline 72
Govenier 73, 145
Mariah 76
Abner 80
Jonas 87
Nathan 89, 133
Maria 89
Letitia 92
Hubbard 93
Moses 97
Derrick 98
Alletta 98
Levi 98
Oliver 100, 103
Johannah 102
Jacob 103
July 104
M̃ascy 110
Conklin 114
Peter M. 115
Mahetable 116
Lewis 118
Nehemiah 119, 133
Ann Mariah 121
Ira 121, 129
Albert F. 127
Bradner 127
Oscar 127, 128
Milton 128

Theophilus H. 133
Gideon P. 138
Mulliner B. 138
Charlotte 138
Harvey M. 147
Sophia 147
Capt. S. 53
L. B. 74
S. G. 130
J. A. 138

TREMBLE, TRIMBLE
Isable 10
Allexander 11
Jane 14
George 17
Sarah 30
William 79

TRYON
Eliud 11, 49, 101, 104, 106, 107, 108, 110, 112, 113, 116
Abigail 20
Bathia 22, 106
Mary 104
Mehettabel 107
Phaneale 108
Ephangele 110
Bradock 112
Thomas S. 116
Jacob A. 113

TEED
Mary 12
Julia Ann 68

TINLEY
Charles 12

TYLAR, TYLER
Mary 13
William 13
John 14, 98
Oliver 98
Bazaleel 98
Phebe 98
Elam 98

TUSTEEN, TUSTEN, TUSTIN
(See Thurston)
Temperance 12, 106
Martha 12
Lucretia 17, 50
Abigail 24, 87, 103
Cornelia 29
Sarah 101

Anna 52, 99
Mary 48
Benjamin 48, 99, 101, 103
Emeline 62, 134
James 80, 99
Catherine 81, 99
Sally 83
Thomas 99
Elinor 102
Else 107
Festus A. 109
Cretia 109
Deziah 121

THOMAS
  Abigail 13
  Rosella 37
  David 16

THOMSON, THOMPSON
  Jonathan 9
  Hannah 9, 24, 35, 68, 101
  Moses 10
  Dorthy 13
  Mary 13, 14, 96, 100, 138
  John 13, 34, 37, 39, 40, 42, 42, 56, 64, 74, 77, 97, 101, 128, 138, 138, 139, 142
  Margarett 13
  Elizabeth 13, 73
  Archibald 14
  James 15, 68, 142, 142, 143
  Robert 17, 18, 49, 98, 98
  Phebe 18
  Isaac 19
  Letty 19, 101
  Elioner 22, 48, 106
  William 10, 21, 51, 94, 100, 100, 101, 103, 106
  Christian 25, 100
  Ann 25, 31, 37, 70, 74, 142
  Annie 42
  Sarah 25, 65, 74, 100, 138, 138, 139
  Oliver 26
  Gabriel 28, 90
  Keturah 30
  Hiram 32
  Frances E. 34
  Henry 34, 83, 89
  Harrison 35
  Ezra 36
  Capt. J. 38
  Charles 37, 101
  Martin 39, 42
  Edna 43, 43
  Georgee 43

Catherine A. 42
Horace 44, 45
Virgil 45, 143
Alexander 49
Nancy 68, 74
Maria 70, 70
Abjah 70, 70
Benj. 73
Sally M. 82
Charity 85
Julianah 103
Martha 121
Polly 111
Grace 139
George H. 142
Howard 138
Mrs. 91
T. D. 65

TUCKER
  Charles 14, 99, 112, 112, 115, 123
  Keturah 15
  John 16
  Henry 18, 115
  Mary 20, 115
  Elizabeth 23, 99
  Samuel 52, 112, 123
  Reuben 99
  Julianah 112
  Lott H. 123
  Sally 123

TAYLOR
  John 17, 86, 137
  Jane 20
  Zarah 24
  William 25
  Eliza 27
  Mary 29, 64, 136, 137, 137
  Josie 46
  Sarah 55, 87, 130
  Jno. 55
  Morrison 64, 88, 89, 137, 137
  Sally 58, 90
  Caroline 73
  Tinah 92
  Morris 136
  James W. 137

TRAVERSE
  Sarah 15

TERRY
  Uriah 15, 42, 43, 50, 112, 118, 119, 119, 120, 121
  Constance 17

Norton 18
Mathetable 20
Gilbert 20
Anna 20
Julia 23, 119
Galen 29
Parshall 48
Bethiah 50, 112
Azubah 56
Austin 56, 68, 91, 96
Elsa 65, 138, 139
Eliza Ann 74
Nathl. 65, 74, 138, 139
Mary 70, 118
Abigail 71, 119, 144
Wilmot 71, 144
Haven 94
Joshua 112
Ichabod 112
Hiram 119
Elizabeth 119, 119, 121
Hannah 120
Adelina 121
William J. 139
Mrs. 96

TRIMPON
Elizabeth 15

TALMAGE
Sarah 72, 74, 144
Helen L. 144

TURNER
Jane 16, 57, 133
Sarah 16
James 24
Elsa Jane 133

TOTTEN
Phebe 16
Sarah 18
Lydia 18
John 20
Joseph 21

TEARS
Jacob 17, 25

TOWNSHEND, TOWNSEND
Peter 10
Margarett 17, 46
Robert 21
Sarah 23, 51
William 26, 40, 52
Cornelia 28
Kezia 52

Roger 52
Hannah 117, 120, 122, 123, 124

TOPPEN
Unice 18

TENTS
Catherine 18

TERWILLAGER, TERWILLIGER
Levi 18
Peter A. 21

THACKER
Rachel 19

TRACY
Lucy 19

THORN, THORNE
Daniel 21, 83, 120, 122, 122
Mary 59, 89, 92
Richard 61, 76, 122
Wm. E. 88, 120
Sarah Ann 122
Thomas 23

THOM
William 22

TIBBITS
Obediah 23
Sarah 125
Esther 125
Phebe 125

TREDWELL
Charles 24

TOULON
Elizabeth 24

THEW
Letty 25
Elizabeth 40

TOOKER
Elmira 25
Charles 51
Samuel 51
Hannah 55, 95, 127
Rachel 58, 91
Danl. 55, 127
Jacob 64, 75, 127
James B. 84
William 127
Mary L. 127
D. 28

TELLER
  Oliver 29

TITTYBALL
  Horace 29

TERBELL, TERVELL, TERVELE
  Josephus 39, 42, 146
  Jeremiah 58, 77, 130

TELLEBALL
  Christopher 83

TOMPKINS
  John 30

TALLMAY
  Sally A. 31

TUPPER
  Abigail 33
  Abba 66, 139

TIFFANY
  L. O. 38

TINKEY
  Wm. H. 39

TILSON
  Mary Jane 41

TRAPHAGER
  John 42

TOLMAN, TALMAN, TALLMAN
  Ann 60, 132, 135, 136
  Joseph 60, 60, 76, 76, 84, 132, 132, 135, 136
  Mary 76, 87, 135
  Burnitt 89
  George G. 132
  William H. 136

TUNN
  Jane 77

TITUS
  Patience 88
  Azuleah 90

TICE
  —— 93

TOPPING
  Susan 69

TUTHILL
  Francis 11, 12, 37, 91
  Jeremiah 11
  John 12, 17, 17, 28, 40, 42, 45, 56, 78, 119
  Rachel 12
  Mary 13, 17, 30, 38, 45, 54, 108, 111, 113, 117, 126, 146
  Jonathan 15, 16, 52
  Abigail 18, 50, 86
  Benjamin 18
  Thomas 21
  Nathaniel 17, 19, 25, 40, 43, 61, 117, 119, 126
  William 20, 38, 43, 70, 126, 146, 146
  Freegift 22, 27, 34, 85, 95, 101
  Joshua 21, 96, 101
  Elizabeth 24, 61
  Harriet 28, 71
  Joseph 28, 42, 117
  Daniel 30, 93, 141
  Nancy 32
  Oliver 36, 65, 71, 74, 143, 144, 144
  James 26, 36, 38, 40, 42, 44, 46, 70, 71, 144
  George 39
  Horace 39, 73
  Charles 41, 44, 46, 97, 146
  Jane E. 43
  Sarah 46, 52, 83
  Rosilla A. 47
  Hiram P. 46
  Mehitable 50
  Catherine 72, 141
  Martha 73, 144, 145
  Anna 83
  Edward E. 83
  Andrew 89
  Hector 89
  Widow 95
  Caroline 141
  Ezra F. 143
  Frances J. 144
  Elimra 65

TUTTLE
  Mary 14
  Mehitable 15
  Nathan 16

THURSTON (See Tusteen)
  William P. 39, 92
  Robert C. 45
  Sarah 46
  Anna 47
  John D. 47

UTTER
  Moses 22
UPSON
  Hannah 31
UPPER
  Francis L. 33

VANTYLE, VANTILE
  Charity 9
  Catharine 9, 106
VANTASSEL, VANTASSAL
  Rhebeckah 10, 106
  Mary 12
  Huldah 14
VANBUMEL
  Thomas 10
VECTUR
  Martha 11
VANATTA
  Aaron 12

VANDUSER, VANDUZER
  Isaac 12, 54, 82, 132
  James 23, 94
  William 25
  Lucretia 30
  John S. 36
  Arron 37, 38, 73, 96, 137, 137, 138, 146
  Henry T. 42
  Martha 40, 54, 138
  Benjamin 25, 60, 60, 76, 76, 131, 132, 132
  Almira 60, 131, 132
  Susan 73, 137
  Christianna 73, 74
  Frances Emily 132
  Frances 137
  Amelia 76
  Caroline 39
  Walter H. 132
  Sally 137, 137
  Hannah 137
  Sarah 138, 146

VANORSDOLL, VANORSDOL, VANOSDOL
  John 14
  Cornelius 18
  Christopher 22

VAIL
  Asa 9, 103, 105
  Hannah 9, 20, 29, 30, 49, 55, 57, 59, 103, 125, 125, 130
  Elinor 10, 20, 55, 99, 127
  Josiah 11, 49, 108, 112, 116, 121
  Phebe 12, 17, 17, 18, 49, 64, 65, 80, 99
  Alsup 12
  Patience 13
  Mary 13, 47, 48, 50, 67, 72, 81, 99, 99, 101, 121, 140
  Julianna 14, 114
  Julia Ann 30
  Irene 14
  Samuel 14, 20, 55, 80, 97, 116, 125, 125
  David 14, 112
  Nathaniel 16
  Abigail 16, 101
  Joseph 16, 101
  Sarah 17, 38, 72, 105
  Abraham (Abram) 18, 28, 127, 136, 137, 139
  Absolom 18, 101
  Hester 19
  Elizabeth 21
  Deborah 22
  Dolly 25
  Azuba 26
  Jacob 28, 58, 125, 134
  Hiram 29, 65
  Julia 30, 125
  Horace 31, 62, 125
  Esther 34, 67, 140
  Peter 34
  Oliver B. 40
  Sally Ann 40, 70, 80, 144
  Isaiah 48, 51, 101, 101
  John 52, 58, 82, 91, 99, 101, 125
  Lydia 56, 88, 89, 101
  William 57, 99, 101, 101, 105, 108, 125, 136
  Christian 58, 129
  Jane 58
  Harriett 61, 136, 137, 139
  Maria 62
  Fanny 64, 75
  Almina 66, 139
  Eliza 70, 78, 144
  Richard M. 72
  Wickham 82
  Emeline 87
  Nathan 87, 139
  James 89, 125, 134, 136, 139, 146

VANDERHOOF
  Jacob 24, 80
VAN CLEFT
  Levi 31
VAN DYCK
  Henry 33, 69
VANDERWORT
  Hannah 34
VAN GUISHING
  Myndert 35
VAN KLEECK
  George D. 38
VANBUREN
  Martin 38
VANORT
  Teressa S. 41
VAN SICKEL
  A. Addie 42
  Nathl. 42, 44
  Daniel 42, 45
VAN HOOSEN
  Dr. J. B. 42
VANDEWATER
  Hattie H. 43
VANBRANER
  James L. 45
  Mary 45
VERNON
  Alice J. 45
VAN INVEGIN, VAN INVIGIN
  Julia Ann 65, 97
  George 97
VANRIPER
  Mary L. 73, 145
VAN BRUNT
  Ruliff 79
WATERS, WATER
  Hannah 9
  Conelia 39
  John 39, 93, 138
  Eliza 63, 74, 135, 137, 138
  Henry 63, 92, 135, 137, 138, 138
  Elizabeth 71, 115, 118, 138
  Catherine 71, 74

  George W. 101
  Benjamin 101
  Joannah 101
  Anna 105
  Moses 108
  Martha 108, 136
  Jonah 110
  Luther 110
  Gilbert 114
  Hilah Ann 134
  Margaret 136
  Jonathan 136
  R. M. 40
VOLENTINE, VALENTINE
  Ananias 16, 53, 89, 120, 124, 126, 126
  Stephen 25, 69, 86, 92, 96, 120, 142
  Mary 26, 120
  Kezia 27, 120
  Hannah 28, 124
  Elizabeth 29, 69, 89, 124, 124, 126, 126, 142
  Louisa 33
  John 37
  Clara E. 44
  Flemming H. 64, 68, 75
  Flemmon 126
  Harriet 68
  Jarvis 85
  William 87, 126
  Phebe 124
  Sarah 124
VANESS
  Peter 16
VAN SCOIT, VANSCOIT
  Patience 16
  Millicent 17
VAN WYCK
  Theodorus 17
  Theodore 122, 122
  Abraham 122
  William 122
  Sally 122
VAN LEVER
  John 20
VAN KEUREN
  Esther 21
VAN CURAH
  Hannah 115, 117, 118, 120

Bridget 81, 138
William S. 137
Thomas 27, 53, 83, 90, 92, 128
H. W. 71

WILLSON, WILSON
   Andrew 9, 32, 39, 63, 134
   William 23, 24, 101, 108, 113
   Nancy 24, 89
   John 32, 33, 34, 66, 66, 87, 92, 96, 96, 140, 140, 141, 145
   Pierson 31
   Deliah 36
   Agnes 38, 72, 94, 140
   Caroline 39, 73, 140
   James 45, 140
   Sarah L. 63
   Ann 66, 90, 140, 140, 141
   Samuel 99, 100, 106, 108
   Mary 99, 99, 100, 106, 108, 140
   Martha 100
   Margaret 101
   Isabel 113
   Jane 140

WILLIAMS, WILLIAM
   Margaret 9, 115
   Thomas 10
   Henry Abraham 14
   Isaac 22
   George 22
   Fanny 29
   Samuel 61, 76, 134
   May 76
   Nicholas E. 39
   Sally 56, 78
   Gilbert 56, 78
   Mercy 61, 134
   Susan Maria 134

WELLER
   Hannah 10
   Henry 19
   Andrew 20
   Hiram 85

WOODHULL
   Abel 50
   Jesse 51
   Sally M. 78

WHITAKER
   Mary 10, 105
   Benjamin 14

WEILY
   Millecent 10

WOODWARD
   Hezekiah 10
   Mary 12

WARD
   James 11
   Elizabeth 29

WITTER, WITTERS
   Isaac 11, 49, 107, 109, 113
   Ezrah 107
   Hannah 109
   Anna 113

WARNER
   Margaret W. 39
   Dr. J. 92

WILLCOX, WILCOX
   Unice 12
   Wm. Henry 39
   Sarah 41, 45

WELLING
   Richard 14, 112, 114
   Thomas 39
   John 40, 114
   Hezekiah D. 112

WALDRON
   Benjamin 14

WHITMAN
   Elener 12
   Annanias 18
   George 36, 59, 131, 132
   Mehitable 30, 63, 132
   Maria 30, 63, 132
   Mary H. 42
   Thomas 31, 132
   Samuel 42
   Judah 56, 90
   Joshua 56, 85
   Bethiah 59, 87, 132
   Daniel 61, 76, 133
   Hannah 61, 76, 133

WHITE
   James 13
   John 19, 52, 117, 119, 121
   Amos G. 22
   Sally 24
   Jonathan 26, 64, 75
   Julia 27
   Gilbert H. 36
   Dolly 64, 75
   Nancy 92

Samuel 119
Jane 119
Jannet 121

WEST BROOCK, WESTBROOK
　Sarah 13
　William 92

WALKER
　William 15
　Andrew 19

WINAN
　Ichabod 15

WEBSTER
　Sarah 15
　Clarissa 35
　Hosea 39
　John 62, 92
　Ethelinda 82

WESTOVER
　Naomi 15

WILKISON, WILKINSON
　Esther 15
　Mary 47

WEEKS
　Elizabeth 16
　Joseph 34
　Johannis 82

WYLEY
　Mary 18

WELLS
　Mary 9, 11, 19, 39, 64, 69, 77, 95, 118, 135
　Sarah 10, 26
　Abijah 12, 48, 86
　Catherine 14, 64, 96, 135
　Lydia 15
　Lydea N. 71
　Martha 15, 111
　David 16
　Henry 19, 117, 147
　Nathaniel 21
　John 22, 28, 44, 98
　Joshua 22, 36, 62, 64, 81, 85, 85, 98, 102, 104, 104, 135
　Daniel 22, 65, 103
　Dolly 25
　Julia 66, 135
　Christian 25
　Jerome 34, 35, 70, 97, 135
　William 35, 36, 50, 110, 116, 116

Adeline 36, 61, 134
Theodore 39
J. Edward 40, 44
Kate R. 41
Charles A. 42
Jennie E. 42
Frances 44, 64, 135
Charlotte 44, 70, 143
James E. 44
Keziah 50, 116
Elijah D. 59, 76
Jane 65, 138
Elizabeth 67, 98, 117, 135
Alfred 71, 135, 145, 145, 147
Rhoda 90
Abigail 92
Hannah 98
Thanna 105
George 102
Lewis A. 145
Eugene F. 145
Samuel 116
Israel 98, 103, 105, 109, 110, 112
Dr. 96, 143

WEB, WEBB
　Abigail 9, 84
　Chales 11
　Mary 11
　Joseph 15
　Benjamin 17
　Sarah 21, 48, 71, 74, 82, 120
　Hannah 21
　Elioner 22
　David 22, 23, 55, 56, 78, 80, 127
　Andrew 29, 89, 90, 146
　Emeline 30
　Hudson 30
　Moses 31
　John 39, 43
　Richard T. 40
　Festus A. 42
　M. Frank 44
　Nathaniel 48, 69, 70
　Fanny 56, 78, 127
　Louisa 70, 144
　Eusibius A. 71, 74
　Susan 84
　Gabriel 84
　Samuel 86
　Thomas E. 86
　Margaret 102
　Julia 146

WEEB
　Elizabeth 12

WICKHAM
  Matthew 9, 104, 108, 110
  Isreal 9, 20, 60
  Julianah 13
  Margrett 13, 112, 113, 114, 116
  Mary 14, 18, 111, 117
  Martha 19, 117, 119
  Frances 20, 103
  Abigail 21, 22, 60
  Joseph 24, 44, 87
  George 25, 27, 114
  Albert 38
  John 47, 85
  Samuel 48, 105, 111, 113
  Hilinda 62, 75
  Sarah 86
  Richard 87
  Thomas 88
  Tamer 88
  Caesar 88, 89
  William 24, 82, 103, 105, 114
  Anna 104
  Eunice 108
  Jesse H. 111
  Elizabeth 113
  J. E. 45

WILLKIN, WILKIN, WILKINS
  John 10
  Sarah 10, 42, 63, 105, 136, 136, 137, 137, 139
  Daniel 17
  Joseph 22
  Samuel 27, 32, 34, 39, 40, 42, 63, 91, 117, 136, 136, 137, 137, 139
  Elizabeth 14, 28, 43
  Anna 19
  James 28, 58, 60, 64, 66, 70, 75, 85, 93, 94, 117, 120, 122, 123, 124, 126, 135, 137, 139, 140
  Caroline 30
  Frances 34, 123
  Ann Eliza 36, 140
  Alexander 37, 136
  Theodore 38, 39, 140
  Henry 43
  Dewitt 43
  Hannah 55, 93, 126, 135, 139
  Janson 60
  Jason 89
  Clarissa 66, 70, 70, 139, 140
  Mary 73, 136, 140
  William 13, 89, 117, 137
  Sally Ann 94, 120
  Eliza Maria 120

  Charles 97, 136
  Roger T. 122
  Townsend 126
  Westcott 136
  Jane 137
  J. W. 81, 141
  Marcellus 137

WATKINS
  Thomas 13, 111, 115, 119, 120
  Elizabeth 16, 143
  Phebe 17, 127
  Dolly 17
  Abel 18, 22, 54, 127, 131, 132, 133
  Samuel 18, 132
  Submit 20
  Hezekiah 23, 28, 33, 43
  David 25
  Hannah 28, 54, 87, 127, 131, 132, 133
  Deby Ann 31, 127
  Victor M. 32
  Mary 32, 65, 94, 127, 138
  Sally M. 33
  Albert G. 33, 80
  James 25, 40, 65, 138, 143
  Ila 65, 95, 138
  Milicent 67, 74
  Margaret 67, 127
  John 73, 78
  Joshua 82
  Rhebeeka 111
  Joseph 112, 127
  Else 119
  Sarah 119
  Lydia E. 120
  Benjamin H. 127
  Cornelia 127
  Emeline 127
  George W. 133
  Mrs. 143
  ———— 112

WADKINS
  Sarah 15

WISNER
  Sarah 14, 22, 100, 103, 103, 109, 110, 113
  Temperance 16
  James 17
  Elizabeth 18, 102, 105
  Henry 10, 20, 49, 51, 57, 77, 82, 100, 103, 107, 109
  Robert 41
  Anna 52

John 52
Prime 95
Harriet 100
Gabriel 109, 118
Mary 107
Tempe 113

WEED
John 19

WAUGH
Sarah 19

WHEAT
Salmon 19

WILLOUGHBY
John D. 22
Widow 86

WOOD
Richard 10, 19, 50, 54, 78, 80, 101, 101, 128
Sarah 10, 32, 73, 128, 128, 137
John 10, 19, 38, 40, 58, 77, 80, 81, 81, 90, 100, 100, 102, 102, 129, 131, 137
Keziah 11, 35, 66, 140
Isreal 17
Alexander 17, 50
Hannah 18
Jane 18, 131, 144
Johannah 19
William 18, 34, 41, 67, 68, 97, 128, 143
Phebe 21
Silas 21
Simeon 22, 52
Timothy 22, 56, 80, 84, 84, 87, 88, 90, 92, 101, 104, 128, 128, 133
Andrew 23
Joshua 24, 146
Elsa 24, 53, 85, 107, 131
Anna 24, 68, 141
James 25, 42, 55, 61, 68, 75, 78, 104, 127, 129, 132, 134, 134, 136, 143
Benjamin 25, 63, 75
Ruth 28
Frances 29, 59, 73, 76, 127, 128
Mary 29, 59, 77, 128, 129, 137
Matilda 29, 62, 128
Solomon 29, 40
Anthony 30, 68, 94, 131, 142
Deborah Ann 31
Juliette 34, 67, 109, 128, 145

Joseph 25, 27, 35, 53, 56, 60, 64, 79, 83, 90, 100, 101, 102, 104, 107, 109, 128, 137, 144
Gabriel 39, 133, 146
Susan 40
——— 39
Lewis 41, 44, 62, 137, 141
Abby M. 41
Robert 53, 81, 102, 136
Lucretia 50
Christian 54, 78, 80
Charlotte 55, 78, 127, 129, 131, 132, 134, 136
Dolly 56, 128, 128, 133
Abigail 56, 104, 111, 114, 118, 123, 128, 131
Catherine 58, 77, 129, 131, 137
Avis 63, 75
David 67, 72, 78, 96, 128, 144, 145
Elizabeth 68
Cornelia B. 72, 74
Margaret S. 78
Juliann 94
Joanna 101
Oliver 101
Henry 101
J. Lewis 94
Isaac L. 68, 72, 75, 128
Samuel 86, 128
Eleanor 89, 100
Julia 100
Nelly 104
Suzannah 104
Asa D. 127
Ann Maria 132
Martha C. 134
J. L. 74
J. T. 77
R. L. 144

WELSH
William Henry 23
J. W. 46

WYCOFF, WYCOUGH (See Wynkoop)
Sarah 23, 73

WHITNEY
John 23
Abby 27

WHEELER
Nathan 24, 41, 41
Sally Maria 25
Joel 25

Elijah 86
Henry 91

WADE
　Eliza 27
　Calvin 27
　Uzal H. 28
　Maria 30
　Tabitha 57, 77
　Benj. 57, 77, 92
　Richard 91
　Harry 94

WILMOT
　Allen 27

WESTCOTT
　Sarah 27, 122
　Nathan 34, 35, 126
　Catherine 35, 125
　Mandeville 43
　Kezia 54, 86, 124, 125, 125, 126, 128
　David 54, 97, 122, 122, 123, 124, 124, 125, 125, 126, 128
　Jane 60, 94, 122
　William 70, 127
　Anna M. 122
　Benjamin G. 122
　Elizabeth 123
　Charlotte 124
　Henry 124
　Ency 124

WIGGINS
　Samuel 28
　William H. 29
　Catherine 58

WRIGHT
　Samuel 28
　Dr. 35
　S. P. 41
　Helen 41
　Mary B. 43
　Sarah A. 45
　Jacob 50
　Margaret 50

WATSON
　James 29

WILLIS
　Wilmot 29
　Mary A. 59

WALLACE
　John 29, 31, 34, 37, 39, 40, 41, 41, 43, 45, 47, 68, 69, 89, 93, 143, 143
　Frances B. 36
　Harvey 39, 40
　Fannie C. 45
　Wm. T. 47
　Emma 47
　Robert 47, 47, 69, 72, 74, 97, 97
　Jane 65
　Elizabeth 69, 69, 143, 143
　Phebe 92
　Mary 95
　Jack 82, 90

WARDEN, WORDEN
　Daniel 32
　E. 37

WYNKOOP, WYNCOOP (See Wycoff)
　William T. 37
　Sarah J. 78

WALL
　Alonzo C. 38

WINFIELD
　Charles H. 40, 41, 42, 43
　D. C. 43
　W. H. 44

WISE
　Capt. 42

WETMON
　D. O. 45
　Augusta J. 45

WOODRUFF
　Arthur M. 45
　Sarah A. 45
　Dr. 46

WYKER
　Wm. H. 45

WILKES
　George M. 47
　Chas. B. 47
　R. L. 84

WEYMER
　Cornelia 47

WAIT
　Wesley 47

WOODEN
　Wm. 92

WESTERVELT
   Daniel 95

WINNE
   Lavinia 95

YOUNGS, YONGS, YOUNG
   Esther 9
   Rhoda 9, 103
   Phebe 9
   James 12
   Henry 15, 18, 59, 77, 131
   Mary 20, 24, 66, 104, 107, 139
   Zechariah 21
   Abimel 22
   Lueia 23
   Deborah 26
   Sarah 28
   Eunice 29
   Henrietta L. 38
   Joseph S. 38, 42
   Robert 40, 44
   Mrs. Denton 43
   Alice C. 46
   Laura 62 ,134
   Lura 75
   Matilda 80
   Sally 122
   Colvin 66
   Calvin 139
   Susan E. 146

YERKS
   Elizabeth 12

YELVERTON
   Anthony 13
   Hannah 14, 108, 110, 114
   Phebe 17
   Abijah 100, 100
   Margarett 100
   Mary 108, 112

YONKER
   Simon 25

ZIMMER
   Peter 43

www.ingramcontent.com/pod-product-compliance
Lightning Source LLC
Chambersburg PA
CBHW050147170426
43197CB00011B/1991